P

ARUBA, BONAIRE & CURAÇAO

Lynne Sullivan

HUNTER

HUNTER PUBLISHING, INC,
130 Campus Drive, Edison, NJ 08818
☎ 732-225-1900; 800-255-0343; fax 732-417-1744
www.hunterpublishing.com

Ulysses Travel Publications
4176 Saint-Denis, Montréal, Québec
Canada H2W 2M5
☎ 514-843-9882, ext. 2232; fax 514-843-9448

Windsor Books
5, Castle End Park, Castle End Rd, Ruscomb
Berkshire, RG10 9XQ England
☎ 01189-346-367/fax 01189-346-368

ISBN 978-1-58843-647-4

© 2007 Hunter Publishing, Inc.

Cover photo: © *Explore/Dreamstime.com*

Maps by Toni Carbone, © 2007 Hunter Publishing, Inc.
Index by Jan Mucciarone
Printed in China

1   2   3   4

Contents

MAPS

INDEX   371

About the Author

Lynne Sullivan is passionate about Caribbean islands. As the author of a dozen best-selling travel guides on locations throughout the eastern Caribbean, she spends much of her time hopping from one island to another scouting out a variety of activities, attractions, shops, accommodations and restaurants. Her goal is to steer independent vacationers on any size budget to the best each island has to offer.

Readers can check for updates and new information on each island at **www.caribbeanguide2.com**. This is the author's website.

Questions?

If you have a question about the eastern Caribbean or one of the individual islands, send your inquiry through the website, and the author will answer as quickly as possible.

We like to receive email from readers. Opinions, experiences and reviews that may be of interest to others will be posted on the author's website.

Introduction

Aruba, Bonaire, and Curaçao are tucked into a secure pocket of the Caribbean that is rarely invaded by hurricanes. Their shared Dutch heritage unites them culturally, but

each island is in a different stage of development, and their topographies vary enough to be distinctive.

Aruba became autonomous in 1986 when it seceded from the Netherlands Antilles, but it remains an autonomous part of the Kingdom of the Netherlands, and its history, customs, language, and location link it inextricably with nearby Bonaire and Curaçao.

Curaçao is the largest and most economically developed of the three islands. It is also the trio's cultural and political hub. Bonaire, second largest, is an eco-traveler's dream and a scuba diver's wonderland. Of the three, Aruba is the smallest, has the best beaches, and draws the most tourists to its flashy resorts and glittering casinos.

Savvy travelers often divide their vacation days among each of the ABC islands. Several tour operators run day trips and overnight excursions between the islands. Do-it-yourself planners may prefer to book transportation on one of the inter-island airlines.

The Top Temptations

- *Endless summer weather with little rain.*
- *Dutch colonial charm.*
- *Ideal tradewinds for sailing and windsurfing.*
- *Excellent underwater reefs and magnificent sea life.*
- *Super duty-free shops.*

Facing page: Willemstad, Bonaire

Catamarans at sunset (Fernando Arroniz)

- *Championship golf courses on Aruba and Curaçao.*
- *International cuisine served at a wide variety of restaurants.*
- *Genuine hospitality offered by friendly residents.*
- *Accommodations, from basic to luxurious, at reasonable prices.*
- *Miles of trails and dirt roads for hiking and biking.*
- *Intriguing national parks and nature preserves.*
- *Curaçao's capital, Willemstad, a UNESCO World Heritage Site.*

Tips on Using This Book

- *General information about Caribbean travel and facts that apply to all three of the ABC islands is covered at the front of this convenient take-along guide.*
- *Specific information about Aruba, Bonaire and Curaçao follows in separate sections.*
- *If you plan to visit only one of the islands, rip out just the relevant sections from this book, place them inside a zip-lock bag and tuck them into your carry-on luggage. Leave the unneeded pages at home.*

- Most attractions, hotels and restaurants have web sites, and web addresses follow the phone numbers given in this book. Use them to gather additional information or make reservations.
- Prices change seasonally in the Caribbean, so use the cost information given in this book as a guide to a price range, rather than a specific cost.
- Check Island Facts and Numbers at the end of each island section for important information that will be helpful both during the trip-planning stage and once you arrive on the island.
- Every listing in this book is recommended and considered above average in its category. Listings with one star (★) are highly recommended, and those earning two stars (★★) are considered to be exceptional. A few resorts and restaurants rate three stars (★★★), which means the establishment is worthy of a special occasion splurge.

High Points in History

4000 BC-1499 AD: Earliest archeological evidence of nomadic tribesmen, probably **Taino/Arawak** from South America, inhabiting the Lesser Antilles. These tribes were

Early Indian rock painting (Arikok National Park)

later joined by other Amerindian subgroups, such as the **Caribs** and **Caiquetios**, also from South America. They migrated in waves through the Caribbean for thousands of years, competing for food and land.

1499: Spaniard **Alonso de Ojeda** and Italian **Amerigo Vespucci** arrive and claim the islands off the coast of South America for Spain. Finding little of commercial value, the Spanish decide not to develop the islands, but capture the natives and move them to Hispaniola (Haiti/Dominican Republic) to work on plantations.

1526: Governor Juan de Ampues starts cattle ranches on Bonaire.

1634: The **Dutch West India Company**, a quasi-private, government-backed company, lays claim to Curaçao and makes Dutch explorer **Peter Stuyvesant** the governor in 1642. Plantations and the lucrative slave trade flourish on Curaçao, and to a lesser extent, on Aruba and Bonaire.

1732: The Jewish community establishes the **Mikve Israel Emanuel Synagogue** in Willemstad, Curaçao. The structure is still standing and is one of the oldest synagogues still in use in the Western Hemisphere.

1800-1815: The British twice wrestle control of the islands from the Dutch. The 1815 Treaty of Paris returns the ABC islands to the Dutch. Social and economic conditions are harsh.

1824: Gold is discovered on Aruba and becomes a major export, along with phosphate, divi-divi pods (used in leather tanning) and aloe.

1837: Bonaire becomes a thriving center of salt production and exportation.

1920: Oil is discovered off the Venezuelan coast. Curaçao and Aruba become centers for distilling crude oil imported from Venezuela.

1939-1945: During World War II, the Allies establish an American military base at **Waterfort Arches**, in Willemstad, Curaçao.

1954: The ABC islands, along with St. Maarten, Saba and St. Eustatius, become part of the Kingdom of the Netherlands.

1986: Aruba is granted "*status aparte, and becomes an autonomous part of the kingdom.*

2007: Bonaire (along with St. Maarten, Saba and St. Eustatius) signs an agreement with the Netherlands to dissolve the Netherlands Antilles by December 15, 2008.

 Did You Know? Citizens of the ABC Islands are Dutch nationals and carry passports issued by the European Union.

Land & Sea

Location & Layout

Aruba, Curaçao, and Bonaire line up west-to-east just off the north coast of Venezuela, safely south of the Caribbean hurricane belt. Of the three, Aruba is closest to South America (15 miles), and smallest (approximately 110 square miles). Curaçao, 40 miles east of Aruba and 44 miles north of Venezuela, is the largest, at 182 square miles. Bonaire encompasses 112 square miles and lies 30 miles east of Curaçao and 50 north of Venezuela.

Geography & Topography

First-time visitors are surprised by the arid landscape of the ABCs. Each of the islands has somewhat varied topography, but all are basically flat, dry, and rugged – more like the southwestern United States than a typical Caribbean Island.

What makes the islands compellingly attractive to travelers is their leeward beaches and their spectacular underwater reefs.

Climate

 Summer never ends here. The temperature difference between June and December or midnight and noon is rarely more than four degrees either side of 82°F. A dependable cooling trade wind blows from the east, and fewer than 22 inches of rain fall anywhere on the three islands during a year.

Since the equator runs about 12° to the south, the sun is strong, especially between 11 am and 3 pm, and visitors enjoy morning sunrises and evening sunsets at roughly the same times each day, regardless of the season. (The sun rises at 6:45 and sets at 6:15 during December, while it rises at 6:15 and sets at 7:05 during June, making summer days only a few minutes longer than winter days.)

From January through March, the trade winds provide ideal windsurfing conditions off the windward coast. Since the terrain is almost flat, these same winds sweep clouds quickly over the islands without allowing moisture to build into rain showers. Therefore, the sea off the leeward coasts is rarely stirred up by a storm, and visitors may count on ideal conditions for scuba diving, snorkeling, and swimming.

 Did You Know? Current weather reports can be found online at www.intellicast. com/LocalWeather/World – or the National Oceanic & Atmospheric Administration at www.noaa.gov.

Plants

 Landscapes on the ABCs resemble those of the southwestern United States. Cacti outnumber palm trees and aloe plants thrive where ferns won't grow. But, the countryside is lovely in a dramatic minimalist sense, and the plants that struggle to grow in the arid windswept soil deserve recognition for their ingenious tenacity.

Cacti (Fernando Arroniz)

A dozen types of cactus grow on the islands. Most impressive are the tall pillar varieties, which islanders call **datu** (straight-limbed plants that are sometimes made into privacy fences) and **kadushi** (an organ-pipe variety that is used in soups). The kadushi can grow to a height of 40 feet and live as long as five years without water. After a rain shower, flowers spring forth from the dense thorns.

Unaware hikers may come into contact with the prickly pear **infrou**, which makes a pleasant-tasting jam, but also delivers a nasty sting to bare skin. Less dangerous plants include the large **agave** (century plant) that sends out a 30-foot stem and blooms only once before it dies, and the prickly **bromeliads** that attract thirsty birds to their red-centered white flowers. **Aloe** plants are cultivated for their medicinal uses, and islanders recommend their gooey sap

Agave (Fernando Arroniz)

as a balm for sunburned or cactus-gashed skin.

Watapana tree (Fernando Arroniz)

The most recognized and photographed tree on the ABC Islands, and the national tree of Curaçao, is the **divi divi** or **watapana**. It always bends toward the southwest at almost a right angle, pointing away from the easterly trade winds. Divi divi seed pods were once a valuable ingredient in leather-tanning products, and plantations on Bonaire and Curaçao profited from exporting the crop to Europe.

Brasilwood trees (also called dyewood) are recognized by their twisted, deeply grooved trunks. At one time, Europeans heavily logged the tree and used its timber to produce a red dye for the textile industry. Today, only a few hundred Brasilwoods grow wild on the islands. Look for them on the west side of the Bubali Bird Sanctuary on Aruba. You'll recognize them by their sinuous trunks, thorny branches, small round leaves, and small yellow flowers that appear during dry periods.

The indigenous **matapiska** tree produces a substance that is harmless to humans but deadly to fish. Caiquetio Indians put leaves and berries from the tree into the sea to poison nearby fish, then scooped up the dead fish when they floated to the surface. Unlike the matapiska, the **manchineel** tree is harmful to humans. Most of the trunks have been marked with red paint, but uninformed tourists sometimes pick up the yellowish-green apple-like fruit, with painful results. The sap, leaves, and fruit are highly acidic and easily irritate broken skin and mucus membranes.

Tourist-pleasing **palm** trees and flowering bushes have been imported to resort areas on the three islands. Desalinated water is used to irrigate familiar tropical plants such as **frangipanis**, **bougainvilleas**, **oleanders**, and **hibiscus**. Fruit trees produce mangoes, lemons, and papaya for restaurant tables.

Frangipani (Fernando Arroniz)

Wildlife

The ABCs have a surprisingly large number of critters, considering their sparsity of vegetation and fresh water. **Iguanas** and **lizards** come in many sizes and colors, including the **Caribbean anolis**, a lizard noted for its ability to cling to smooth surfaces, such as tree leaves and hotel walls.

Iguana (Fernando Arroniz)

Frogs, whose ancestors probably arrived on the islands as stowaways on cargo ships, can be heard croaking their love songs after an infrequent rain shower. Several species of harmless **snakes** (only Aruba has poisonous rattlesnakes, the indigenous **cascabel** or *Crotaluds thurissus*) and a variety of land **snails** make themselves at home under the islands' limestone rocks.

As for mammals, **bats** find shelter inside caves and under rocky outcrops along the coasts, and benefit the islands in several ways. Insect-eating bats devour as many as 600 pesky mosquitoes an hour, and nectar feeders pollinate night-blooming cacti that provide fruit for the birds.

Curaçao has a few **white-tailed deer** living in the thickets of Christoffel Park. All three islands have a problem with **goats** and **donkeys**, both originally brought to the Antilles by Spanish settlers. They run wild on public lands, often darting into the path of motorists and getting hit. While the donkeys have outlasted their usefulness as transportation animals, the goats are still raised for food. However, many break out of their fences and roam wild, grazing in private gardens and gobbling up the scant vegetation.

Curious goat on Aruba (Fernando Arroniz)

Birds

Native and migrating birds are the islands' true wildlife treasure. On Bonaire, **flamingos** are the national symbol. These captivating birds flock around the salt ponds at the Pekelmeer Sanctuary, one of the few places in the world where flamingos breed. The rare and endangered yellow-shouldered **lora parrot** (*Amazonia Barbadensis Rothchild*) also lives on Bonaire and is protected by international treaty. This mostly green parrot is recognized by yellow feathers on the shoulders, thighs, and around the eyes. Adults measure about 13 inches from head to tail, and the shy birds congregate in flocks to feed on wild fruit, including cactus fruits.

FANTASTIC FLAMINGOS

These long-legged long-necked birds have distinctive pink plumage, with black flight feathers. An adult may grow to a height of five feet and weigh as much as eight pounds. Most live 20 to 30 years, but records indicate a life span of up to 50 years. In the wild, flamingos eat algae, aquatic invertebrates, and small seeds. They feed with their head upside down and their bill in the water so that they can pump water through their bill with their tongue in order to sift out food.

Flamingos in flight (Susan Swygert/Tourism Bonaire)

While flamingos are shy around people and will run or fly away when they feel threatened, they are quite social and prefer to live in large flocks. They walk gracefully and balance delicately on one leg when at rest.

Flamingos mate for life, and the monogamous pairs build volcano-shaped nests for their young. Females typically lay one egg during a breeding season; each egg incubates for 28 days. Hatchlings are covered with gray down that remains through several molts before the bird becomes pink.

Curaçao's national bird is the **yellow-breasted oriole** (*trupial kachó*). Locals say its relative, the **orange-breasted oriole** (*trupial*), is a messenger of good news and a sign of good luck. Orioles can be spotted perching on top of pillar cacti, and their bottle-shaped nests may be seen hanging from high tree branches.

Approximately 160 other species of birds live on Curaçao, including the talkative bright green **Caribbean parakeet** with a distinctive yellow face (*prikichi*). While these birds are beautiful and a delight to visitors, farmers dislike them because they feed on crops and destroy gardens.

Aruban owl (Fernando Arroniz)

A more beneficial bird is a white subspecies of the **barn owl** (*palabrua*) that is unique to Curaçao. They live in the narrow band of limestone caves and plateaus that surround the island and feast on bats and mice. Probably, fewer than 50 breeding couples remain, and the species is listed as endangered.

Aruba claims two exclusive bird species: the **Aruban parakeet** (*Aratinga pertinax arubensis*), and the **Aruban burrowing owl** (*Athene cunicularia arubensis*). The offshore keys are major breeding grounds for **black** and **brown noddies** and **sooty terns**. **Brown pelicans** and **cormorants** live in the island's mangroves and along the coast, and the Bubali Ponds (man-made lakes used for storing treated water) attract 80 species of migratory birds.

The most common bird on these islands is the cute **yellow-bellied bananaquit** (*barika hel*). It brazenly snatches crumbs from outdoor dining tables and is not shy about coming indoors when it finds an open window. **Tropical gray mockingbirds**, known on the islands as chuchubis (a term also used to describe a snoopy, chatty person), are famous for their incessant calling. Along the coasts, you'll see several species of **herons** and **egrets**. The most impressive sea bird is the **magnificent frigate bird** (magnificent is part of its name). Also known as the man-o'-war because of the way it badgers other birds, it is easily identified by its split tail and tremendous wing span, the largest in relation to body weight of all birds.

Brown pelican
(Susan Swygert/Tourism Bonaire)

Visitors' centers on all the islands will direct tourists to the best places for birdwatching.

 Serious birders will want to pick up a copy of *Birds of the Caribbean* by Lucy Baker or *A Checklist of the Birds of Northern South America: An Annotated Checklist of the Species and Subspecies of Ecuador, Colombia, Venezuela, Aruba* by Clemencia Rodner.

Marine Life

The waters surrounding Aruba, Bonaire, and Curaçao sustain a vast assortment of fish and plants. Dozens of varieties of coral have formed reefs over millions of years, and much of the underwater area around Bonaire and Curaçao is protected by the government as national parks. Aruba is noted for its outstanding wrecks. Underwater visibility off all three islands is routinely more than 60 feet, and frequently up to 150 feet.

CRABBY CRITTERS

Hermit crab (Dirk van der Made)

Hermit crabs live on land but lay their eggs in water, so during spawning season, hundreds of them dash down the hillsides to become parents on the coast. After the baby crabs hatch, they spend a few months in the ocean before trudging onto land carrying enough water in their shells to sustain themselves for a while. When they grow too big for their backpack homes, they look about for larger dwellings – sometimes killing and eating other hermits so they can steal the deceased's shell. If a suitable shell isn't available, they will move into almost any kind of container. And, they will eat almost any kind of garbage – including sewage.

Ghost crabs never leave the beach. They tunnel into the sand, then dart out of their holes, zip a few feet across the wet beach, then burrow down again and disappear like a ghost. At night, they emerge to feed, and during a full moon hordes of them can be seen scooting around the beach.

Bonaire is expressly recognized for its spectacular underwater treasures, and the entire island is maintained as a Marine Park. Two sea areas are designated research fields with no diving allowed, and Lac Bay is a restricted area because of its mangroves. Islanders are serious about safeguarding nature, and visitors are cautioned not to remove or harm anything in the protected areas. No one is allowed to feed the fish, touch the coral, capture a critter, kick up the sand, or drop litter. That said, divers and snorkelers are warmly encouraged to jump in and enjoy.

Sponges & orange cup coral (Susan Swygert/Tourism Bonaire)

Sponges

Much of the color on Caribbean reefs is provided by sponges. These simple multi-cellular animals are called **Porifera**, which means pore-bearing and refers to the organism's many ostia (surface holes) and oscula (internal openings). Approximately 5,000 species of sponges have been identified world-wide.

Most sponges attach themselves to hard surfaces on the ocean floor where they use their flagellum to capture tiny organic particles that are floating in the water. Nutrients from these particles, as well as oxygen, are absorbed, and wastes are filtered out.

A single sponge may be either male or female, as the situation requires. Living young that resemble plankton are released through the hermaphrodites' outgoing oscula and attach themselves to a nearby surface. The life span of a sponge ranges from a few months to 20 years, and each organism can regenerate from microscopic fragments of the original.

Orange elephant ear sponge, deep water sea fan, black & white crinoid (Susan Swygert/Tourism Bonaire)

Sea sponges come in a rainbow of colors, various shapes, and all sizes. Some resemble a vase, others look like a fan, while others take on the appearance of a tulip. Under favorable conditions, sponges form gardens that become a habitat for other sea creatures. These fragile environs are easily destroyed by pollution, rising water temperatures, over-harvesting, and human carelessness.

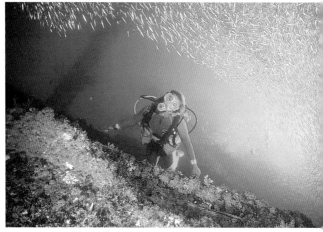

Diver with anchovies (Susan Swygert/Tourism Bonaire)

The Reefs

Curaçao is surrounded by a gently sloping reef composed of magnificent coral formations. Much of it is protected as an underwater park. Dozens of colorful fish feed here, and observant divers often spot eels, lobsters, turtles, and rays. While the reef drops off sharply, snorkelers may still see brain coral, sponges, and sea fans at shallow depths.

Aruba's reef system runs along the western and southern shoreline. Off the south coast, the coral reef slopes steeply from a water depth of 35 feet to about 130 feet, where it meets a sandy floor scattered with bits of coral. On the long stretch of well-developed western coast, the reef is flatter and less dramatic, but it protects the island's best beaches.

Snorkelers find large schools of tropical fish living among the beautiful coral formations at Boca Grandi, Palm Beach and Baby Beach.

Bonaire is well-known among divers for its pristine fringing reefs that support diverse marine life. Since all water surrounding the island is designated as an official marine park, dive areas are relatively undisturbed and undamaged, a situation that is unequaled in the Caribbean. Reefs extend from the high water mark down to a depth of 200 feet, which creates excellent conditions for snorkeling, shore diving and deep-water boat dives.

Sea Turtles

Following a turtle underwater or spotting its large head poking up out of the surf is always a thrill. These huge air-breathing reptiles differ in size, shape, and color, and some adults weigh up to 1,300 pounds.

Sea turtles do not have teeth, but use beak-like snouts to grasp and maneuver their food. Their sense of smell is excellent and, although they don't have visible ears, they can hear low frequencies with eardrums hidden just beneath

Hawksbill turtle (Susan Swygert/Tourism Bonaire)

their skin. Underwater, their vision is sharp, but they become nearsighted on land.

Females come ashore to dig nests and lay eggs in the sand, but males rarely return to land after they crawl into the sea as hatchlings. Typically, females lay eggs twice during a mating season, usually on the beach where they were born. Some females nest up to 10 times in a single season, but all skip at least a year between mating seasons, and some skip two or more years. Depending on the species, turtles may be 15 to 50 years old before they reach reproductive maturity, and some live over 100 years.

All sea turtles, except the leatherback, have hard scales covering their upper shell. Over the past 100 years, entire species of sea turtles have become extinct, and more are now endangered from destruction of habitats, pollution, and demand for turtle meat, eggs, skin, and shells.

CONCH

Queen conch (Ryan Shell)

One of the most popular shelled creatures in the Caribbean is the conch (pronounced konk). Its meat is the key ingredient in many island recipes, and collectors covet the large shells, which have a pearly pink interior and echo the sound of ocean waves. It's not unusual to see islanders cleaning and selling the more perfect shells near busy piers.

Talk the Talk

Snorkel and dive information throughout this book often refers to marine life that may be unfamiliar to novice underwater explorers. The best fix is a good book with lots of pictures identifying various common fish and plants that inhabit the

Southern Caribbean Sea. Next best is a good imagination and the following brief descriptions:

Sea anemone (Stuart Cummings)

■ **Anemones** (say ah-nem-oh-knees) stick to reefs and have tentacles that protrude from cracks and coral heads (like flexible, round-tipped tubes). They retract if touched. Anemones come in several varieties and colors.

Fire coral & anthias reef fish (Jon Hanson)

■ **Fire coral** is unlike other varieties of coral and is recognized by its drab beige color. It often grows upright like misshaped dinner plates or flattened boxes, and it stings, so don't touch it. (Remember that you are prohibited from touching anything in a protected marine park, and you shouldn't touch living plants and animals anywhere in the sea.)

■ **Stinging hydroids** are similar to fire coral and grow on things that divers often touch, such as chains that have been in the water a long time, the sides of wrecked ships, and inside caverns. Recognize them by their black ruffled shape. Don't touch. They give an electric-like sting that can cause large blisters.

■ **Gorgonians** (say gor-go-knee-ans), like corals, come in several varieties and grow in colonies. They are sometimes mistakenly called soft corals because of their flexible skeletons and bushy appearance. **Sea fans**, **sea plums**, **sea rods**, **sea fingers**, and **sea whips** are all gorgonians.

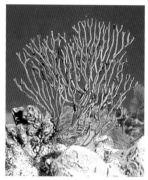
Sea fan

Sea urchin (Raphaël Rigo)

■ **Sea urchins** are those spiny black things you might have stepped on in the sea. The **long-spined sea urchin** is sometimes white, or black and white, but the spines puncture skin, regardless of color. Other common varieties include the **pencil urchin** (with thick, blunt spines) and the **West Indian sea egg** (a large, round, black body covered in short, white, dull-tipped spines that are blunt enough to be touched safely).

Feather star crinoid (Richard Ling)

■ **Crinoids** (say crynoids) have feathery, long arms that stick out of cracks. The arms of the **orange crinoid** are sticky and curl at the end. The **black-and-white crinoid** moves about and looks similar to a tall bouquet of shellacked white-tipped black feathers. Other varieties of crinoids include the **sea lily** and **feather stars**.

The People

Residents of the ABC Islands descend from more than 40 different ethnic groups and 80 nationalities. The fully integrated society is made up primarily of descendants of early settlers from the Netherlands, Britain, Spain, France, and Portugal, as well as descendants of South Americans, Southeast Asians, and Africans who came to the islands as workers or slaves.

Through years of intermarriage, most locals are an attractive mix of several races who speak numerous languages and pay little attention to social status. The majority of the population is happy to live on a prosperous island and eager to share their paradise with international tourists, who make their lifestyle possible. Since each island is small, the people enjoy a unique spirit of community and take every opportunity to celebrate a variety of cultural, religious, and ethnic events.

Introduction

If a distinction must be made, Arubans are the most Americanized, Curaçao's citizens are the most cosmopolitan, and Bonaire's population is the most typically Caribbean. But visitors won't notice much difference between locals living on the three islands. All are genuinely amicable, well-educated, hardworking, and open-minded.

Language

 Dutch is the official language, but most residents prefer to converse with one another in **Papiamento**, the local language. However, most people are also fluent or conversant in English and Spanish, and many also speak French and Portuguese.

Papiamento (also spelled Papiamentu) is especially interesting to linguists because it is spoken at all levels of society, while most Creole languages are used mainly by the lower classes. Also, Papiamento is a recognized language with a large vocabulary and formal grammatical structure, whereas the pidgin or patois spoken on many Caribbean islands is a diminished language with a limited lexicon and simple syntax.

> *Did You Know? In the Papiamento language, the word papia is a verb meaning "to speak." The ending or suffix -mento is the method of making a verb into a noun. So, Papiamento means "a way of speaking."*

Papiamento is a well-organized mix of Portuguese, Dutch, Spanish, English, and French, with hints of Arawak and African inspiration.

Residents of the ABCs use Dutch for official business and government dealings, but Papiamento is widely spoken and often used in newspapers, public signs, songs, and literature. Small variations in spelling and vocabulary exist between the islands, and the language is still being standardized, but anyone who understands Spanish,

Dutch, Portuguese, English, or French will grasp many familiar words.

Local Lingo

Papiamento	*English*
Bon bini	Welcome
Bon dia	Good morning
Si	Yes
No	No
Danki	Thank you
Masha danki	Thank you very much
Dushi	Sweetheart
Bebe	Drink
Ayo	Good-bye
Kuanta e ta kost?	How much does it cost?
Kon ta bay?	How are you?
Por fabor	Please
Despensa	Excuse me
Ki yamabo?	What's your name?
Mi yama...	My name is
Pasa un bon dia	Have a good day

Cuisine

Native dishes make good use of locally available seafood, imported Dutch cheeses, and Venezuelan fruits and vegetables. Menus often feature island specialties such as iguana stew, fried cactus or cactus soup, and funchi (a cornmeal mush that resembles polenta). Hot sauces made of onions, peppers, and vinegar add a bit of fire to many dishes, and Arubans often put a bottle of papaya-based salsa on the table.

Since the islands are affluent and Curaçao is a major port, the ABCs enjoy a variety of imported foods. Supermarkets are well-stocked, restaurants serve all types of international cuisine, and bakeries sell traditional sweets made mostly of coconut, peanuts, and sugar. On Bonaire, ice cream is considered an essential food group.

Menus in most restaurants are in English, or English and a couple of other languages, but it helps to be familiar with the local words for basic dishes.

Papiamento	*English*
Kabrito/Kabritu	Goat
Galiña	Chicken
Baka	Beef
Yanbo	Gumbo
Kesio	Flan
Karko	Conch
Piska	Fish

Music

 The Caribbean is well-known for distinctive music, and residents of the ABCs enjoy a rich mix of island sounds, Latin rhythms, and gospel songs. **Aruba** hosts several annual music festivals and features a Calypso Road March during Carnival. The local star, **Claudius Philips**, also known as

Claudius Philips

Mighty Talent, has won Carnival's Music Man of the Year award many times, and is a great influence on musicians from all three islands.

Curaçao is home to many talented musicians, who play at local clubs and perform at the island's music festivals. Folkloric shows, Carnival, and radio programs feature the hot African drumming patterns of tambú, and its musical cousin, tumba. **Aurelius "Boy" Dap** is the island's local music celebrity and has won the Carnival title King of Tumba several years in succession.

On **Bonaire**, music is so integrated into daily life that shoppers are treated to a live show outside the island's largest supermarket every Saturday morning, and many restaurants and clubs feature weekly live entertainment by the island's most talented musicians.

Tipico Bonairiano has been entertaining audiences for more than 40 years with music played on a variety of unusual instruments, such as the ukulele-like kuarta and the cheese-grater-like wiri. Newer arrivals on the local music scene include Florida transplant soloist **Ralph "Moogie" Stewart**, and the group **Glen I Su Gang**. Moogie is known for his original funky-Caribbean songs, while the 12-member Gang draws a crowd with a mix of charisma and rocking folk songs.

*For information on where to catch performances of local music celebrities, pick up a free copy of **Bonaire Nights**, **Curaçao Nights**, or **Aruba Nights** at hotels and other tourist spots on the islands.*

Travel Information

When to Go

Everyone imagines being on a Caribbean island during the winter when the weather is miserable most everywhere else. While winter is an ideal time to visit, summer, spring, and fall have advantages, too. Since temperatures remain steady in the 80s year-round, smart travelers often come here during the summer off-season when more bargains are available.

Airfare and hotel rates begin to drop around mid-April, just in time for the Queen's Birthday. Queen Beatrix, the current monarch of the Netherlands, was actually born in January, but that's a lousy time of year in Holland, so citizens (including those living in the Netherlands Antilles) celebrate on the birthday of the former Queen (Juliana), April 30.

The islands' biggest event of the year is Carnival, so if you want to join this parade-studded high-energy pre-Lenten celebration, book your reservations early. All the best resorts will be fully occupied, every rental car will be taken and dinner reservations at popular restaurants will be in short supply.

Celebrations & Events

No matter when you travel, your trip may coincide with a local celebration. Pick up copies of free publications in the tourist areas and hotels on each island to find out what's scheduled while you're there.

Grand Carnival parade in Oranjestad, Aruba (Fernando Arroniz)

Summer is packed with celebrations and events. Aruba hosts a culinary exhibition, a music festival, and an international golf tournament. Curaçao has salsa, jazz, and classical music festivals, and Bonaire hosts a couple of bike races, an art exhibition, and an international sailing regatta that includes windsurfing competitions and fishing tournaments. Since the ABCs are well out of the hurricane belt, late summer and early fall are an ideal time to visit.

Winter is high season throughout the Caribbean, and tourists are treated to a heavy schedule of activities. Locals begin the new year with elaborate parties: Bonaire holds a costume parade known as **Maskarada**; Arubans are serenaded by groups of roaming troubadours known as **Dande**; and Curaçao throws a **Tumba Festival**. Then the islands move directly into pre-Carnival preparations and festivities. **Carnival** itself takes place during the week before Lent begins on Ash Wednesday.

Holidays

On official holidays, islanders take a day off. All government offices and banks, most businesses and shops, and many restaurants are closed. If your trip coincides with a holiday, plan to spend your time enjoying community events, visiting public beaches, and eating in hotel restaurants.

All three islands celebrate the following official holidays:

January 1 . . . . New Year's Day
April 30 . . . . Queen's Birthday
May (1st Monday) . . . . International Labor Day
December 25 . . . . Christmas Day
December 26 . . . . Boxing Day

Floating holidays celebrated on all three islands include the Christian holy days of **Ash Wednesday**, **Good Friday**, **Easter Sunday**, **Easter Monday**, **Ascension Day**.

On Curaçao, **Rosh Hashanah** and **Yom Kippur** are observed in September/October by Jewish-owned shops and banks.

Check these websites for a current calendar of coming events:

- *Aruba*: www.aruba.com/calendar/month.php;
- *Bonaire*: www.infobonaire.com/calendar.html;

- **Curaçao**: *www.curacao-tourism.com/ActivitiesEvents/
FestivalEvents/Calendar.aspx.*

Documentation

 Immigration officials require that all visitors to the ABCs possess a round-trip or onward-transit ticket, sufficient funds for their stay on the island, and the necessary documents for returning to their country of origin. For US and Canadian citizens, a valid passport is required.

Make two copies of the data page of your passport, your driver's license, all airline and cruise ship tickets, hotel and rental car confirmation numbers or vouchers, phone numbers for offices that refund lost or stolen traveler's checks, and prescriptions for essential medication. Leave one copy with a dependable person at home and carry the other with you in a safe place apart from the originals.

Passports & Visas

The Western Hemisphere Travel Initiative requires all travelers, including US citizens, to present a valid passport when entering or re-entering the US by air, land or sea.

Americans, Canadians, Australians, New Zealanders and nationals of EU countries may visit Aruba, Bonaire and Curaçao for up to three months without a visa. If you plan to stay longer, you must apply for a visa through the Department of Foreign Affairs in Aruba (☎ 297-583-4705) or through the Dutch embassy in your home country.

If you don't have a passport, find out where to apply for one by entering your zip code or state into the search box at www.iafdb.travel.state.gov, or call toll-free ☎ 877-487-2778.

Citizens of countries other than the US must check with their country's department of foreign affairs for re-entry information. The islands will accept EU Travel Cards or national identification cards from citizens of most countries other than the US.

 Scan all your important travel papers, driver's license and credit cards into your computer and e-mail the document to yourself. If something is lost or stolen, you can print a copy from any Internet café in the world.

Protect the Kids

The ABC Islands strive to prevent international child abduction by requiring anyone traveling with a minor to provide documentary evidence of relationship and permission for the child to travel from the parent or legal guardian, if they are not present. Travelers may also be asked to present these documents when they return to their own country. Carrying these documents when you vacation with a child may prevent travel delays and inconveniences.

Help

If you lose your passport, contact the local police and the embassy or consulate of your country in the Netherlands Antilles. Citizens of the United States may contact the US Consul General at J.B. Gorsiraweg #1, Willemstad, Curaçao, ☎ 59-99-461-3066; fax 59-99-461-6489.

Canadian citizens can contact the Consulate of Canada, located at Maduro and Curiels Bank, N.V., Plaza Jojo Correa 2-4, Willemstad, Curaçao, ☎ 59-99-466-1115; fax 59-99-466-1122.

For Customs regulations, contact the **US Customs Service**, ☎ 202-354-1000; www.customs.gov.

Entering the ABCs

The ABCs have strict laws concerning illegal drugs, including marijuana. Possessing even a small amount of these substances will land you in jail and cost you more than you'll want to pay to get out.

If you take prescription medications, carry them in the original labeled container, and if they contain narcotics, get a note from your doctor or carry a copy of the prescription.

Visitors who are 18 years old or older may bring in two liters of liquor, 200 cigarettes, 50 cigars, and 250 grams of tobacco. You probably will not be questioned about specific items that you're bringing into the islands, but Customs officials have the right to look through your bags and ask about unusual articles or large quantities of items. They may also charge duty, between 7% and 22%, on goods valued at more than $250. Plants must have a disease-free certificate, and no meat products or birds (living or dead) are allowed.

 Save the immigration card that you receive on arrival in the islands. You will be asked to return it to officials when you depart.

For additional or updated information on entry requirements and limits on length of stay, contact Aruba's Department of Immigration, ☎ 297-582-8946.

Duty-Free Allowances

Make your return trip quick and hassle-free by packing all items that you bought on the islands together in the same bag and having all receipts readily available for Customs officials. Remember that you must declare everything that was given to you as a gift as well as everything that you bought. If you had merchandise shipped home, you must declare the item when you go through Customs.

Each country has its own regulations for taxing and exempting purchases made by residents traveling to a foreign country. If you think you may buy more than a T-shirt, request a copy of rules from the Customs Service before you leave home.

Citizens of the **UK** may obtain a copy of regulations by contacting the National Advice Service of The UK Customs and Excise Center, ☎ 0845-010-9000; www.hmce.gov.uk.

Australian residents may request a copy of *Know Before You Go* from Custom Services, ☎ 1-300-363-263, or check the Customs Information for Travelers on the www.customs.gov.au.

Canadians living in all provinces may get a summary of regulations by contacting the Canada Customs and Revenue Agency, ☎ 800-461-9999; www.ccra-adrc.gc.ca.

Each resident of the **US** is allowed to return home with $600 worth of duty-free goods every 30 days, and families traveling together may fill out a joint declaration form. If you arrive with new items worth more than the allowable credit, you will be charged a flat rate of 10% on the excess.

Citizens who are at least 21 years old may reenter the country with one liter of duty-free alcohol, and all residents may bring back 200 cigarettes and 200 cigars, as long as they are not from Cuba.

Up to $200 worth of duty-free merchandise may be sent home from abroad, but only one package may be sent to each address per day, and alcohol, tobacco products, and perfume valued at more than $5 are not allowed. Each parcel must be labeled "Personal Use," and an itemized list of the contents and the retail value must be provided on the shipping form.

Duty-free gifts to friends and family may be sent from foreign countries, but the limit is only one package per address per day, and the value must not exceed $100. Mark parcels "Unsolicited Gift."

DRUG DO'S & DON'T'S

Security and Customs officials are suspicious of pills, powders, and syringes, so if you are carrying such things, leave them in their original container and carry a copy of the doctor's prescription or instructions, especially if medications contain narcotics.

Request a copy of *Know Before You Go* from the US Customs Service, ☎ 202-354-1000; www.customs.gov.

Money Matters

Currency

 Just to make things amusing, Aruba uses different currency from Bonaire and Curaçao. All three islands graciously accept US dollars and Venezuelan Bolivars, but don't try to use Aruban bills on Bonaire or Curaçao, and expect Arubans to be outright surly when presented with money from their sister islands.

Aruba's official currency is the Aruban guilder (AWG), also known as the florin (Afl). Bonaire and Curaçao use the Netherlands Antilles guilder (ANG) (not the same as the Dutch guilder that was used in the Netherlands before the euro). Exchange rates may vary slightly at stores, hotels, and restaurants, but both the AWD and ANG are pegged to the US dollar and worth about 56¢ ($1=1.79ANG/AWG).

All prices in this book are quoted in US $.

On Aruba most prices are listed in both US dollars and Aruban guilders, but Bonaire and Curaçao are more likely to post prices in only the local currency. All three islands accept traveler's checks and most major credit cards, but small establishments in rural areas may require cash, and some may insist on local currency. Always carry enough cash for taxis, buses, snacks, and tips.

 On Aruba, don't bother changing US dollars into guilders. On Bonaire and Curaçao, simplify your life by exchanging a small amount of money. On all three islands, plan to charge as much as possible to your credit card. The exchange rate will be exact, you'll have a detailed record of where your money went, and you won't have to carry large amounts of either currency.

When you pay for goods or services with US dollars, expect change in local currency, and assume the exchange rate will not be in your favor. Also, be sure which currency prices are in before you buy, and become familiar with the paper bills and coins so you can quickly calculate your change.

 Did You Know? *Although the Netherlands began using euros when they were introduced to the European Community in January, 2002, the Netherlands Antilles continue to use their own guilders.*

The Aruban guilder is divided into 100 cents, and coins come in denominations of five, 10, 25, and 50 cents, as well as one, 2½, and five guilders. The square silver yotin is worth US 50¢ and makes a good souvenir. Paper bills come in denominations of five, 10, 25, 50, and 100 guilders.

The Netherlands Antilles guilder also is divided into 100 cents, and coins come in denominations of one, 2½, five, 10, 25 cents, as well one and 2½ guilders. The old square five-cent piece and the new square 50-cent piece are popular souvenirs. Paper bills come in denominations of 10, 25, 50, and 100. Both old- and new-style coins are in circulation.

Larger-denomination notes are available in AWG and ANG, but they, like large US-dollar notes, are hard to exchange, and many establishments refuse to accept them. Convert US bills larger than $20 into smaller denominations.

Double-check the amount on all charge slips. Most stores record the amount using the currency of the country issuing the card. However, occasionally the charge will be written in AWG or ANG. Before you leave the store or restaurant, make sure the use of local currency is clearly marked on the bill. Merchants who bill in local currency generally use a special charge slip that allows them to designate a type of currency.

PAY ATTENTION

On Bonaire, numbers are written with a decimal point between thousands and hundreds. Guilders are separated from cents by a comma. Visitors may find it difficult to read large prices, since five thousand six hundred guilders and 56 cents is written ANG 5.600,56.

Credit Cards, Banks & ATMs

ATMs are located at all banks, the airports and cruise-ship docks, and in many tourist areas on all three islands. The machines accept international bank and credit cards, and dispense cash in either local currency or dollars. Your account will be charged in the currency of the country where the card was issued.

Most major credit cards are accepted by the majority of businessess, but many require purchases to be more than $20. Supermarkets usually accept credit cards, but small grocery stores and mini-marts may not.

Banks are normally closed weekends and holidays. On Aruba, general banking hours are 8 am-noon and 1:30 pm-4 pm. Some banks stay open as late as 6 pm on Fridays, and **Aruba Bank**'s Mainstreet Branch, at Caya Betico Croes #41, is open Saturdays from 9 am until 1 pm. **Caribbean Mercantile Bank**'s airport location is open 8 am-4 pm, Monday-Friday, and 10 am-6 pm, Saturday-Sunday.

On Bonaire and Curaçao, some banks operate straight through the lunch hour, usually from 8 am until 3:30 pm,

Monday-Friday. The airport bank on Curaçao stays open from 8 am until 8 pm, Monday through Saturday and 9 am until 4 pm on Sundays. On Bonaire, the airport bank opens on Saturday mornings.

Electricity

 On Aruba, electricity operates at 110 volts/60 cycles, while on Bonaire and Curaçao the electricity operates at 110-130 volts/50 cycles. This doesn't pose a problem for most US- or Canadian-made small appliances, but European- and South American-made products that operate at 220 volts will require a voltage converter and a plug adapter.

Travelers are advised to use a surge protector for sensitive equipment, such as computers, and to be cautious about allowing equipment to overheat. Appliances with internal timers may not keep the correct time, and dive equipment, such as strobes, should be charged at the regulated outlets available at dive shops.

See pictures of various international plugs and find voltage information by country online at www.franzus.com.

Time

All three of the ABC Islands are on Atlantic Standard Time, one hour later than Eastern Standard Time in the US, and four hours earlier than Greenwich Mean Time. The islands do not observe Daylight Savings Time.

Health & Safety

The ABC Islands are clean, modern, and safe. That said, you should take responsibility for your own health and safety, as well as assume certain precautions.

- The **water** that comes from indoor taps is desalinated and purified directly from the sea. It tastes delicious. Water from outdoor taps is meant for irrigation, not drinking.

- **Food** in most eating establishments is free of disease-causing bacteria and contamination. Eat hot foods hot and cold foods cold. Do not eat from a buffet that has been sitting out more than two hours, unless the food has been kept covered and at the correct temperature with heating or cooling apparatus. Avoid prepared food sold by street vendors, and wash all fresh fruits and vegetables before eating.

- Most **health-reporting agencies** include all Caribbean islands in one general category without considering the conditions on individual islands. The ABC Islands are more healthful than less developed islands, so keep that in mind when you check the following agencies for information about infection outbreaks, health concerns, and suggested vaccines:

  The US Centers for Disease Control and Prevention, ☎ 404-332-4559 (in the US), or internationally at 1-877-394-8747 (1-877-FLY-TRIP); fax 1-888-232-3299; www.cdc.gov/travel.

  The Bureau of Consular Affairs, http://travel.state.gov/.

  Medical Advisory Services for Travelers Abroad (MASTA) provide health tips and useful links for minimizing risks while traveling; www.masta.org.

  The World Health Organization, www.who.int/homepage.

  Health Canada, www.hc-sc.gc.ca.

- The **sun** here is very strong year-round. Wear a high sun-protection-factor (SPF) cream containing zinc oxide or titanium dioxide, sunglasses, and a hat or visor during daylight hours. If you get burned, drink plenty of water to prevent dehydration and smooth on a coat of cream containing aloe vera. If you feel dizzy or develop a fever, headache, or nausea, you may have experienced sunstroke and should seek medical attention.

■ **Mosquitoes** are usually kept away by the steady winds, but at night and on calm days, you may want to use an insect repellent containing DEET. Some people claim that Avon's Skin-So-Soft is the best insect repellent, but scientists can't duplicate results in the lab. Try the nontoxic stuff and decide for yourself. If precautions don't work and you are bitten, use a product such as Sting-Eze to relieve the itch.

If you do become ill or injured while here, your country's consular or embassy office in the Caribbean may be able to assist you. Also, your health insurer and most major credit card companies can suggest names of qualified doctors and certified hospitals in the Caribbean.

Citizens of the United States may contact US Consul General, J.B. Gorsiraweg #1, Willemstad, Curaçao, ☎ 59-99-461-3066; fax 59-99-461-6489.

Canadian citizens may contact the Consulate of Canada, Willemstad, Curaçao, ☎ 59-99-466-1115; fax 59-99-466-1122.

 For hospitals and medical clinics on the ABC Islands, see Island Facts & Contacts at the end of each island's section in this book.

Getting Here

Air Service

 The ABCs constantly vie for increased air service from Europe and the Americas. For the best fares and most direct routing, search the Internet in addition to checking with a certified travel agent specializing in the Caribbean.

More than 60% of visitors come from North America; air service is frequent from several Canadian and US cities and from San Juan, Puerto Rico. Within the Caribbean, scheduled flights travel between the ABCs and Jamaica, Dominican Republic, Trinidad, St. Maarten, and Suriname. Charter flights operate from additional US cities and Toronto. Visitors from the UK fly overnight to the US, then on to the ABCs. Tuesday, Thursday, Saturday and Sunday flights go nonstop from Amsterdam, the Netherlands to all three islands. (See *Package Vacations*, page 43.)

NONSTOP FLYING TIMES	
Aruba-New York	4½ hours
Aruba-Miami	2½ hours
Aruba-Atlanta	4 hours
Aruba-San Juan. Puerto Rico	1½ hours
Aruba-Bonaire	30 minutes
Bonaire-Curaçao	15 minutes
Bonaire-Caracas, Venezuela	30 minutes

Airline Contact Information

Air Canada, ☎ 800-776-3000 (US), 888-247-2262 (Canada), 08705-247226 (UK); www.aircanada.ca.

Air Jamaica, ☎ 800-523-5585 (US/Canada); 0208-570-9171 (UK); www.airjamaica.com.

American Airlines/American Eagle, ☎ 800-433-7300 (English worldwide); www.aa.com.

British Airways, ☎ 800-247-9297 (US); 800-268-0288 (Canada), 0845-773-3377 (UK); www.ba.com.

Caribbean Airlines, ☎ 800-920-4225; www.caribbean-airlines.com.

Continental Airlines, ☎ 800-523-3273 (US/Canada), 800-231-0856 (international); www.continental.com.

Delta Air Lines, ☎ 800-221-1212 (US/Canada); www.delta.com.

Divi Divi Air, ☎ 599-9-888-1050; www.flydivi.com.

Dutch Antilles Express, ☎ 599-717-0808; www.flydae.com.

Insel Air, ☎ 599-9-888-0444; www.fly-inselair.com.

Jet Blue, ☎ 800-538-2583 (US); www.jetblue.com.

KLM, ☎ 0870-507-4074 (UK); 800-447-4747 (US/Canada); 31-20-4-747-747 (Netherlands); www.klm.com.

Lufthansa, ☎ 800-399-5838 (US), 800-563-5954 (Canada), 0870-837-7747 (UK); www.lufthansa-usa.com.

United Airlines, ☎ 800-241-6522 (US), 0848-844-4777 (UK); www.ual.com.

US Airways, ☎ 800-428-4322 (US), 0845-600-3300 (UK); www.usairways.com.

Charter Air Service

The following companies offer seasonal or charter air service to Aruba:

Vacation Express, ☎ 800-309-4717; www.vacationexpress.com.

Apple Vacations, ☎ 800-517-2000; www.applevacations.com.

GWV, ☎ 800-225-5498; www.gwvtravel.com (flights and packages from Boston and Hartford, CT).

Fun Jet Vacations, ☎ 888-558-6654; www.funjet.com.

TNT Vacations, ☎ 888-468-6846; www.tntvacations.com.

Cruising

 To find a cruise to the ABC Islands, contact one of the following:

The **National Association of Cruise Oriented Agencies** (NACOA) is an organization of certified travel agents who have made a serious commitment to helping travelers find the cruise vacation that best suits their expectations. To find a cruise-travel specialist in your area, go online to www.nacoaonline.com.

The website for the **Cruise Lines International Association** (CLIA) gives cruisers information, current news, and ship profiles. Find them at www.cruising.org.

The following websites provide additional information for cruise passengers:

- Find descriptions of cruise ships, destinations, and schedules from **i-cruise.com** at www.i-cruise.com; ☎ 888-427-8473.
- Check out *Cruise News Daily* for information, rates, and tips on shore excursions at www.cruisenewsdaily.com.
- Up-to-the-minute news and reviews for travel-savvy cruisers from www.cruisediva.com.

 Windjammer Barefoot Cruises allow you six laid-back days in the ABC region on a multi-masted sailboat. For information on upcoming cruises, call a travel agent or contact Windjammer directly, ☎ 800-327-2601; www.Windjammer.com.

Island Hopping

Jumping from one island to another is fun and easy. Small airplanes offer scheduled service and tour operators offer day-trips and multiple-island vacations.

Package Vacations

Many travelers come here on an unescorted package deal that includes transportation and accommodations. Often, these bundled arrangements cost less than separately booked hotel and airfare.

Start with the airlines. They frequently throw in multi-night hotel arrangements at a great price when you book your flight. Or go the other way and check with the hotel of your choice for a package deal that includes airfare.

Tour-scan computerizes all the published package trips to the Caribbean according to season, then selects the best values for each island. Travelers may search for their vacation by destination, cost, hotel rating, or preferred activity. This can save you a lot of time, but if you want to search for yourself, you may find unpublished packages at even better rates. ☎ 800-962-2080; www.tourscan.com.

Yachting

Insurers often require boat owners to head south, below latitude 12° N, when hurricane season arrives in order to protect their vessels. Aruba is at 12° 30 minutes N. Bonaire and Curaçao are even farther south. But many captains come to the ABCs simply because they offer a terrific boating experience. They are close to the Venezuelan coast, offer safe harbors, and the friendly locals welcome visiting yachts and their crews.

Sailing between the islands is often difficult because of the strong trade winds and ocean currents, and most crews avoid the 70-mile trip between Aruba and Curaçao. However, the 35-mile journey downwind from Bonaire to Curaçao takes an average of six hours, and sailors enjoy the ride. Visitors who do not own a boat can take advantage of the many day sails and party cruises offered on each island.

For contact information on day sails, party cruises, inter-island ferry, and yacht rental, see Adventures on Water in each island section.

Getting Around

Hotels do not operate shuttle service to and from the ABCs' airports, but if you're on a charter flight or package vacation, transfers to and from your hotel are often included. Taxis wait for arriving passengers just outside the terminal, and most car rental companies have offices on the airport grounds.

Driving

- Driving is on the right-hand side of the road, as in the US and Canada.
- International road signs are posted, along with local road signs written in Dutch or Papiamento.
- Speed limits are set in kilometers at 40 (25 mph) in urban areas, and 60 (37 mph) in rural areas.
- Most rental car speedometers register in kilometers.
- Right turns are not allowed on red lights anywhere on the islands.
- If you plan to rent a car, you must present a valid international permit or a valid license from the US, Canada, or Europe. Either must have been held for a minimum of two years.
- Plan to pay with a major credit card and ask before you leave home about included insurance on rentals charged to the card.
- If you pay cash, you will be required to leave a $500 deposit. Age restrictions for renters vary somewhat among companies, but in general, the minimum age is either 21 or 25 and the maximum age is 65 to 70. If you fall at ei-

ther end of these age groups, verify the company policy before you book a car.

■ Most gas stations close early in the evening, and few open on Sunday.

■ Watch out for roaming goats, donkeys, bikers, and pedestrians.

■ Your rental car will have a "V" on the license plate, so petty thieves know who you are. Lock the doors and use any theft-prevention device the rental company supplies.

INTERNATIONAL CAR RENTAL COMPANIES		
Avis	☎ 800-331-1212	www.avis.com
Budget	☎ 800-527-0700	www.budgetrentacar.com
Dollar	no toll-free number	www.dollar.com
Hertz	☎ 800-654-3001	www.hertz.com
National	☎ 800-227-7368	www.nationalcar.com
Thrifty	☎ 800-847-4389	www.thrifty.com

See Getting Around in each island section for local numbers of international companies and listings for local rental agencies.

Taxis

Taxis are plentiful in tourist areas on all three islands. Fares are not metered, but prices are fixed at government-approved rates between many common destinations, such as from the airport to major hotels. Each driver is supposed to carry an official rate schedule, so ask to see it. If your destination isn't listed, negotiate a price before you get into a cab, and confirm that the rate is quoted per trip, not per passenger.

Surcharges are added late in the evening and on Sundays and holidays. There should not be additional charges for luggage, unless a bag is very large or there are too many pieces to allow the trunk to close securely.

Do plan to tip extra if the driver helps you with your luggage, usually 50¢ to $1 per bag, depending on the size and weight. Unless the driver overcharges, is rude, or takes you out of your way, plan to add at least a 10% tip to the fare. US dollars and local currency are accepted, but don't expect the driver to have change for large bills.

Most drivers will not allow you to get into their taxi wearing wet swimsuits, so make sure you're dry and wearing some type of coverup.

TAXI DISPATCH	
Aruba	☎ 297-582-2116
Bonaire	☎ 599-717-8100
Curaçao	☎ 579-869-0747

Buses

Aruba has an excellent bus system, but public transportation is limited on Curaçao and almost nonexistent on Bonaire. See *Getting Around* in each island's chapter for specific information.

Accommodations

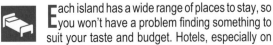

Each island has a wide range of places to stay, so you won't have a problem finding something to suit your taste and budget. Hotels, especially on Aruba, go all out to attract patrons with features such as fitness clubs, casinos, health spas, constantly-irrigated gardens, and oversized swimming pools. Some resorts offer all-inclusive packages that cover meals, drinks, and activities. If you're looking for seclusion, you'll find it at smaller inns, villas, apartments, or condominiums.

Rates drop around mid-April, and this is when families and budget-minded travelers fill the hotels. Regardless of season, you can probably get the best rates if you opt for a package deal, either through a tour operator or from the resort itself.

Expect hotels to add government taxes and service fees to the bill. Some also add an energy fee. Ask if the quoted rates include these charges before you book accommodations.

The section for each island includes an accommodation price range for individual hotels. Use these prices as a guide to the average high-season rate per standard double room. If the review is for an all-inclusive or all-suites resort, the listed price is the lowest available during high-season for two people sharing a room.

Getting Married

Aruba

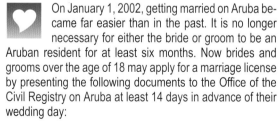

On January 1, 2002, getting married on Aruba became far easier than in the past. It is no longer necessary for either the bride or groom to be an Aruban resident for at least six months. Now brides and grooms over the age of 18 may apply for a marriage license by presenting the following documents to the Office of the Civil Registry on Aruba at least 14 days in advance of their wedding day:

- *birth certificates for each person*
- *a legal document proving divorce or death of a spouse if either the bride or groom has been married before*

- *a written request for a marriage license*

If you won't be on the island at least 14 days before the wedding, it is probably safest to send your documents by courier service. You may also mail or fax the documents to: **Bureau Burgerlijke Stand En Bevolkingsregister**, Schoolstraat #2, Oranjestad, Aruba, Dutch Caribbean, ☎ 297-583-4400, fax 297-839160.

After the documents are verified, both the bride and groom must appear before the registrar with two witnesses in order to pick up the marriage license, which is valid for one year. All the major resorts on the island can help you with plans for the ceremony, reception, and honeymoon.

The simpler way is to get married in a civil ceremony by a justice of the peace or a municipal judge before you leave home, then have a religious service on Aruba. In that case, couples simply contact the church and government officials in advance, and present proof of their marriage once they arrive on the island.

Every religion has a different set of regulations for church marriage ceremonies. Confirm the following information with a church official on the island well in advance of the wedding day.

 A boat captain is not authorized to officiate at a wedding, according to Dutch law.

Catholic Church

The bride and groom must provide proof that they attended pre-wedding preparation at their home parish.

The couple must bring a permit for marriage in Aruba from their parish priest.

The couple must present an official form stating that neither of them has ever been married in a church ceremony.

A minimum donation of $70 must be made to the church.

A priest will not perform a religious wedding outside of the church building.

Contact one of the following priests well in advance of the planned Catholic wedding in Aruba:

Father Ray Nares
St. Franciscus Parish
Irausquinplein 3
Oranjestad, Aruba
☎ 297-821-434

Father Anthony L. Boks
St. Anna Parish
Noord 16
Oranjestad, Aruba
☎ 297-871-409; fax 878-554

Protestant Church

To make advance preparations for a Protestant wedding ceremony, contact:

Pastor Anthony van der Doel PhD
Bilderdijkstraat 7
Aruba
☎ 297-821-435 (church), or 821-961 (home)

Couples may choose to have the ceremony in one of the church buildings, at a hotel, or on the beach. A $200 fee is charged for the ceremony and wedding certificate.

Non-Protestants may ask to be married in the Protestant Church.

Synagogue

Both the bride and groom must submit a verification of Judaism from the rabbi of their home town. In addition, if either the bride or groom has been married in a Jewish ceremony before, they must provide a Jewish divorce certificate to the rabbi.

Also, a petition to the Jewish Community should be submitted to the following address:

Travel Information

Aruba Jewish Community Israelische Gemeente-Bet Israel

Adriaan Lacle Blvd 2

Box 655

Oranjestad, Aruba

☎ 297-823-272

A fee is determined in advance for the ceremony, use of the chuppah, and a call to the Torah on the Shabbat preceding the wedding day. Couples may choose to get married in the synagogue or another location.

 If you are considering an Aruban wedding, request a copy of the new abridged marriage laws from the Aruba Tourism Authority, ☎ 800-TO-ARUBA (in the US), 800-268-3042 (in Canada); www.aruba.com.

Bonaire

Barefoot-on-the-sand weddings are a specialty on Bonaire. Some couples wear traditional formal attire, except for the shoes; others opt for island-casual outfits or even swimsuits. Whatever your preference, make contact with someone on the island and start the preparations and paperwork six weeks before the big day. Here are the rules:

- Either the bride or groom must obtain a temporary residency permit from Immigration by presenting two passport photos plus a photocopy of the signature/photo page of their passport.
- When applying for the official marriage petition, both the bride and groom must present a photocopy of the signature/photo page of their passport, an original birth certificate, and a Declaration of Marital Status by the Civil Registry (☎ 717-5300).
- If either the bride or groom is divorced or widowed, they must show the final divorce decree or the death certifi-

cate for their former spouse in order to get a Declaration of Marital Status.

- It takes four business days to get the marriage license.
- The marriage license costs $150.
- No blood tests are required.
- The location of the ceremony must have government approval in advance.
- Non-resident witnesses must apply for temporary residency.
- Wedding coordinators on the island can arrange for locals to act as official witnesses.

Currently, only Christian churches exist on the island, but an Islamic mosque is being built. A wedding consultant (see suggestions below) can arrange for a church wedding, or you can contact one of the following for information and requirements:

Bonaire Christian Fellowships, ☎ 717-4835.

San Bernardo Roman Catholic Church, ☎ 717-8304.

Seventh Day Adventist Church, ☎ 717-4254.

The Church of Jesus of Latter-Day Saints (Mormon), ☎ 717-8751.

International Bible Church, ☎ 717-8800.

Many couples choose to have their wedding at the courthouse in Kralendijk, then celebrate with friends and family at a reception in one of the hotels. **Buddy Dive Resort** (☎ 717-5080), **Captain Don's Habitat** (☎ 717-8290), and **Plaza Resort** (☎ 717-2500) frequently host wedding ceremonies and receptions.

No matter what type of wedding you plan, the following companies can offer invaluable assistance and advice:

Central Government Offices (call for information, regulations, and business hours, ☎ 717-5300).

ABC-Yachting, ☎ 790-5353; fax 717-5622; www.abc-yachting.com.

Bonaire Sight Seeing Tours, ☎ 717-8778; fax 717-4890; www.bonairetours.com.

Multro Travel & Tours, ☎ 717-8334; fax 717-8834; www. bonaireweddings.com; e-mail info@BonaireWeddings. com.

Scuba Vision Wedding Filming, ☎ 717-2844.

Curaçao

Couples who wish to get married in Curaçao must start the paperwork early. Up to two months is required to get a marriage license after a written request is made by a non-Antillean resident.

All the major resorts have wedding consultants who will guide you through the process, but the basic requirements are:

- Both the bride and groom must be temporary residents of the island for at least three days.
- The couple must apply for a non-resident marriage license and present passports and birth certificates.
- If either the bride or groom have been married before, they must provide an official divorce decree or a death certificate for their former spouse as proof that they are legally eligible for marriage.
- Couples must present return airline tickets as proof that they intend to leave the island.
- No blood tests are required.
- A $167 fee is charged for the marriage license.

Locals follow traditional island rituals when planning a wedding, with civil ceremonies taking place quietly during the day, and church ceremonies taking place in the evening. Formal weddings tend to be very elaborate. This tradition began during the island's early days when slaves were not permitted to marry, and only people with the most money and highest social status held big weddings.

Your resort or wedding consultant will help you arrange for a church wedding, or you can contact one of the following for information:

Antiano Baptist Church, ☎ 437-8262.

Church of Jesus Christ of Latter-Day Saints (Mormon), ☎ 437-2686.

Ebenezer Protestant Church, ☎ 465-3121.

Jehovah's Witnesses, ☎ 461-7528.

Methodist Church, ☎ 437-5834.

Santa Famia Roman Catholic Church, ☎ 462-5627.

Mikvé Israel-Emanuel Synagogue, ☎ 461-1633.

Seventh Day Adventist Church, ☎ 468-7590.

Receptions on the island are usually big, boisterous affairs with a lot of food and drink. One entire table is dedicated to a variety of cakes, including a white multi-tiered cake and the local (and quite expensive) bolo pretu or dark fruit cake. Guests look forward to leaving with a nicely wrapped piece of bolo pretu to enjoy at home.

For a perfect Curaçao wedding, contact:

Wedding Services Curaçao
Ask for Mrs. Violet Nicholas or Mr. Rob Spek
☎ 463 6207; fax 463-6684; www.wsc.an.

Check out the website for **Caribbean Weddings** *at www.caribbeanweddings. com. Information includes which island is right for you, resorts that offer wedding or honeymoon packages, and general island information, including the most romantic spots.*

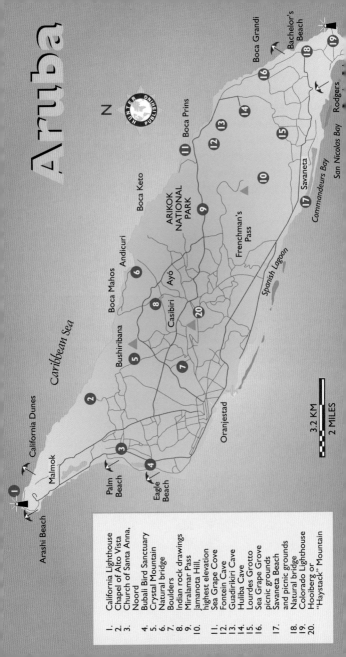

Aruba

Caribbean Sea

N

HUNTER PUBLISHING

ARIKOK NATIONAL PARK

California Dunes

Arashi Beach

Malmok

Palm Beach

Eagle Beach

Oranjestad

Bushiribana

Boca Mahos

Andicuri

Boca Keto

Casibiri

Ayó

Frenchman's Pass

Spanish Lagoon

Boca Prins

Boca Grandi

Bachelor's Beach

Rodgers

San Nicolas Bay

Commandeurs Bay

Savaneta

Noord

3.2 KM

2 MILES

1. California Lighthouse
2. Chapel of Alto Vista
3. Church of Santa Anna, Noord
4. Bubali Bird Sanctuary
5. Crystal Mountain
6. Natural bridge
7. Boulders
8. Indian rock drawings
9. Miralamar Pass
10. Jamanota Hill, highest elevation
11. Sea Grape Cove
12. Fontein Cave
13. Guadirikiri Cave
14. Huliba Cave
15. Lourdes Grotto
16. Sea Grape Grove picnic grounds
17. Savaneta Beach and picnic grounds
18. Natural bridge
19. Colorado Lighthouse
20. Hooiberg or "Haystack" Mountain

Aruba
Overview

Aruba is one of the most popular destinations in the Caribbean. Although it's the smallest of the ABC Islands (just over 19 miles long and six miles across its widest section), it has done the most to promote itself as a tourist destination. Visitors have fallen for the hype and returned again and again for the excellent beaches, perfect weather, superb resorts, and lively nightlife.

California Lighthouse
(Stuart Cummings)

The vivacious capital of **Oranjestad** (oranJUStat) is packed with boutiques, restaurants, casinos, and nightclubs. Its lovely Dutch architecture mixes with bright Caribbean color to create a theme-park-like downtown waterfront area.

Just to the north, a dazzling white beach stretches up the west coast. A string of low-rise hotels and casual restaurants line up along the sand and directly across a narrow road.

Less than a half-mile farther north, the high-rise resorts, glitzy casinos, and chic restaurants begin. The landmark **California Lighthouse** stands at the island's northernmost point.

South of Oranjestad, a good road leads to the fishing village of **Savaneta**, the former capital, and **San Nicolas**, the second-largest town on the island. Inland, the terrain turns rugged, good roads taper into rutted dirt paths, and adventurous tourists discover a wild countryside full of cacti, iguanas, and house-sized rock formations.

The wave-battered **east coast** features sand dunes, limestone cliffs, and a boulder-protected **Natural Pool**. **Arikok National Park**, just south and inland from the pool, covers almost 20% of the island and protects a vast ecological wonderland of exotic plants and animals.

Natural Pool (Aruba Tourism Authority)

A Dozen Reasons to Visit

- Best beaches in the ABCs.
- Colorful Dutch architecture.
- Luxury resorts with all the amenities.
- Friendly residents who welcome tourists in many languages.
- A wild, arid countryside with spectacular geological formations.
- Great dive sites and the largest shipwreck in the Caribbean.
- Constant trade winds for windsurfing.
- An eco-friendly national park.
- A Robert Trent Jones, Jr.-designed championship golf course.

- World-class casinos and nightclubs.
- Shopping malls and designer boutiques.
- Reasonably priced restaurants with international cuisine.

MAKING CALLS

To call Aruba from North America, dial 011-297 + the six-digit local number. To call from Europe or most other countries, dial 00 + 297 and the six-digit number. On Aruba itself, dial only the seven-digit local number.

Unique Celebrations

In addition to the traditional holidays celebrated on all three islands, Aruba observes some of its own:

January 25 is set aside to honor **G.F. (Betico) Croes**, a political leader who helped the island attain *status aparte* in 1986.

March 18, **National Anthem and Flag Day**, features folkloric presentations at Plaza Betico Croes in Oranjestad and sporting events throughout the island.

May 1, **Labor Day**, is celebrated with sports competitions, dances, and picnics.

June 24, **Saint John's Day** or **Deramento Gai** (the burying of the rooster), features lively music, bright yellow and red costumes, and traditional dances. It is celebrated on the

Deramento Gai (Fernando Arroniz)

Feast of St. John the Baptist to give thanks for a successful harvest. At one time, the festival included a game requiring blindfolded men to smash about with heavy sticks until one of them clobbered a rooster that had been buried up to its neck in dirt and covered with a hollow gourd so that it could breathe. Today, the live rooster has been replaced with a toy replica or a ripe calabash gourd.

Annual Events

For information and exact dates on upcoming events, contact the Special Events Department of the Aruba Tourism Authority, ☎ 582-3777, 800-862-7822 (in the US and Canada), or 297-582-3777 (on Aruba). A month-by-month calendar is online at www.aruba.com/calendar/month.php.

Getting Here

By Air

If you arrive by air, you will land at the newly expanded and modernized **Queen Beatrix International Airport (AUA)**, a short distance from the capital of Oranjestad. Unless several planes land at once, you'll get through Customs quickly and in air-conditioned comfort. Free baggage carts are available, and you'll find the Caribbean Mercantile Bank and an ATM to your left as you exit the terminal. New restaurants and shops may be open by the time you visit, but most facilities are located beyond the security checkpoint in the departure terminals.

Tourist information is available inside the arrival terminal, after you leave the baggage claim area. Taxis meet all flights, and car rental offices are directly across the narrow road in front of the terminal.

As part of an agreement with the taxi union, the government prohibits hotels from providing shuttle service from the airport. Tour operators arrange bus transportation

Reina Beatrix International Airport
(Fernando Arroniz)

from the airport to hotels for their package vacationers, but everyone else must take a taxi or pick up a rental car.

 See Getting Here *in the Travel Information chapter for additional airline information.*

Aruba

LOCAL AIRLINE CONTACT INFORMATION	
American Airlines/ American Eagle	☎ 297-582-2700; www.aa.com
Avianca-SAM (AVI-SA)	☎ 297-582-5484; www.avianca.com
Continental Airlines	☎ 297-588-0017; www.continental.com
Delta Airlines	☎ 297-588-6119; www.delta.com
Dutch Antilles Express	☎ 297-588-1900; www.flydae.com
Insel Air	☎ 297-582-2663; www.fly-inselair.com
Jet Blue	☎ 297-588-5388; www.jetblue.com
KLM - Royal Dutch Airlines	☎ 297-582-3546; www.klm.com
Santa Barbara Airlines	☎ 297-588-6441; www.sbairlines.com
US Airways	☎ 297-800-1580; www.usairways.com
United Airlines	☎ 297-582-9592; www.united.com

American Airlines hosts a VIP lounge across from gates seven and eight for their business class departing passengers. It's open daily, 6 am-9 am and 11:30 am-4:30 am.

By Cruise Ship

Cruise ships in the harbor (BC Pictures)

It's not unusual to see two or three large cruise ships docked at Aruba's modern cruise ship terminal in Oranjestad. About half a million visitors arrive by ship each year, and many return.

A tourist information booth and ATM are at the terminal, and Oranjestad's restaurants, shops, museums, and casinos are within walking distance. Most stores open on Sunday and stay open late on week nights when a ship is in port.

If you don't sign up with your cruise line for a shore excursion, you can take a taxi or bus to the beach or hire a driver for a private island tour. Taxis meet arriving passengers at the pier, and the public bus terminal is just across the boulevard.

Tour operators and a selection of scheduled excursions are listed under Touring the Island, *page 67. For a schedule of cruise-ship visits, contact the* **Cruise Authority**, ☎ 297-583-3648; *www.arubabycruise.com.*

Leaving Aruba

Aruba's airport is staffed by agents of US Customs and Border Protection (CBP), so you clear Customs before you board a plane bound for the United States. This means no long reentry lines when you land in the US, but the process of clearing in Aruba is time-consuming, so arrive at least three hours before your return flight is due to depart. You are required to be through Customs an hour before the flight departs.

If you have questions about what you can bring home or the screening procedures, call **US Customs and Border Protection**, ☎ 297-583-1316.

The Aruba airport is independent and sets its own security regulations, even though it is staffed by US CBP agents. The list of prohibited objects has changed several times since the September 11 attacks, so contact your airline or consult the sign posted in the departure terminal for the latest information. For questions concerning prohibited merchandise and duty limits, contact CBP at ☎ 297-588-7240.

For up-to-date information on air travel to and from Aruba, see www.airportaruba.com.

 The $37 international departure tax is hidden in most ticket prices, but check when you make your purchase. If you do any island-hopping, you will be charged a separate airport tax. At publication time, the tax from Aruba to Bonaire had been lowered from $20 to $10, but the tax to Curaçao remained at $20. A transfer charge of $3 applies to all passengers changing planes in Aruba for flights to non-US destinations. Other fees may apply, but most are included in your ticket price.

Aruba

Getting Around

Taxis

Most taxi drivers own their cabs, so they generally drive safely and expect passengers to avoid damage to their vehicle. They won't allow you to overstuff their trunk or sit on their seats wearing wet clothes. Many drive vans that accommodate large groups and diving equipment. Arubans are typically happy people, and most taxi drivers have participated in the government's Tourism Awareness Program, so you can expect a friendly welcome when you step into their cab. Check fares before you accept taxi services, and tip generously if you have a pleasant ride.

Airport Taxi Service . . . . ☎ 297-582-2116
Island-wide Taxi Service. . . . . ☎ 297-587-5900
Best Taxi . . . . ☎ 297-588-3232

Official taxis' license plates are tagged with the letters TX. Also, fares are per taxi, not per person. Up to five passengers are allowed per taxi.

Taxi Rules & Fares

Confirm fares before you get into the taxi. Drivers do not accept $50 and $100 bills. All prices are per taxi, not per person (maximum of five passengers), and subject to change at any time. Surcharges are government-approved on Sundays ($1), official holidays ($3), and after midnight ($2). The minimum charge per ride is set at $4, and the per-hour hire rate is $35. Drivers may also charge $8 per 15 minutes while waiting for you. Expect to pay about $20 for the trip from the airport to any of the high-rise hotels and around $17 to go to one of the low-rise hotels. Taxi fares from the hotels to town range from $8 to $10.

By Car

Car Rentals

 Most airport car-rental offices are open from 8 am to 8 pm, but a few operate from 7 am to 11 pm. Others appear to open and close on a whim. When you make your reservation, verify that someone will be available at the times you wish to pick up and return your car. Some companies have a drop box for after-hour returns; others arrange for an adjacent office to handle the paperwork, if they plan to be closed during your arrival/ departure times.

Rental rates vary season to season, but they average about $40 per day for a small car with manual transmission, air-conditioning and unlimited mileage. You pay about $70 per day for a larger car or one with automatic transmission or four-wheel-drive. Weekly rates are available and may work out to be less per day. Insurance add-ons begin at $10 per day, but you may be responsible for $500 worth of damage, anyway. Check before you sign up.

INTERNATIONAL COMPANIES	
Avis	☎ 297-582-5496; www.avis.com
Budget	☎ 297-582-8600; www.budgetaruba.com
Dollar	☎ 297-583-0101; www.dollar.com
Hertz	☎ 297-588-7570; www.arubarentcar.com
National	☎ 297-582-5451; www.nationalcar.com
Thrifty	☎ 297-585-5300; www.thriftyaruba.com

LOCAL COMPANIES	
2 Plus Car Rental	☎ 297-582-0009, www.aruba2plus.com
Ace	☎ 866-978-5191 (toll-free), 297-583-0840, www.acearuba.com
Amigo	☎ 297-588-3296; amigocar.com

Aruba

Caribbean Car Rental	☎ 297-582-2515; www.caribbeancars-aruba.com
Econo Car Rental	☎ 297-582-0920; www.econoaruba.com
Economy	☎ 297-583-0200; www.economyaruba.com
Explore	☎ 297-582-5496; www.explorecarrental.com
More4Less Jeep & Car Rental	☎ 297-588-7255; www.more4less-aruba.com
Optima	☎ 297-583-2531; www.optimarentacar.com
Ruba Car Rental	☎ 297-583-1020; www.rubarent-aruba.com
Top Drive	☎ 297-587-1729; www.arubatopdrive.com
Toyota Rent A Car	☎ 297-583-4902; www.toyotacarrent-aruba.com
Tropic	☎ 297-993-0788; www.tropiccarrent.com

 If you plan to decline insurance coverage offered by a rental agency, verify in advance that the credit card you will be using covers you if you have an accident or damage the car. American Express and Visa Gold Card customers are not covered when they rent a sports car or four-wheel-drive vehicle.

By Bicycle, ATV & Motorcycle

 The best way to get around the island is by car, but Aruba is flat and many roads are in excellent condition, so biking or motorbiking are also possible. Traffic in Oranjestad is heavy, especially when a cruise ship is in port, and the main highways are busy during rush hours. Unless you're a skilled, experienced biker, stick to side-roads. An all-terrain or four-wheel-drive vehicle is best for the poorly paved or dirt roads in the countryside.

You'll pay about $5 per hour or $25 per day for a basic bicycle, $35 per day for a scooter, and $45 to $100 per day for a motorcycle. To roar around the island on a Harley will cost $150 per day during tourist season.

RENTAL COMPANIES

Aruba Ocean-View Bike & Locker Rental, Kamer lingh Onneststaat 72, Oranjestad, ℅ 297-593-8160.

Big Twin Aruba/Harley-Dividson, L.G. Smith Blvd 124A, Oranjestad, ☎ 297-582-8660; www.harleydavidson-aruba.com.

George's All Terrain Vehicles, Cycle Rental/Yamaha, L. G. Smith 124, Oranjestad, ☎ 297-583-2202.

Melchor Cycle Rental, Bubalbi 106B, Noord, ☎ 297-587-1787.

Road Runner ATV Rental, Kamer lingh Onnestraat 72, Oranjestad, ℅ 297-593-8160.

Semver Cycle Rental, Noord 22, Noord, ☎ 297-586-6851.

By Bus

 You can't get everywhere on Aruba by public bus, but frequent scheduled service runs to many areas Monday through Saturday from 6 am until 6 pm, with less frequent service from 6 pm until midnight. On Sundays and holidays, buses operate a light schedule between 6 am and 6 pm.

Have the correct change when you board. A one-way ticket is $1.30 or 3.25Afl, and round-trip fare is $2.30 or 4Afl. Stops are marked by a yellow *Bushalte* road sign. You can pick up a schedule at the Arubus station behind the Parliament Building on Zoutmanstraat in Oranjestad or at tourist information booths and hotel reception areas throughout the island. Regular routes run between San Nicholas on the southwest coast and the resorts along beaches on the northwest coast, with stops in Oranjestad.

 For information on bus routes contact **Arubus**, ☎ *297-588-2300.*

Touring the Island

You can tour tiny Aruba in one day. However, you will need to abandon the gorgeous leeward beaches for at least part of two or three days to explore the island well.

Many interesting sites can be reached on paved roads in a car, but consider renting a four-wheel-drive vehicle if you want to investigate the untamed windward side of the island. You'll be surprised at the difference between the suave resort areas and the striking outback.

Getting Oriented

 Many paved roads and all unpaved roads on Aruba are not named and have no street signs. Locals give directions by landmarks, which is not helpful if you don't know the island well. Also, Aruba is positioned in the sea at a tilted angle to true north, so the cocoon-shaped island's coastlines are neither north-south nor east-west. The residents of San Nicolas say their town is on the sunrise side (east) of the island. Most people, looking at a map, would say San Nicolas is on the southwestern coast. This book uses the following terms for identification of and directions to various sites:

The longest coasts are east (the **windward outback**) and west (the **leeward developed side**). **California Lighthouse** is on the northern point; **Colorado Lighthouse** is on the southern tip. **High-rise** and **low-rise hotels** are on the sandy beaches of the curved northwest coast.

Highways are numbered and lettered A or B. The letter signifies the direction of traffic, so Highway 1A is the same road as Highway 1B, with each going in the opposite direction. Road signs will differ depending on which direction you are traveling.

Guided Tours

- **De Palm Tours** is the principal tour operator on Aruba. Their representatives will probably greet you as you exit the airport or step off your cruise ship. The 4½-hour Discover Aruba tour stops at most of the major sites and includes a swim and snorkel at Baby Beach. Other half- and full-day tours include sightseeing aboard a large air-conditioned bus, off-road excursions to remote areas of the island in yellow Land Rover Defenders, visits to private De Palm Island, combo land-water-underwater adventures, off-island day-trips, and nighttime jaunts to the casinos, bars, and nightclubs. Most hotels have a De Palm Activities Desk, and there is a De Palm Tours Pier on Palm Beach. Contact the main office for information and reservations, ☎ 297-582-4400 (Aruba), 800-766-6016 (US); www.depalm.com.

- **ABC Tours** takes passengers on an Island Safari in their 24-passenger air-conditioned bus and runs Off Road Safaris in customized Land Rover Defenders that hold six, rather than the usual nine, passengers. Small 1groups, an adventurous spirit, unlimited soft drinks, and stops at often-missed sights make this energetic company a favorite. Most of their business is from word-of-mouth advertising by happy tourists. Give them a call, ☎ 297-582-5600; www.abc-aruba.com.

- **Wix Tours** is owned and operated by Marco Wix. His staff of friendly guides starts your vacation off right with round-trip transfer service from the airport to your hotel for $12 per person. After you're settled in, take the 4½-

hour tour of major sites in their 24-passenger air-conditioned bus. The $30 charge includes a stop at Baby Beach for a swim. The Jeep and Eco Adventure is a full-day-trip by Jeep to remote sites and the National Park, lunch, and snorkeling at Baby Beach. The $57 cost includes snacks and snorkel equipment. Book by phone or online, ☎ 297-586-0347; www.wixtours.com.

- **Pelican Adventures** are known for sea quests, but they also operate a land tour of intriguing sites and best-kept-secret places. Entertaining guides narrate as the air-conditioned bus travels across the island; passengers are encouraged to ask questions and offer feedback. Tours cost $30-$45 and you can book reservations by calling ☎ 297-587-2302; www.pelican-aruba.com.

See Adventures on Water, *page 86, for information on sightseeing by boat, snorkel/scuba trips, and party boats. Evening tours are listed under* Nightlife.

Walking Tour of Oranjestad

Tourists head into the bustling capital city to shop, eat, bar hop, and play the slot machines. But, you'll miss a lot if you don't take the time to stroll aimlessly through the streets and stop to visit the museums and historic sites.

Locate **Wilhelmina Park** on the main waterfront highway, L. G. Smith Boulevard, at the southeast end of down, just before the highway crosses a lagoon. This is an excellent place for rest and orientation. The lush park is named for Queen Wilhelmina of the Netherlands, who reigned for 50 years (1898-1948) and abdicated in favor of her daughter, Juliana, after ruling through two world wars. A statue of the popular queen stands on a green lawn in the center of the landscaped park.

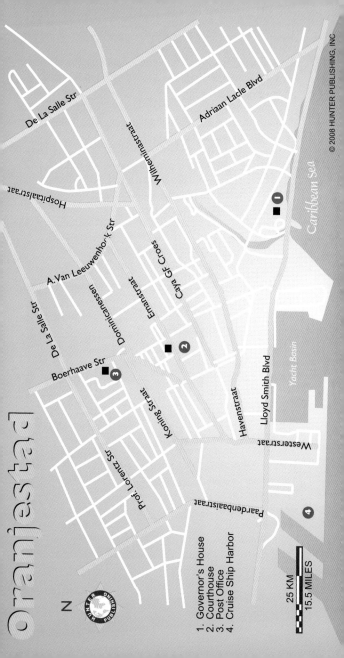

Oranjestad

N

De La Salle Str

Adriaan Lacle Blvd

Willeminastraat

Hospitaalstraat

Caribbean Sea

A. Van Leeuwenhoek Str

Caya GF Croes

Emanstraat

Dominicanessen

De La Salle Str

Boerhaave Str

Koning Straat

Havenstraat

Lloyd Smith Blvd

Yacht Basin

Prof. Lorenzstr.

Westerstraat

Paardenbaaistraat

1. Governor's House
2. Courthouse
3. Post Office
4. Cruise Ship Harbor

25 KM

15.5 MILES

HUNTER PUBLISHING

© 2008 HUNTER PUBLISHING, INC

The **Renaissance Hotel** is beyond the park, on the water at Paarden Baai/Bay, and the popular ★**Seaport Marketplace** (☎ 297-583-9190) is tucked between the north side of the park and the boat-filled yacht harbor. Across the main street, you'll see a sprawling marble World War II memorial set beside the lagoon.

> It helps to have a map, and you can pick up a free **Aruba Road Map** at any tourist information center, car rental office, or hotel reception desk. (A better choice is the laminated island and city map published by Berndtson & Berndtson. You may purchase one at hotel gift shops, or order it from a bookstore before you leave home.)

Walking toward town on Smith Blvd, you'll come to the **Historical Museum** (Museo Arubano) located inside the Willem III Tower at ★★**Fort Zoutman**, the oldest building on the island. It was built in 1796 and named after a rear admiral in the Dutch navy who had an honorable fighting record against the British.

Willem III Tower at Fort Zoutman
(Fernando Arroniz)

Did You Know? *The capital was named for the royal Dutch house of Orange-Nassau in the 1800s.*

The coastline ran alongside the fort until the harbor was filled in during construction in 1930, so the fort's four cannon were well placed to protect the island from 19th-century pirates and foreign navies. It's worth the $2 admission just to get inside the building. The haphazardly arranged displays include fossils, tools, furniture, and other items from the island's earliest times to the present.

Today, you can visit the Historical Museum inside the restored fort's walls weekdays, 10 am-noon and 1:30-4:30 pm. ☎ 297-582-6099.

If you want to take a break or do some shopping, continue past the yellow Parliament Building and Government Offices to the ★**Seaport VillageMall** and the businesses along **Main Street**, directly behind the Renaissance Resort.

Otherwise, turn inland on Oranjestraat and walk a block northeast to Zuidstraat 7 (near the Chamber of Commerce building and parking lot). Here you'll find the **Numismatic Museum of Aruba** (☎ 297-582-8831), also known as Mario's Worldwide Coin Collection. You don't have to be a coin collector to appreciate the 35,000 pieces in this treasury owned by Mario Odor and run by his daughter. It represents 400 countries, including ancient Rome, Greece, Egypt, and China, and is said to be much larger and more complete than the distinguished American collection in Colorado Springs. Facts and background are displayed with the coins, so if you have an interest in world history, put this stop at the top of your sightseeing list. The museum is open 7:30 am-3 pm; $5 admission fee. ☎ 297-582-8831.

Work your way north along Wilhelminastraat (behind the Renaissance Resort), to the **Protestant Church**, which was established in 1846 and is the island's oldest house of worship. Although the present building was built in 1952, it stands on the site of the original chapel. A small no-charge Bible Museum is open here on weekdays from 10 am until

noon, and services are held at 10:30 am on Sundays,
☎ 297-582-1435.

Turn right off Wilhelminastraat onto Emmastraat and head
east toward the best gallery on Aruba, the **Archeological
Museum** (Museo Archeologico Aruba). It's a bit of a walk,
but well worth it. The museum is in a courtyard behind San
Francisco Catholic Church (☎ 297-582-1434), near the
University of Aruba and the central post office. Inside the
small museum you'll find pre-Columbian pottery, burial urns,
tools, and cooking implements that have been uncovered
by both organized digs and random backyard encounters.
Some of the objects have been carbon dated to 500-900
AD. All the documentation is written in both English and
Papiamento. History/archeology buffs should allow plenty of
time for this small well-organized collection. Admission is
free, and the museum is open weekdays, 8 am-noon and
1 pm-4 pm, ☎ 297-582-8979.

Island-Wide Sightseeing

Don't miss the
★ ★ ★ **Butterfly
Farm**, just south of
the high-rise hotel
area. It's a 3,000-
square-foot mesh-
enclosed garden
with waterfalls and
stocked fish ponds.

Hundreds of majestic butterflies from all over the world flut-
ter freely to new-age music and land weightlessly on visitors. Try to visit when the doors first open in order to witness
new babies being born and get in on the most active part of
a butterfly's day. The $12 admission fee includes compli-
mentary return visits, so make this stop early in your vacation. Take the guided tour to learn amazing facts and hear
amusing stories about these gorgeous little creatures. Be-

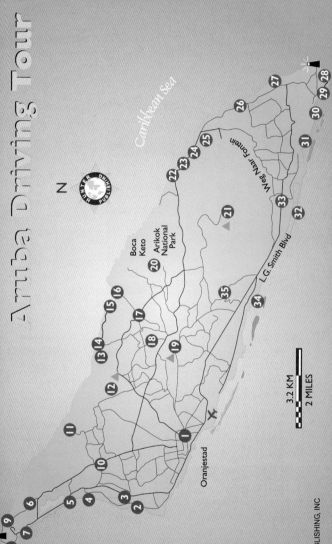

Aruba Driving Tour

Caribbean Sea

Boca Keto

Arikok National Park

Weg Naar Fontein

L.G. Smith Blvd

Oranjestad

3.2 KM

2 MILES

fore you leave, scoop up a couple of unique souvenirs from the gift shop and linger in the outside courtyard to enjoy refreshments in the company of liberated butterflies. The farm is open daily, 9 am-4:30 pm, with the last tour at 4. Located on Irausquin Blvd, across from the Divi Phoenix Hotel, ☎ 297-586-3656.

Bubali Plas Bird Sanctuary (Fernando Arroniz)

As long as you're in nature mode, stop by the **Bubali Plas Bird Sanctuary** to spy on local and migratory species that live and breed in the marshy vegetation around two man-made lakes. You can get into the area at any time, but the birds are most active just after sunrise and around sunset. Look for a dirt access road (marked Bubaliplas) to the observation tower. The road is about a mile north of town on Irausquin Boulevard. At the busy intersection near the Wyndham Beach Resort, turn east toward the big red windmill and watch for the dirt road on your right within 200 yards. The observation tower is visible several hundred yards farther along. A climb to the covered deck allows you a good view of the interconnected lakes and lush greenery where blue heron, egrets, ducks, terns and up to 80 other species of birds feed. There are no signs to help you identify what you're looking at, so bring a birdwatchers' book if you want to know. No charge, no set hours, no phone.

The little ★★ **church of Santa Anna** in the village of Noord is a popular place for weddings because of the beautiful light that pours through stained-glass windows into the high-ceilinged sanctuary. Originally constructed in 1766, the building was rebuilt in 1831, 1886, and 1916. You can see a portrait of the last builder, F a t h e r Saddelhoff, at the 12th station of the cross. The altar, pulpit, and communion rails are solid oak and were carved in neo-Gothic style

Church of Santa Anna

by Dutch craftsman, Hendrik van der Geld. The work received high praise when it was displayed at the Vatican Council exhibition of 1870, and Aruba received the masterpiece in 1928. You may be able to get inside on weekdays, and Catholic mass is held Monday, Wednesday, Friday at 6:30 pm, Saturday at 7 pm, and Sunday at 7:30 am and 6 pm. Look for the church on Caya Francisco D. Figueroa, south of Highway 3A/B, inland from Palm Beach, ☎ 297-587-1409.

From Santa Anna Church, take Smith Blvd (Highway 1A/B) north, past the high-rise hotels and the village of Malmok, to an elevated stretch of land on the far north end of the island. This isolated area is known by its Caiquetio name, Hudishibana, but most people call it the California Dunes because of the mounds of white sand that surround the focal point, the ★★**California Lighthouse**.

The stone lighthouse was designed by a French architect in 1910 and then constructed on Aruba between 1914 and 1916. It's named after the S.S. *California*, a wooden-hulled

Aruba

California Lighthouse (Fernando Arroniz)

barquentine (or barkentine, a three- to five-masted sailing ship) that sank near shore more than a century ago. The coral-encrusted wreck is popular among underwater photographers, but rough seas and strong currents make it difficult to reach and advisable only for advanced divers on a calm day.

Did You Know? You may read elsewhere or hear tour guides claim that the S.S. California *was the ship that disregarded distress signals from the sinking* Titanic. *In fact, the captain who failed to respond to the "mayday" signals was aboard another liner, named simply* California. *That vessel was hit by a German torpedo during World War I and sank near southern Greece.*

You can't go inside the lighthouse, but stand on the plateau and look out over the sea, down the coast at a string of fabulous beaches, and across the sand dunes to the irrigated greens of Tierra del Sol Golf Course. Plan to be at the foot of the lighthouse late in the afternoon for a beautiful view of the sun setting to the west. You can grab a pizza from 3 until 6 pm at **La Trattoria El Farro Blanco**, the nearby Italian restaurant. The trattoria serves dinner after six. See *Where to Eat,* page 159, for a full review.

The prestigious residential/vacation golfing neighborhood of **Tierra del Sol** is just south and east of the lighthouse.

Tierra del Sol golf course (Fernando Arroniz)

Golfers should consider staying at the resort here or signing up for tee times on the championship course. Farther south, the windward east coast turns into a wild countryside called the *cunucu.* You'll need a four-wheel-drive vehicle to travel some of the roughest dirt roads and paths.

 If you don't have a vehicle that will handle off-road and poor-road driving, check your map for inland roads that lead from Noord, Paradera, and Santa Cruz to some of the most interesting east-coast sites.

Traveling to the Chapel of Alto Vista from Noord, look for a paved road on the left leading to a water tank on top of a 200-foot hill. The view from the top takes in the entire north end of the island and includes the high-rise hotels on Palm Beach, the California Lighthouse, and the golf course at Tierra del Sol.

Your first stop should be the peaceful ★**Chapel of Alto Vista**. It is often called the pilgrim's church, and you'll feel as though you're making a pilgrimage when you ramble up the winding cross-studded road to the tiny yellow chapel. The white crosses marking the stations of the cross along the road indicate this is a Catholic/Christian site, but people of

Aruba

Alto Vista Chapel (Fernando Arroniz)

all faiths come here to think, meditate, or pray. A priest says mass in the church once a week, and locals stop by regularly to offer adoration to the statue of the Virgin Marie of Alto Vista.

Venezuelan missionary Domingo Antonio Silvestre supervised the construction of the original church in 1750, with the help of Spanish settlers and Caiquetio Indians. The present building was erected in 1952 with funds collected on the island, and it is so tiny, stone pews had to be put up outside to accommodate all who wished to attend services.

> **Did You Know?** *The statue of the Virgin that is on display today is a replacement for one that was built in 1950 in the Netherlands with funds donated by Arubans. The original statue was destroyed by a vandal in 1997. A 200-year-old cross that is now at Santa Anna Church originally adorned the altar at Alto Vista. One of the two graves near the chapel holds the remains of the missionary Domingo Antonio Silvestre.*

A bit farther down the coast are the ruins of **Bushiribana Gold Mill** above the surf at Boca Mahos. Gold was found on Aruba in 1824, supposedly by a boy playing in a dry creek bed, and for several years locals were allowed to collect the precious metal and sell it at a government-fixed price. Thirty years later, the Aruba Island Gold Mining Company was

Bushiribana Gold Mill ruins (Mitsy Rae & Donald Rosborough)

granted all rights to the cache and built the large smelting works at Bushiribana. Today, you can climb around the tumbling-down heap of rocks that once housed the mill. Photographers love to take pictures of the impressive coastline from the highest points. The tapped-out gold mines are located inland near Cero Gerard.

> **Did You Know?** *The word "boca" or "boka" is both Spanish and Papiamento for mouth, and you will see it on maps wherever the sea has carved a bay or inlet.*

Just to the south is **Boca Andicuri**, until recently the site of Aruba's famous **Natural Bridge**. The stunning 25-foot-high, 100-foot-long natural limestone bridge toppled into the surf before dawn on September 2, 2005. The collapse was unexpected, but not at all surprising, since the bridge was actually all that remained of a cave that had crumpled long ago. Take time to walk down to the black-sand beach below the cliffs, but be aware that the ocean currents at Andicuri are powerful, and only good swimmers should venture into the water.

The Natural Bridge before it collapsed (Fernando Arroniz)

Another, shorter natural bridge is still standing on the southern curve of the bay, where the pounding surf has worn caves into the cliffs. It's well worth stopping there to watch the hypnotic spray that spews from the caves' hollows as the ocean crashes wildly against the bluffs.

 Driving Tip: Official road signs are rare, but you may be lucky enough to spot small, hand-lettered markers pointing in the general direction of the island's major sightseeing attractions, including Ayo Rock and the Boca Andicuri Natural Bridge. It helps to have a map, but not much, since there are few street signs. Maintain a pioneer spirit and you'll have a great adventure, even if you never get to your destination.

Make an inland detour to see the bizarre and intriguing rock formations at nearby Ayo. Regular cars must make a loop back toward Bushiribana, then south (veer left at "Ys" and intersections) to the ★**Ayo Rock Formations**, which are less than three miles west of the Boca Andicuri. These huge wind-carved boulders are like something out of a space fantasy, and geologists have not been able to explain how

Ayo rock formations (Fernando Arroniz)

these massive stones appeared on the otherwise flat and sandy island. Paths meander around through the area, and lead to a small cave with pictographs left by the Caiquetio Indians. Views from the top are spectacular, and you'll probably spot parrots in the trees. Open daily at no charge from 9 am to 5 pm.

Similar boulders are located at ★★**Casibari Rock Formations**, about two miles farther inland, off Hwy 4 A/B. Here, steps lead to the top of the rocks and a panoramic view of the countryside. Tunnels and narrow ledges make the climb interesting, but a bit tricky for very young children and those who are unsteady on their feet. Snacks, souvenirs, and drinks are sold at the refreshment stand, and the site is open at no charge from 9 am to 5 pm every day.

From the top of Casibari, you'll have a good view of 541-foot **Hooiberg** (Dutch for haystack), a local landmark that indeed resembles a stack of hay. Steps lead to the top and the climb is worth the effort. Try to visit on a clear morning when you'll have cooler air for climbing. If the visibility is good, you may be able to see the Venezuelan coast to the south.

Back on the east coast, south of Boca Andicuri, the fit and adventurous can hike over sand dunes along the coast. Everyone else will need a four-wheel-drive vehicle or a horse to reach spectacular **Boca Daimari** and **Boca Ketu**.

Aruba

When you see palm trees swaying in the breeze, don't assume you're delirious from too much sun. **Rancho Daimari**, now a horseback-riding establishment, was once a thriving coconut plantation. The first trees were planted in the 1600s – one of the first coconut plantations in the Caribbean.

 See Horseback Riding, page 111, for information on rides along the coast and through the national park.

A short distance to the south, just beyond Boca Ketu, is ★★★**Cura di Tortuga**, a natural pool. This small rock-enclosed seawater pool is difficult to enter and exit, and not worth the trouble, unless you just want to cool off. However, it is worthwhile to climb up onto a boulder to watch the ocean surf break over the rocks and cascade into the basin. Forget about snorkeling on most days. The water is too churned up. Visit the pool for the magnificent views.

Arikok National Park (perfectpicturesaruba.com)

★★★**Arikok National Park** is Aruba's ecological treasure. It protects a large triangle-shaped portion of land bordered on the east by the sea from Boca Daimari to Boca Prins. The apex of the triangle is inland, just west of Mount Arikok, near the center of the island. Follow signs for Parke Nacional Arikok from the town of Santa Cruz to the entrance of the park located on the left a short distance beyond the paved road.

The enclosed wilderness preserve has 21 miles of marked hiking trails that showcase the island's native plants and animals, as well as early Indian rock art and historic structures. Among the desert vegetation in the park, are divi-divi trees, rare and exotic cacti, aloe plants, and colorful tropical flowers. Critters living in the reserve include the local conejo rabbit, indigenous Kododo Blauw lizards, and the endemic Cascabel rattlesnake. The park is open daily from 8 am to 4 pm; ☎ 297-582-8001.

Cunucu Arikok (Fernando Arroniz)

A path from the national park parking lot leads to **Cunucu Arikok**, a somewhat restored farm at the foot of 500-foot Cero Arikok. (Look for the airport radar station on the top.) Follow the walking trail through the outdoor exhibit that includes a typical *cunucu cas di torto* (a country house made of mud-and-grass adobe), planting areas that once grew a variety of crops, and stone walls and cactus fences that were built to keep out farm animals. The farmland is a popular hangout for rabbits, reptiles, and birds, and they will keep you company as you rest on one of the shaded benches along the path.

Gardeners may be interested in the aloe exhibit at **Masiduri Cunucu House and Experimental Gardens**, an area made fertile by intersecting creek beds in the hills west of Mount (or Cero) Jamanota. During the 1950s, the experimental garden grew a variety of plants, but today primarily aloe and eucalyptus provide sanctuary for lizards, iguanas, snakes, and wild donkeys. Before you leave the area, drive to the top of 564-foot **Cero Jamanota**, the highest point on the island. The views are terrific.

Geology buffs and nature lovers should schedule time to explore the unique rock formations, sand dunes, and coastal limestone cliffs between **Dos Playa** and **Boca Prins**. Strong currents make the water unsafe or unpleasant for swimming on most days, but photographers will find glorious landscapes and sea vistas, especially at Boca Prins where the ocean has carved a natural bridge known as Dragon Mouth. The young at heart will want to slide down the sand dunes at Boca Prins; sunbathers prefer the wide span of sand at the more northen of the two beaches at Dos Playa.

Fontein, **Guadirikiri**, and the **Tunnel of Love Caves** are worth a visit, but come early in the morning or late in the afternoon because the caves are hot and airless. **Fontein**, just south of Boca Prins, has perhaps the island's best Indian art and early-European graphics on the walls and ceiling. A guide will point out limestone stalactites and stalagmites that resemble animals and religious figures. You may need a strong imagination to appreciate the similarities.

Guadirikiri Cave (Fernando Arroniz)

Guadirikiri is a two-chamber cave with skylights, so there is more air and natural light inside. A long tunnel here is home to hundreds of bats that sleep during the day. Come at dusk to see them swarm out of the cave in search of dinner. The **Tunnel of Love** gets its name from the heart-shaped stone entrance. Pick up a flashlight from the stand at the entrance (you'll be charged a $6 fee) because the 300-foot-long tunnel is totally dark. A guide will point out various formations as you inch your way along, and will entertain you with tales of pirates' treasure.

The road from the Tunnel of Love takes you south and west past the International Raceway Park, where it becomes Highway 7A/B, leading to the town of San Nicolas.

San Nicolas

The rich aroma of oil once again hangs over Aruba's second-largest town. At one time, the world's largest refinery produced crude oil from Venezuela in San Nicolas, but a world-wide glut closed that plant in 1985. Texas-based Coastal Oil bought out the former owners and reopened in 1990, but by that time the entire island had turned from oil to tourism as its economic mainstay. Today, San Nicolas is looking pretty good as a slow-paced free-thinking village. New residents are moving in, building lovely homes, and demanding more creature comforts, such as restaurants, shops, and churches.

Aruba's Carnival got its start here, and each year the streets ring with music as costumed residents from all over the island parade through the streets behind

Charlie's Bar

tambú bands. The rest of the year, the town is quieter, and tourists enjoy wandering the uncrowded streets to view the 1950-ish art deco buildings. **Charlie's Bar** is unquestionably the most famous landmark and has been drawing a crowd since 1941. Take time to have a drink and look at the museum of jumbled treasure that covers every inch of the restaurant and bar. Scuba divers, fishermen, sportsmen, and entertainers have left a half-century of memorabilia stuck to the walls and ceiling. ☎ 297-584-5086.

Savaneta

Heading back towards Oranjestad along the west coast, you'll pass through the village of Savaneta, the island's first Dutch settlement and original capital. Today, the town is populated by fishermen and tourists stop for a sunset drink or dinner at the popular **Brisas del Mar** and **Flying Fishbone** restaurants (see pages 161). The new-age **Cosmos Day Spa** has a loyal following among those who enjoy pampered beach-side seclusion.

> *Did You Know? While driving through the old settlements south of Oranjestad, watch for cas di torto homes that date back 150 years. These traditional Aruban houses were constructed of mud-and-grass adobe smeared on supports made of braided branches. Most of the originals have been destroyed by time and weather, but a new cas is being built using authentic techniques and materials on a dirt road near Boca Prins in the national park.*

Adventures on Water

Warm, crystal-clear seas make Aruba the ideal vacation destination for watersports fans. Swimming and snorkeling are safe all along the leeward coast, and outfitters provide equipment for every type of water activity. Calm coves allow for leisurely kayaking, and constant trade winds across open water provide excellent conditions for sailing and windsurfing. Fishing charters, sightseeing cruises, and party boats guarantee guests a good time. Beneath the surface, divers explore Aruba's reefs and wrecks, and non-divers share their enthusiasm from a dry underwater observatory or the *Atlantis* submarine.

Best Beaches

You won't find a bad beach anywhere along Aruba's leeward side. All are public, clean, and easily accessible. Many are outfitted with lounge chairs, tables, and shade umbrellas intended for use by guests of the nearby resorts. Others have no facilities, but offer more privacy.

Porthole Cruise Magazine recently ranked Palm Beach and Eagle Beach as the best in the world. Referred to as the Turquoise Coast, the two beaches are noted for their seven-mile stretch of beautiful white sand conveniently located just 10 minutes by car from Oranjestad. Try to visit several beaches during your stay on the island. Each has a different ambience and you will need to sample a few to find the one that suits you best.

 Public nudity is illegal and offensive to Arubans. There are no official clothing-optional beaches, but you won't be bothered if you disrobe and stretch out on a sandy spot in a secluded cove. In the resort areas, you will see topless sunbathing on the beaches (particularly at Manchebo, Druif, and parts of Sonesta/Renaissance Island), but not around the pools.

★**Palm Beach** is lined with luxurious high-rise resorts that offer watersports equipment, chairs, and shade huts for guests. Mature palm trees provide additional shade, and the sand is groomed daily. The water is calm and excellent for swimming, but motorized water toys and crowds of people make this a busy, noisy area.

Palm Beach (Fernando Arroniz)

★**Eagle Beach** is directly south of Palm Beach, but a rocky outcrop separates the two and prevents foot travel between them. *Travel + Leisure Magazine* says this mile of soft white sand is one of the 10 best beaches in the world. Low-rise hotels and time-share resorts occupy the area, but the beach is wider than at Palm, so it is less crowded, quieter, and more laid-back. Locals take over the shaded picnic area on weekends, so arrive early to stake out your spot.

Punta Brabo & Eagle Beach (Fernando Arroniz)

Manchebo Beach is a continuation of Eagle, just to the south, and offers the widest unspoiled stretch of soft white sand on Aruba. Because the beach curves outward into the sea, the surf can be stronger than at Eagle or Palm. No motorized watersports are allowed, so the beach is quiet and uncrowded.

Arashi, **Boca Catalina,** and **Malmok Beaches**, near the California Lighthouse, are all part of the Arashi Underwater Park. Calm water, gentle currents, shallow reefs, and superb visibility make them popular swimming and snorkeling sites. There are a few shade huts at Arashi, but no other facilities. Snorkelers spot large elk horn coral, sponges, and schools of colorful fish six to 30 feet below the water's surface. Steady winds at Malmok draw windsurfers.

Hadikurari Beach, directly south of Malmok, is also called Fisherman's Huts, and is well-known for terrific windsurfing. The Hi-Winds Pro-Am Windsurfing Competition is held here each June, but colorful sails and accomplished surfers entertain spectators year-round. Shade huts and picnic tables are provided for public use. The water is clear and shallow enough to be good for swimming and snorkeling, but access is a bit hard on bare feet because of rocks near the water's edge.

Druif Beach, south of Manchebo Beach, is just beyond a curve in the island where the sand narrows, the surf becomes stronger, and pebbles make barefoot strolls more difficult. Nonetheless, several fine low-rise resorts are located here, and guests en-

Druif Beach (Fernando Arroniz)

joy windsurfing, swimming, and lounging on palm-shaded white sand.

Bushiri Beach is on the northern edge of Oranjestad, next to the container port of the Aruba Free Zone. While the industrial area to the south is unappealing, the beach itself is nice and the water is protected by a sea wall. The only way onto the beach is through the Bushiri Resort, and no motorized watersports are allowed, so it's a quiet and uncrowded spot.

Surfside Beach is on the southern edge of Oranjestad. While there are far better beaches, the location makes it convenient for locals who work in the capital city and tourists who need a shopping break. The water is calm and perfect for a refreshing swim.

De Palm Island is a private strand of luxurious white sand off the west coast, five minutes by ferry. De Palm Tours offers several package tours to the island, but it's possible to simply show up at the ferry terminal near Spanish Lagoon and purchase a ticket to the island for $10, which includes a beach-side drink. (Take Hwy. 1A/B south from Oranjestad, pass the airport, turn right at the first traffic light, then follow signs to the ferry terminal.) Once there, you can swim, snorkel, feed the sociable blue parrot fish, and sunbathe with lazy iguanas. The island has three snack bars, equipment rental shacks, a fishing pier, locker rooms, beach lounges, snuba tours (like scuba diving without wearing a tank) and sea trek adventures (similar to snuba, but with a watertight helmet instead of a breathing regulator and goggles). The ferry runs every half-hour from 10 am-6 pm daily; ☎ 297-582-4400.

Mangle Halto Beach is just south of Spanish Lagoon and its close-in reef is part of the same superb formation that extends to De Palm Island. Locals often picnic on the beach. The water is shallow, and nice for swimming, but rocks make entry into the water a little tricky.

Roger's Beach is adjacent to the oil refinery south of San Nicolas, and this is a turnoff for many. However, if you can

Roger's Beach (Fernando Arroniz)

overlook the smoke stacks and ignore the occasional smell of petroleum, this is a fabulous beach. Too bad the oil companies weren't concerned with environmental aesthetics back in 1924. Nothing seems to have leaked into the sea, and the water is fine for swimming and snorkeling. The beach itself is narrow, but the sand is white, and there's a snack bar that brings in local bands on the weekend. Boats belonging to local fishermen are anchored near the shore.

Baby Beach sits in a lovely lagoon at the island's southern tip, and, as its name implies, it is an ideal swimming beach for children. The water is shallow and calm; local families turn out on weekends to grill burgers and listen to music on their boom boxes. During the week, the area is fairly quiet. Strong swimmers and experienced snorkelers may want to go beyond the protected lagoon to the outer reef where the coral and fish are magnificent, but the water can be quite choppy. **Jads Beach Shop** sells snacks, drinks, and ice cream. The shop also rents snorkel equipment during business hours, Sunday-Friday, 9 am-5 pm; ☎ 297-582-6070.

Baby Beach (Fernando Arroniz)

As you round the southern tip of Aruba to the windward side of the island, the beaches become dramatically beautiful and wild. The water's edge is generally rocky, and the sand may be mixed with pebbles. **Bachelors Beach** and **Boca Grandi** are typical windward beaches. Both are often deserted, especially on weekdays, but you may see a few windsurfers, if the water isn't too rough. Snorkeling is excellent, and some tours stop here because of the magnificent elk horn coral on the protective reef, but the current and surf are frequently too robust for all but the strongest swimmers.

Boca Prins, inside the boundaries of Arikok National Park, is a popular spot for picnicking and sand-dune sliding, though not for swimming. Wear long pants if you plan to slide, and sneakers with good traction if you're going down the rocky cliffs to the surging surf at the water's edge. Since there are no paved roads, you will need a four-wheel-drive vehicle to reach the dunes, but the scenery is worth the trip.

Dos Playa does indeed have two beaches, as the name suggests. Turtles nest in the sand, and therefore vehicles are not allowed in the area. You must leave your jeep at Boca Prins and walk about 15 minutes north along the coast. The scenery is desert-stark and spectacular along the way. Crashing waves make it all but impossible to enter the water, so plan to simply enjoy the view.

Andicouri, near the natural bridge, has a black pebble beach that is considered one of the most beautiful in the Caribbean. Strong wind and big waves prevent most from entering the water, but avid body surfers sometimes plunge right in.

Adventures Underwater

French angelfish (Stuart Cummings)

The underwater world off Aruba's 17 miles of coastline is excellent for scuba diving, snuba, sea trekking, submarine tours, and glass-bottom boating.

Snuba is a step above snorkeling; a step below scuba diving. Participants breathe underwater, up to 20 feet below the surface, through an air-supply hose connected to a tank that floats on the surface. Using the snuba apparatus, divers as young as eight years of age can explore one of Aruba's colorful coral reefs or the *Antilla*, the largest shipwreck in the Caribbean. No experience necessary. Expect to pay about $60-$80 for a guided underwater snuba tour.

Snuba (Aruba Tourism)

For snuba and sea trekking information and reservations, contact De Palm Tours at your hotel or at their pier on Palm Beach, ☎ 297-582-4400.

Sea trekking is the newest underwater adventure. Participants wear an apparatus like a space-helmet that allows them to breathe underwater while their hair and face stay dry. It's not even necessary for trekkers to know how to swim. They simply put on the helmet, descend a ladder into the water, and walk around the sea floor. Tours are guided and narrated.

Onboard the Atlantis (Atlantis Submarines)

The *Atlantis VI* is an authentic 65-foot-long submarine that takes up to 48 passengers 150 feet below the surface to view shipwrecks, reefs, and sea creatures. Tickets are $74 for adults and $35 for children four-16. Trips leave every hour between 9 am and 2 pm daily.

For Atlantis VI and Seaworld Explorer reservations, contact the activities desk at your hotel or ☎ 888-546-7820 (in the US) or 297-588-6881 (on Aruba); www. atlantissubmarines.com/aruba.

The *Seaworld Explorer* is a semi-submarine. The upper portion remains above water while the air-conditioned observation deck is five feet below the surface. Passengers look through large windows at the *Antilla* shipwreck and the Arashi Reef. Tickets are $37 for adults and $20 for children two-12.

Scuba

Aruba is known as the Ship Wreck Capital of the Caribbean because of the number, quality, and accessibility of wreck sites off its coast, but the island also has intact natural reefs. Novices can shallow-dive with an instructor in placid waters during a resort course, while experienced divers take on swifter currents and greater depths. The strongest and most advanced divers will want to tackle crashing waves off the windward coast to explore the famous *California* wreck and the boulders near the Boca Andicuri Natural Bridge.

Aruba is surrounded by a shallow sandy embankment of reefs that are easily reached by boat from the west side of the island. Experts can shore dive off the northeast and southern coast. When cruise ships are in port, the most popular sites often get crowded with divers, boats, the *Atlantis* submarine, and the *Seaworld Explorer* all jockeying for a favorable position at the same time. Plan ahead so that you can dive these sites during off-season or at off-times. If you can't choose your time, elect to dive one of the less-visited sites.

Since visibility ranges from 60 to 100 feet, many of Aruba's underwater sites can be seen from the surface with only a mask and snorkel. Parts of the *Antilla*, the largest shipwreck in the Caribbean, stick out of the water or are close to the surface, so snorkelers enjoy exploring it almost as much as divers who descend up to 60 feet. Most dive operators will allow non-divers to go out with an organized group, if there's room on the boat.

Boat Dives

The ★**Antilla** wreck is famous. Its 400-foot-long hull sits in 60 feet of water about a half-mile off Aruba's north-

Diver at Antilla (Stuart Cummings)

At the Antilla *wreck (Stuart Cummings)*

west coast. Parts of the huge ship stick up above the water's surface, and more experienced divers may explore the wreck's large compartments in deeper water. Colorful sponges and corals attract schools of bait fish, colorful angelfish and yellowtail snappers; eels, octopus, and lobsters are there, but hiding in crevices, so they're more difficult to spot.

Locals refer to the *Antilla* as the ghost ship because it seemed to disappear when anyone tried to pursue it. The ship didn't have much history. It was a new German freighter anchored in Dutch territory off the northwest coast of Aruba when Germany invaded Holland in May, 1940. Aruban authorities became interested in the freighter near its shore, and speculated that the ship might be supplying German U-boats in the Caribbean. Whatever its purpose, the Allies didn't want the ship near Aruba, and the captain was given notice that he must surrender his ship in 24 hours. Before the one-day grace period was over, the captain charged the boilers and flooded the engine room. The resulting explosion almost blew the *Antilla* into two pieces. Then the freighter quickly sank below the surface near Malmok beach.

The ★*Pedernales*, a US flat-bottomed oil tanker, was hit by a German submarine in 1942 while it was bringing crude oil from Venezuela to the distillery on Aruba. The most damaged mid-section of the ship lies in 25-35 feet of calm water, so it's a favorite with novice divers. The forward and rear sections of the tanker were recovered and taken back to the US, where they were welded into a new smaller vessel that was

The Pedernales *(divewithjay.com)*

used to transport troops to Europe for the Allied invasion of Normandy in 1944.

Today, divers explore large pieces of the ship's crossbeams, wash rooms, and cabins that have been covered in coral formations. Various fish, such as groupers, trumpet fish, squirrelfish, and angelfish, feed on the artificial reef. Peek below large metal pieces to find colorful corals protected underneath.

The Aruba Watersports Association submerged a DC-3 and an oil tanker in 30 feet of water near the Pedernales *a few of years ago. Artificial reefs are growing up around them and will become interesting shallow dives soon – perhaps by the time you visit.*

Between the *Antilla* and the *Pedernales* wrecks, you'll find **Malmok Reef** and another wreck, the ★*Debbie II*. This is the area to photograph lobster, eels, and stingrays against a purple and orange background. The current is swift over the 70-foot-deep reef that features brain and leaf corals and large sponges. *Debbie II* was intentionally sunk in 1992 to form an artificial reef, and the 120-foot fuel barge attracts schools of barracuda.

The wooden-hulled **SS *California*** sank in 40 feet of water when it ran aground in choppy seas off the northeast coast about 50 years ago. As with the site near the Boca Andicuri Natural Bridge, also off the east coast, only experienced divers should attempt the descent due to very strong currents and rough seas. Photographers who do make the 30- to 45-foot dive return with colorful shots of sponges, anemones, and large corals. Sharks are sometimes seen in the area, but grouper and barracuda are more common.

Beginning divers find safe, calm seas around the northern tip of the island at Arashi Beach. Here, a twin-engine Beechcraft known as the **Arashi Airplane** sits in about 30 feet of water. The small plane once had the company of a Lockheed Lodestar, but that aircraft has deteriorated over the years. Brain corals and sea fans grow around the algae-encrusted fuselage, making it a popular hangout for hungry grunts, sergeant majors, and goatfish. Schools of colorful angelfish and round-faced pufferfish congregate in and around the cockpit, where eels take refuge during the day.

Near Oranjestad and the outer Sonesta and De Palm islands, several reefs and wrecks draw divers to depths of 40 to 90 feet. **Harbour Reef** and the nearby **Tugboat** wreck are directly out from the city's Seaport Casino. The water is typically calm here, and beginners can see a lot of color at shallow depths. Experienced divers can continue down the slope to look for rare eagle rays, stingrays, and seahorses. The old tugboat is overgrown with lovely coral and sponges, and colorful feeding fish create a rainbow of color around the hull.

Snorkelers can see plenty of fish around the disintegrated body of a sunken **Beechcraft** airplane near **Sonesta Island**. The water is normally calm in this area, and elkhorn, staghorn and fan corals grow among scattered pieces of the aircraft about 15 feet below. At around 40 feet, divers explore a still-intact **Convair-400**. Like the Beechcraft, it once belonged to drug runners. Now, curious divers explore its doorless cockpit and photograph the coral and algae encrusted propellers, which are still attached to the engines. Non-divers may get a look at the

Convair-400 at 60 feet (Stuart Cummings)

wreck through the windows of the *Atlantis VI* submarine.

South of the airplanes, four reefs provide excellent dive sites at various depths and with diverse conditions. **Sponge Reef** is perhaps the most colorful of all the reefs. Orange elephant ear sponges stand out against purple and yellow tubs sponges and turquoise vase sponges. Bring an underwater camera. **Barcadera Reef's** healthy corals can be viewed from depths of 20 to 80 feet, making it a versatile dive for a snorkel-dive group with mixed skills. Fish in the area include parrots, puffers, angels and the occasional barracuda. Waving sea fans on the sandy bottom create an undulating fantasy land.

Kantil Reef drops from 40 to 110 feet. Descend down the wall viewing huge brain and star corals, large gorgonian sea fans, and a variety of sea creatures, including eagle and manta rays. **Skalahein Reef** begins shallow, at about 15 feet, then slopes gently to 120 feet. Bring your camera to capture shots of barracuda with a backdrop of large brain and star corals. Lucky divers may spot seahorses.

★ *Jane Sea* wreck is considered one of the best dives because the freighter rests in an upright sloped position in a thicket of colorful corals and sponges. The 250-foot hull is totally encrusted with fire coral, orange cup coral, black coral, and red sponges. Sunk intentionally after it was

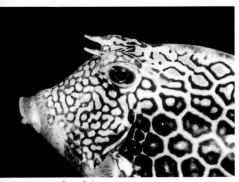

Cow fish (Stuart Cummings)

caught hauling cocaine, the Venezuelan ship's anchor lies at the bottom of an AWA-placed mooring rope. Divers swim with schools of fish along the anchor's rigid chain to a reef that leads to the bow of the ship in 50 feet of water. Watch for lobsters, barracuda, green moray eels, and colorful tropical fish. It's possible to enter the ship's compartments and the propellers provide great photo ops.

De Palm Island is considered the best snorkeling site off Aruba. Parrotfish are accustomed to being fed, and they come in mobs begging for handouts from anyone who gets into the water. Divers enjoy the drift dive and can go out from De Palm Island's shore or by boat from the main island. The coral reef starts 30 feet from De Palm in shallow water and quickly slopes to 120 feet. Moderately strong currents in clear water carry divers past magnificent coral formations and vast numbers of fish, including surgeons, grunts, blue tangs, and the occasional barracuda or nurse shark.

Mike's Reef is perhaps the best reef dive off Aruba. It's a rocky garden of gorgonians, purple and orange sponges, and various corals. Divers can photograph the outstanding formations then drift along to another nearby reef called **The Fingers**, so named because the coral seems to "point" downward to deeper water. Schools of colorful fish swim along and a lone barracuda often follows at a distance.

Mangel Halto Reef is excellent for snorkelers and divers. Located off a beach with the same name, between Pos

Chiquito and Savaneta on the southwest shore, the beautiful corals are visible in 15 feet of water about 300 yards from shore. From there, the reef slopes steeply to 110 feet, where the coral, sponge, and fan formations grow dense and draw huge numbers of fish, lobsters, and rays. Octopi and seahorses are frequently seen around the reef. Conditions are normally calm, so

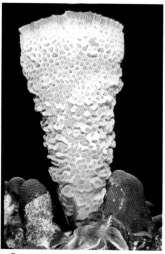

Deep sea gorgonia (Stuart Cummings)

divers may enter from the shore and swim out along the slope. This is considered one of the best deep-water dives on the island.

Pos (Porto) Chiquito is a terrific night dive, especially during coral-spawning season in September and October. Special dive trips are scheduled to coincide with the annual renewal of the reef, but conditions are excellent for shore excursions year-round. Sea turtles and manta rays live in the area, and the sloping reef supports an abundance of fish. Locals call the spot Snapper City because of the nocturnal snappers that are spotted in large numbers during night dives.

Isla di Oro Reef begins in 20 feet of water around the mangrove-lined shore near Savaneta. When the current is weak, it is an excellent snorkeling spot featuring brain, staghorn, star, and plate coral. Schools of parrotfish feed in the area. At greater depths (up to 120 feet), moray eels hide in caves, and divers spot lobsters, Spanish hogfish, and coral crabs moving among the sea fans.

Commandeurs, **Lago**, **Indian Head**, and **Cross Reefs** parallel the shore beginning just south of Savaneta. All three are excellent boat dives. Commandeurs drops from 40 to 90 feet and features ample marine life among sheet and leaf corals. Lago is a deep dive (100-120 feet) that shows off sea anemones, branching gorgonians, and many crustaceans. Indian Head has a large formation that resembles a human head and creates an ideal home for colorful fish. Star and brain coral are at 80 to 120 feet below the surface. The Cross Reef actually has a 10-foot memorial cross dedicated to San Nicolas embedded in the sand beside the reef. Lovely corals and sponges act as a backdrop to schools of fish as divers ride the current along the formations to depths of 60 feet.

Baby Beach Reef is off bathtub-like Baby Beach, with its warm, placid, shallow water. Snorkelers won't see much inside the lagoon, but if they tackle rougher seas outside the breakwater, they may spot lobsters and crabs hiding among large elkhorn and sheet corals at depths of 20 to 40 feet. At depths over 60 feet are more spectacular formations and greater marine life.

Expert divers may want to try drift diving from **Santana Di Cacho Reef** back to Baby Beach Reef. Entry at Santana is rough, but once divers are under water, the current takes them west, at a depth of 40 to 50 feet, along large formations with active and abundant marine life. The dive ends at calm Baby Beach.

Cabez Reef is located south of Colorado Point, at the southern tip of Aruba, where the surf is choppy and the current is swift. Expert divers enter from the shore and are rewarded for their battle with the sea by large numbers of fish that find the rapidly moving water delightful. Amberjacks, rainbow runners, barracudas, and stingrays are among the sea creatures commonly seen around Cabez.

*The nearest **recompression chamber** is located on Curaçao. In an emergency, dial 911 or go immediately to **Dr. Horacio Oduber Hospital**, across from Eagle Beach on L.G. Smith Blvd, ☎ 297-587-4300. Patients requiring hyperbaric treatment will be airlifted to Curaçao.*

Dive Operators

Snorkelers who wish to join a dive boat excursion will pay about $40 for the trip and $15 for equipment rental. Snorkel-specific outings begin at around $20.

One-tank dives run $40 (two-tank dives are $60), including tank and weights; other equipment is extra. Multi-dive and multi-day packages are available at a lower rate. Inclusive dive vacation packages are offered at many resorts.

If you would like to give scuba a try, resort courses cost approximately $75 and include a shallow dive. Complete certification courses run about $375.

DIVE OPERATORS

Dive Aruba
Bushiri Beach Resort, ☎ 297-582-7337; www.divearuba.com
A native Aruban owns and operates this shop. Classes are given mornings at Bushiri Resort, and morning and afternoon trips go out with small groups.

Red Sail Sports
Nine locations, including Hyatt, Marriott, Renaissance and La Cabana resorts, ☎ 877-733-7245 (toll-free in the US), 297-583-1603; www.redsailaruba.com
The largest watersports operator on the island, Red Sail offers a variety of trips and departure times. They have two custom-outfitted dive boats and four luxury catamarans.

Unique Sports
Aruba Grand Resort, ☎ 297-586-0096; www.visitaruba.com/uniquesports
The specialty here is tailored trips for small groups using two customized dive boats.

Aruba

Pelican Water Sports

Holiday Inn, La Cabana, and Wyndham Resorts, ☎ 297-587-2302; www.pelican-aruba.com

This large operation has three dive boats and offers trips to a variety of sites at diverse times.

Windie's Watersport

Palm Beach, ☎ 297-586-4026 (shop); 297-562-9740 (cell); www.windieswatersport.com

Look for husband-and-wife team Rene and Windie inside their dive shop on Palm Beach, across from Bella Luna Restaurant. They're experts in scuba instruction and snorkeling expeditions. Take time to browse through the large selection of books on underwater wildlife and take home one of their souvenir T-shirts.

Mermaid Sport Divers

Bubali 112-J, between the high-rise and low-rise hotels, ☎ 297-587-4103; 297-993-3920 (cell); www.scubadivers-aruba.com

Learn to scuba in record time with these PADI and NAUI instructors. Already certified? Check out their unlimited-diving packages. You get up to 20 boat or shore dives throughout the week at prices that average about $20 per dive.

S.E. Aruba Fly 'n Dive

L.G. Smith Boulevard, ☎ 297-588-1150; www.searuba.com

As one of the newest dive operators, this facility takes divers in small groups from Havana Beach. Fly-and-drive tours are available to Bonaire and Curaçao.

Native Divers

Noord (office location), ☎ 297-586-4763, 297-993-3960 (cell); www.nativedivers.com

Let this small operator take you to the reef off Pos Chiquito to watch the coral spawning in September and October. Other times of the year, check with them for well-organized boat and shore excursions to interesting sites.

Aruba Pro Dive

Costa Linda Resort, ☎ 297-582-5520; www.arubaprodive.com

They pick up at all the hotels in Aruba. Groups average six divers, and the boats visit two or three top sites each day. They run two-tank dives in the morning and one-tank dives in the afternoon. Baby Beach and the surrounding southern reefs are a specialty. Guides also lead customized land/sea combination tours.

Glass-Bottom Boating

You don't have to get wet to view Aruba's fabulous underwater treasures. Take a sightseeing cruise in a glass-bottom boat. Rates for 1½-hour cruises are $25-$35 for adults and about half-price for children four-12 years of age. For information and reservations, call **Discovery Tours**, ☎ 297-587-5875, or **Rainbow Runner**, ☎ 297-593-4707.

Windsurfing

Flat seas and dependable trade winds guarantee ideal conditions for sailing and windsurfing. Winds typically blow at a steady 20 to 25 knots year-round, which makes Aruba the natural location for annual events such as the Hi-Winds Windsurfing Competition (June) and

Windsurfing (Aruba Tourism)

the Aruba Catamaran Regatta (November).

Drop by **Malmok Beach**, called Fisherman's Huts by the locals, to watch beginners struggle with their sails inside the protective reef and experts glide at amazing speeds across the one- to two-foot chop about a half-mile out on the blue highway.

Malmok, north of Palm Beach and south of the California Lighthouse, has shallow water as far as 200 feet from shore, so when you fall off your board, there's little chance of drowning. Out past the lighthouse, moderately windy days produce a six-foot rolling swell. Experts like the challenge off east-coast beaches where the winds are fierce. **Boca**

Grandi is a favorite for daredevil surfers, and spectators enjoy watching their amazing feats.

If you'd like to try this sport, several outfitters rent equipment and give lessons. Instruction rates are approximately $50 for a two-hour beginner lesson, including equipment. Those who know how to handle a board may rent equipment for about $35 per two-hour session, or $45 for half a day and $50 for a full day. For a week, rent the works for about $245.

WINDSURFING OPERATORS

Aruba Sailboard Vacations
Aruba Beach Villas, Malmok Beach, ☎ 800-252-1070 (in the US); 297-586-2527; www.arubasailboardvacations.com

This company has a US office and runs programs on several islands, including the Aruba Windsurfing Academy. The beach villas and adjacent shop, at Malmok Beach, is operated by and for windsurfers.

Aruba Active Vacations
Malmok Beach, ☎ 297-741-2991 (cell) or 297-586-0989; www.aruba-active-vacations.com

See Wim Eelens at Active Vacations if you want an enthusiastic water-fun coach. He'll teach you to wind, kite or board surf in record time. If you're already skilled, he'll rent you top-notch equipment and point you toward the best waves on the island.

Sailing

One of Aruba's most popular adventures is the cruise to nowhere. This is a terrific way to see the leeward side of the island from the water while relaxing with a cool drink aboard a yacht or catamaran. Some tours include snorkeling, lunch or dinner, entertainment, open bar, or a combination package. If you want the ultimate trip, charter your own boat and plan your own itinerary.

Perhaps the most important difference between a good cruise and a fabulous cruise is the amount of open space on the boat. Even large vessels feel cramped when they're filled to capacity, so ask how many people the boat is licensed to carry and how many are expected at various times. Then sign up for the boat with the best passenger-to-space ratio.

Costs vary, depending on the length of the trip and the extras that come with it. A five-hour snorkel, lunch, and open-bar trip will run about $70 per person. Trips without an open bar

Catamaran off Palm Beach
(Fernando Arroniz)

(they usually serve rum punch and soft drinks) may save you $20. Sunset dinner cruises cost approximately $60 per person. Two-hour snorkel trips are in the $30 range. The activities desk at your hotel can give you some information and point you in the right direction, but do a little comparison shopping before you book. The following have a reputation for excellence.

SAILING TOURS

De Palm Tours
☎ 800-766-6016 (in the US); or 297-582-4545; www.depalm.com
Get information at the activities desk of major resorts or at their pier on Palm Beach. They offer every imaginable type of cruise. You can book through them or contact individual operators directly.

Red Sail Sports
Palm Beach. Wednesday-Monday day sails; daily sunset cruises, ☎ 877-733-7245 (in the US), 297-583-1603; www.redsailaruba.com
Two catamarans sail from De Palm Pier on Palm Beach each morning for four-hour snorkel, sightseeing, lunch trips. Shorter afternoon sails and the sunset cruise include snacks.

Pelican Adventures

Palm Beach. Day sails and sunset crises every day; ☎ 297-587-2302; www.pelican-aruba.com

Two catamarans sail from Pelican Pier near the Holiday Inn on Palm Beach for day sails, sunset booze cruises, and special full-moon outings. Depending on time of day, the tour includes snacks or brunch and drinks.

Jolly Pirates

Moomba's Bar & Restaurant, Palm Beach. Daily trips, ☎ 297-586-8107; www.jollypirates.com

These two 85-foot Brazilian schooners are the most popular party boats in the Caribbean, and every trip features an open bar. Lots of noise. Lots of fun.

Mi Dushi and *Tattoo*

De Palm Pier, Palm Beach. Daily excursions, ☎ 297-586-2010; www.arubaadvertures.com

Mi Dushi is an 80-foot oak-and-mahogany sailing vessel that was built in 1925. It offers daytime tours with lunch or snacks and an open bar, as well as a champagne sunset sail with an open bar and snacks. *Tattoo* is a huge adults-only party boat that pretends every night is Carnival. Dancing, dinner, cheap-drinks bar, and entertainment keep passengers busy and happy from 8 pm until midnight, Monday-Saturday.

Wave Dancer

Eagle Beach, near Costa Linda Resort. Daily trips, ☎ 297-582-5520; www.arubawavedancer.com

You can take half-day snorkeling trips to the *Antilla* shipwreck or cruise at sunset on this 42-foot trimaran. All outings include open bar and either snacks or lunch.

Tranquilo

Aruba Grand Hotel, Palm Beach. Monday-Saturday sails, ☎ 297-586-1418; www.tranquiloaruba.com

Captain Anthony Hagedoorn and his family operate this 43-foot sailing yacht that runs daytime snorkeling/sightseeing trips and sunset crises. Private charters and small-group trips to out-of-the-way places is the specialty.

*Boat owners dock at **Seaport Marina** at Seaport Marketplace in Oranjestad. Some offer private charters. Phone numbers are posted in the windows of boats that are available for crewed rental.*

Kayaking

Kayaking is a relatively new adventure on Aruba, and visitors are taking to it with enthusiasm. You will search out hidden caves and get up close and personal with the island's mangrove forest growing in clearwater **Spanish Lagoon**, where juve-

Kayaking (Fernando Arroniz)

nile fish feed. Then paddle over to **De Palm Island** for lunch and a bit of beach time. Later, you can snorkel over a coral reef. No experience is necessary. A well-informed local guide leads you through the basics and handles all the details from pick-up to drop-off at your hotel. The six-hour package costs $82 per person.

ARUBA KAYAK ADVENTURE
Costa Linda Resort/Eagle Beach
☎ 297-582-5520
www.arubakayak.com

Water Thrills & Toys

Several outfitters on Palm Beach offer Jet Skis ($45 per half-hour), banana-boat rides ($15), waterskiing ($70 per half-hour), paddleboats ($15), and parasailing ($45).

WATER TOYS	
Aruba Water Sport Center	☎ 297-586-6613; www.arubawatersportcenter.com

De Palm Tours	☎ 297-582-4400; www.depalm.com
Pelican Watersports	☎ 297-583-1228; www.pelican-aruba.com
Red Sail Sports	☎ 297-586-1603; www.aruba-redsail.com
Unique Sports	☎ 297-586-0096; www.visitaruba.com/uniquesports

The **Master Blaster** is the ultimate thrill on water. You climb aboard a twin-engine, 1,000-horsepower turbo-charged boat and spend an hour doing wild, squeal-inducing high-speed runs, turns, spins and tilts. Not for the squeamish, but if you crave an extreme adrenaline rush, reserve a $49 seat ($30 for kids) on this **Atlantis Adventure,** ☎ 297-588-6881, www.atlantisadventures.com.

Deep-Sea Fishing

Deep-sea fishing boats at Oranjestad marina (Stuart Cummings)

You can count on reeling in a big one when you go out on a half- or full-day fishing expedition in the deep waters off Aruba's coast. Primary catches include snapper, grouper, barracuda, amberjack, wahoo, and yellowfin tuna. Join a group or charter your own boat with a captain and crew to show you the best places to fish. The rate for full-day-trips is about $600, including tackle, bait, and soft drinks. Half-day-trips with everything included run $300.

DEEP-SEA OPERATORS

Mahi Mahi
Seaport Marina, ☎ 297-587-0538 or 297-594-1181 (cell); www.aruba-mahimahi.com

Captain Peter Creutzberg is a seasoned Aruban fisherman who will show you where to catch mahi mahi, sailfish, and other game fish. Join him on his 42-foot Hatteras Sportfisherman outfitted with Caterpillar engines. Bring your catch to dinner at **Driftwood Aruba Seafood Restaurant**, and co-owner Franchine will cook and serve it for $15 per person.

Teaser Charters
Seaport Marina, ☎ 297-582-5088; www.teasercharters.com

Check with Captain Kenneth Pichardo about fishing from one of his two 35-foot Bertram Sportfisherman yachts, *Kenny's Toy* and *Teaser*.

Adventures on Land
Horseback Riding

Riding on the North Coast (Fernando Arroniz)

Aruba's outback lends itself to exploration on horseback. Choose early morning or sunset rides for the coolest breezes and most active wildlife. Several stables arrange group rides along the wild east coast, along beaches, and over inland terrain that cannot be covered by car.

Wear a hat, sunglasses, knee-length or longer pants, and sunscreen. If you want to ride in shorts or swimsuit, bring a thick beach towel to protect the front of your legs from sunburn, and the back of your legs from saddle sores.

Rates vary depending on length and destination, but you'll pay about $45 for a two-hour group ride and $60 for a private two-hour tour.

THE GOLD MINE RANCH
Matividiri 60
☎ 297-585-9870; www.thegoldmineranch.com
With only a dozen horses, this ranch offers nothing but small-group and private rides. Look for their sign on the main road leading to the Boca Andicuri Natural Bridge.

RANCHO NOTORIOUS
Noord
☎ 297-586-0508
www.ranchonotorious.com
They say this is the home of happy horses, and it would appear that Al Capone, Jesse James, Evita, and friends are thriving and pleased to be of service. Every horse is well groomed, easy to handle, and a pleasure to ride. Various 2½- to three-hour tours leave mornings and afternoons for rides into the outback, over to Malmok Beach, and up to Alto Vista Chapel. The sunset rides are especially popular. Call to arrange pick-up at your hotel.

 TIP: A new Ticket Outlet has opened in a small hut on Palm Beach, selling a wide range of land and water activities provided by owner-operated businesses. Book online at www.arubaticketoutlet.com or call ☎ 297-586-8107.

RANCHO DAIMARI
Tanki Leendert
☎ 297-586-6284; www.visitaruba.com/ranchodaimari

Sign up for a private group ride or private couple sunset ride to the Boca Andicuri Natural Bridge. It will be an adventure you'll never forget. Scheduled group rides include galloping over hills in Arikok National Park, leisurely tours of deserted beaches, and a stop at the Boca Andicuri Natural Pool. Call for directions to the ranch, or ask about pick-up at your resort.

RANCHO DEL CAMPO
Santa Cruz
☎ 297-585-0290
www.ranchodelcampo.com

Goldie, Flash, and Chiki invite you to mount up and take a ride out to the National Park and Natural Pool. If you have more time, sign up for the longer trip out to the Ayo Rock Formations and the Boca Andicuri Natural Bridge. You can also organize a private guided tour to secluded spots along the east coast. Call for directions.

Golf

Tierra del Sol (Fernando Arroniz)

TIERRA DEL SOL
Northwest end of the island
Tee times 7 am-5 pm daily
☎ 866-978-5111 (international toll-free), 297-586-0978;
www.tierradelsol.com

Aruba has only one championship golf course, and it's a beauty, with 18 holes overlooking Aruba's northwest coast. Designed by Robert Trent Jones II, Tierra del Sol is a splash of green in the desert countryside – a Palm-Springs-in-the-Caribbean experience.

Tee times are available at a prime-time high-season fee of $159. During the afternoon, fees drop to $124, and low-season play is priced at $112 in the mornings and $92 in the afternoons. The real bargain is five days of golf from May through October for $460. If you plan to spend a lot of time on the golf course during your vacation, compare package deals offered by many of the major resorts.

As a full-service country club and residential development, Tierra del Sol's facilities include a full-length practice range, putting greens, chipping areas, a luxurious clubhouse, a well-stocked pro shop, a full-service gourmet restaurant, and a grill off the 18th green. (There's a $10-per-day fee for unlimited practice.) Views from almost any area of the club include turquoise sea, rolling terrain, and desert vegetation growing around huge boulder formations. The picturesque California Lighthouse is in the distance and is particularly stunning from the third hole.

Wind is the major obstacle on this par-71, 6,811-yard course. But, the constant breeze also makes play comfortably cool most of the time. A few water hazards add a bit more challenge, but the fairways are wide and planted in lush, well-groomed Bermuda grass.

Callaway clubs ($55) and shoes ($15) may be rented, and a storage locker is available ($5) for the entire length of your vacation. Golf carts are outfitted with a Parview GPS satellite dish and a 10.4-inch color screen that projects green overviews and gives the exact distance from the cart to the center of the green, electronic scoring, and two-way communication with the clubhouse.

Divi Golf Club

DIVI GOLF CLUB
Divi Village Golf and Beach Resort
Druif Beach
☎ 297-581-GOLF; www.divigolf.com

This new nine-hole golf course, owned by Divi Resorts, is bordered by luxurious private villas, but the public is welcome. Preferred tee times go to resort guests and villa owners. Fees range from $60-$80 for nine holes of high-season play (guests of Divi resorts get a discount) to $90-$115 for 18 holes of high-season play. You can learn to play or improve your game with lessons from the Johnson & Wales Golf Learning Center, which features video swing analysis and practice areas. In addition, the resort complex has a well-stocked pro shop and an open-air restaurant that serves meals and drinks from 7 am until 11pm daily. The upscale **Windows on Aruba** is a glass-walled, two-level restaurant with panoramic views of the ocean and golf course. Lunch and dinner are served daily, and the Sunday brunch is a popular weekend event.

ARUBA GOLF CLUB
East of San Nicolas
7:30 am-5 pm
☎ 297-584-2006

The greens are Astroturf, and goats sometimes get in the way, but this odd little golf course is a lot of fun. And, the fee is only $10. Water hazards and sand traps add a challenge to the nine-hole course, which can be played from different

Aruba

tees during 18-hole rounds. Golf carts and clubs are available at the pro shop, and a restaurant is open for breakfast and lunch.

ADVENTURE GOLF

L.G. Smith Blvd/Main Hwy.
Across from La Cabana Resort/Eagle Beach
☎ 297-587-6625
www.blackhogsaloon.com

Golf is only half the fun at this something-for-everyone entertainment center. Two excellent 18-hole miniature courses are laid out around a moat filled with paddle and bumper boats. Elsewhere on the property, there's a batting cage, a bank of video games, and a mini-car race track.

Meals, snacks, and drinks are served at a casual on-site restaurant and a lively bar. The **Black Hog Saloon** throws a BBQ Bash every Tuesday and Thursday from 6:30-9:30 at a cost of $35 for adults and $20 for kids 12 and under. The price includes a barbecue dinner, unlimited draft beer and soft drinks, a round of golf, and a paddleboat ride. Entertainment stars the Magnificent Horse and Harley Show with horse celebrities from Rancho El Paso (see *Horseback Riding*, above). **Alfredo's Restaurant** offers nightly specials with an Italian flavor that they claim is "just like Boston's North End" – an area famous for having more than

100 authentic Italian restaurants in a space of five-blocks. Make a reservation for casual outdoor dining nightly from 6 to 10:30 pm.

ATV Tours

The best way to see the rugged Aruban "outback" is on a self-drive all terrain vehicle (ATV). Per-person rates are $65 for a three-hour guided

Rancho Notorious ATVs

tour of the rocky northeast coast with stops at Alto Vista Chapel, the ruins of an old gold mill at Bushiribana, Wariruri Beach, Ayo Rock Formations and the Donkey Sanctuary. Before you head back to your hotel, you'll have a chance to cool down and wash away the dust with a swim in the ocean.

RANCHO NOTORIOUS

Borancana Noord, near the high-rise hotels
☎ 297-586-0508; www.ranchonotorious.com

Three-hour tours leave at 9 am and 2 pm. Call for reservations and to arrange free round-trip transportation from your hotel.

Biking

Flat terrain and deserted back roads make ideal conditions for bike enthusiasts. Traffic is too heavy in the tourist areas and on the main road along the western coast, and wind can be a deterrent for some. However, the paved roads and smoother dirt paths along the northern coast are scenic and enjoyable when the wind is calm.

Rancho Notorious bike tour

Basic bikes rent for about $15 per day. Two-hour tours run about $45 per rider with a group and $90 per rider with a private guide through Rancho Notorious.

TRI-BIKE ARUBA (rental only)

Macuarima 88-F, Oranjestad
☎ 297-585-2734

MELCHOR CYCLE RENTAL

Bubali 106B
☎ 297-587-1787

ARUBA OCEAN VIEW BIKE & LOCKER (rental only)
LG Smith Blvd 234
☎ 297-587-8655

RANCHO NOTORIOUS (guided tours).
Borancana Noord, near the high-rise hotels
☎ 297-586-0508; www.ranchonotorious.com

 For motorcycle and scooter rental, see *Getting Around, page 64.*

Hiking

Arikok National Park has already laid out 20 miles of trails and more are planned. Some of the rock-bordered dirt paths lead to formal presentations and learning centers; others branch out to the isolated undeveloped areas along the park's north and south boundaries. Rangers can provide maps and information at the Visitor's Center east of Santa Cruz.

 Directions: Coming from the beach resorts toward Santa Cruz on Highway 4A/B, turn left at a sign marked Parke Nacional Arikok, just before you reach the center of town. When the paved road ends, look for another sign and the park on the left. Parking is adjacent to the Visitor's Center.

Climbing

If you are an experienced rock climber and want a different type of Caribbean experience, hook up with the **Club Active Aruba**. Its members have cleaned and set up a climbing area at **Grapefield**, on the eastern point of the island, near Seroe Colorado. This section of the island was once covered in seagrape trees, but they

Club Activ Aruba

have been destroyed by refinery waste products that were dumped here in the past. Three climbing enthusiasts visiting from the Netherlands and members of the local climbing club have cleared away much of petroleum waste. The Aruban government has plans to return the area to its original state and protect it as an ecological preserve.

Directions: Get there from San Nicolas by following the refinery walls southeast out of town to a large anchor at an intersection. Turn left, and follow the road through Grapefield toward Boca Grandi Beach. Watch for signs to Boca Grandi. Look on your left for the island's prison on top of a cliff. Travel past the prison on the dirt road (four-wheel-drive is a good idea) until you see a small white wooden sign pointing to the climbing area.

Contact Club Active Aruba for important information about needed materials and the best times and areas for climbing. ☎ 297-585-3433; www.climbing.nl/aruba.

Tennis

Aruba Tennis Academy

Major resorts have lighted tennis courts, and there's a racket club off Caya Francisco D. Figaroa, north and inland from the Marriott Beach Resort. For a fee of $10 per hour, you may use one of the eight lighted courts. The facility also has a pro shop, fitness center, swimming pool, restaurant, and bar.

Aruba

ARUBA RACKET CLUB
Rooi Santo 21
Monday-Saturday, 8 am-11 pm
Sunday, 3 pm-8 pm
☎ 297-586-0215

ARUBA TENNIS ACADEMY
Aloestraat #14, Ponton
☎ 297-583-7074; www.tennisaruba.com

Shopping

Despite the new 3% sales tax and 3.3% duty charge, Aruba is still a good place to buy European luxuries, jewelry, and perfume. Designated duty-free shops are located at the departure terminal of the airport. Dutch treats are, of course, plentiful and well priced; high quality original art, one-of-a-kind fashions, and handmade articles produced by local artisans make sensible souvenirs of your trip.

Oranjestad is the primary shopping area with several open-air malls, a wharf-side market, and a half-mile stretch of top stores along Mainstreet (Caya G. F. Betico Croes). Since the town is small, all the stores are located within a few blocks, and you can easily walk to each. Additional shops are located in the resorts and in the town of San Nicholas, on the South shore.

In the capital, parking can be a problem, and you're not likely to find a spot along the waterfront. On most

Royal Plaza Mall, Oranjestad (Stuart Cummings)

days, spaces are available in the free parking lot in back of the bus terminal on L.G. Smith Blvd, behind the pink and turquoise Royal Plaza Mall at the north end of town. You may be able to find parking in the lot at Seaport Marketplace, on the south side of town, near Wilhelmina Park.

 Taxis are not permitted to pick up or drop off passengers on L.G. Smith Blvd, the waterfront highway, but drivers make stops on all side streets. Buses run frequently between the resorts and town, and are more convenient than hassling with traffic and parking, unless you plan to make heavy or numerous purchases.

During prime cruise-ship season, many stores time their opening and closing hours to coincide with passenger schedules, and most open on Sundays. Otherwise, expect most to open at 9 am and close at 6 pm, Monday through Saturday. A few shops still follow the old-style practice of opening around 8 am, closing during the lunch-siesta hours, and reopening from 2 until 6 pm. Those shops located in resorts follow a whimsical schedule, adjusted seasonally to match occupancy levels and guest activities.

Aruba

GREAT BUYS

- Dutch imports, such as Delft porcelain.
- Cigars (Cuban cigars are not allowed back into the US).
- Designer clothes.
- High-quality original art, pottery, and sculpture.
- Swiss watches.
- English china.
- French perfume.
- Danish crystal.
- German and Japanese cameras.
- Indonesian fabrics.
- Designer jewelry by international artisans.
- Caribbean rum and liqueurs.
- Aruba Aloe beauty and health products.

In the street market, Oranjestad (BC Pictures)

Most stores accept major credit cards, traveler's checks and US dollars, as well as Aruban florins, but no personal checks. ATMs are scattered about the island, and you'll find them at the airport, in all banks, and at most shopping centers. Prices usually are posted in US dollars, but retailers that serve a large number of locals (gas stations, grocery stores, pharmacies) post prices in florins, marked with Afl or AWG after the number. Most restaurants and some shops post prices in both dollars and florins. Expect to receive coin change in florins. Be sure to use it on the island for tips and small purchases, since coins can not be exchanged when you return home.

 Avoid the masses by checking cruise-ship arrivals printed in the newspaper, Aruba Today.

Mainstreet

Aquamarine-colored street signs with a golden sunburst are located at strategic points around town to guide shoppers to Mainstreet (Caya G.F. Betico Croes). This route runs one way, going south. Here you will find:

Gold Palace, a friendly place to shop for gold, of course, but also tanzanite, diamonds, emeralds, rubies, and sapphires. ☎ 297-583-3599.

Mango, an international clothing store featuring original European designs, ☎ 297-582-9700.

Benetton, with its familiar array of colorful clothes for the entire family, fits perfectly into the Aruban shopping scene. ☎ 297-582-8521.

Downtown Oranjestad *(Magalie L'Abbé)*

Maggie's, well known in the Caribbean for beauty products, cosmetics, and perfumes from international companies. ☎ 297-582-2114.

Wulfsen & Wulfsen features a select collection of European-style business wear and casual fashions for men and women. ☎ 297-582-3823.

Artistic Boutique, best on the island for Indonesian imports, also sells jewelry, porcelain, Oriental antiques, handmade Indian rugs, and fine linens. ☎ 297-582-3142.

Art & Tradition must be visited for its folk art, including the amazing mopa mopa works crafted by Colombian Indians. ☎ 297-583-6534.

Aruba Trading Company has good prices on perfume, cosmetics, liquor, and clothing for men and women. ☎ 297-582-2602.

Little Switzerland Jewelers needs no introduction. Visitors are handed fliers at the airport, cruise docks, and hotels touting duty-free jewelry and watches at good prices. ☎ 297-582-1192.

Penha & Sons is a long-time retailer with a good reputation among residents. A Tommy Hilfiger boutique has been added recently, and the main store stocks a large selection of perfumes and cosmetics, with impressive names such as Dior, Givenchy, and Boucheron. ☎ 297-582-4160.

Ecco stocks Delft blue porcelain, a large variety of table linens, and some interesting handcrafted objects, along with a mix of beachwear, sportswear, and T-shirts. ☎ 297-582-4726.

Shooz will cure your aching feet with a pair of fashionably sensible shoes by famous makers such as Nine West, Anne Klein, Nautica, and Dockers. ☎ 297-588-7877.

Boolchand's, a multi-generational family-owned company, has been on the island for almost 30 years and in the Caribbean for more than 70 years. Among the diverse items they stock, you'll find top-brand electronics, cameras, jewelry, and watches. ☎ 297-583-0147.

 Market stalls set up along the waterfront sell local crafts, batik fabrics, T-shirts, and international imports. Haggling is allowed.

Royal Plaza Mall

This open-air mall across from the cruise terminal has several good restaurants (including the Internet Café, where you can check and send e-mail), plus chic shops such as:

Gandelman Jewelers, the place to buy jewelry such as fine gold, top-of-the-market watches, and diamond rings. Their after-sales service claims to be only an e-mail away. The store has branches in the Hyatt, Radisson, and Wyndham Resorts, the Seaport Mall, and inside the departure terminal at the airport. ☎ 297-588-6159.

La Casa del Habano's walk-in humidors are stocked with cigars by Cohiba, Bolivar, Romeo y Julietas, and other famous makers. ☎ 297-583-8509.

Shiva's Gold & Gems, a family-owned operation for three generations, offers a huge diamond collection. They deal directly with suppliers in Israel, Belgium, and Amsterdam to import select emeralds, tanzanites, sapphires, semi-precious gems, and timepieces. ☎ 297-583-4077.

Touch of Gold is well-known on St. Maarten and becoming quite popular on Aruba because of its US customer service centers. Loose stones and fine designer pieces are the specialty. ☎ 297-588-9587.

Vibes, on the second floor, has Aruban-made candles, art, and sculptures, as well as Dutch porcelain and souvenir T-shirts. ☎ 297-583-7949.

Bula Surf Shop serves the local surfing and beach crowd. Find them on the second floor. ☎ 297-583-8458.

Effy Collection, behind Royal Plaza Mall at 26 Havenstraat, is owned by Effy Hematian and noted for high-quality original jewelry art. ☎ 297-582-9812.

Before you buy electronics, cameras, or watches, ask if the warranty will be honored in your home country. Also, charge these purchases on a gold credit card that offers a buyer's protection plan, and save your dated receipts.

Seaport Village Mall

About 90 shops are located here, next door to Royal Plaza on Smith Blvd, across from the cruise terminal. Part of the sprawling complex is under the Renaissance Hotel and includes restaurants and the Crystal Casino and Theater. ☎ 297-583-9244.

Agatha Boutique sells clothes, shoes, and fragrances by Agatha Brown, the well-known New York designer, who now lives on Aruba. ☎ 297-583-7965.

Gimmick is a European fashion boutique selling famous brands. ☎ 297-583-9244.

Little Holland is the place for lovely imported linens. ☎ 297-583-8494.

Confetti on the Beach sells sportswear by the hottest European, South American, and US designers. ☎ 297-583-8614.

Aruba

***Fundacion Artesania Arubiano**, a small shop at 178 L.G. Smith Blvd, across from the Tamarijn Hotel, is great for Aruban and Caribbean articles, such as baskets, pottery, carvings, spices, and art.* ☎ *837-494.*

Seaport Marketplace

Located across Smith Blvd from Seaport Village Mall and next to the Seaport Marina, this casual shopping area has an assortment of shops, restaurants, movie theaters, and even a tiger habitat.

State of the Art features original framed and unframed art by Rene van Nie. ☎ 297-593-0152.

Rage is owned by Marny and Cedric, an energetic young couple who travel extensively to bring terrific new sterling silver jewelry back to their shop, which is located next door to the movie theaters. ☎ 297-588-6262.

Supermarkets

If you're staying in a timeshare unit or private villa with cooking facilities or you want to pack a picnic, seek out the supermarkets north of Oranjestad, just inland from the low-rise hotels. Prices are reasonable, and you can find everything you need for an entire meal or quick snack. Soft drinks, fresh fruits, meat, cheese, eggs, and fresh milk are well stocked, and the larger stores have a good variety of frozen and packaged foods. Many of the stores have an on-site bakery and sell wine, beer and liquor. Things such as sun screen, over-the-counter medicines, toothpaste, and deodorant are priced lower at supermarkets than at hotel minimarts. Prices are marked in Aruban florins, but the registers will convert your total to US dollars, and you can use cash or credit cards to pay your bill.

Large supermarkets are open Monday-Saturday, 8 am-8 pm. Two to try:

Kong Hing, at Havenstraat 16, has wonderful Dutch imports, including coffee and cheeses. ☎ 297-582-1219.

Ling & Sons, at Italiestraat 26 behind Sun Plaza Mall, has a large variety of deli foods, a good bakery, and fresh produce. ☎ 297-583-2370.

Where to Stay

 Do not stress over where to stay on Aruba. The entire island is dedicated to tourism, and you won't end up in a dump, even if you go with the cheapest accommodations.

Concern yourself, first, with location. Most of the resorts line up along the waterfront (or across a narrow coastal road) on the island's northwest shore. Top-of-the-line accommodations are found in glittering complexes on **Palm**, **Eagle**, **Manchebo**, and **Druif Beaches**. If you find a good package deal at one of these resorts, take it.

High-rise resorts line **Palm Beach**, at the far north end of the island's white-sand strip. Roadside and beach-side walkways connect these closely clustered hotels, so guests may conveniently stroll to restaurants or other public facilities at adjacent resorts. Low-rise complexes extend from Eagle to Druif Beaches. These resorts are more low-key, less glitzy, and a wider expanse of sand separates each property from the water and each other. This is the place for upscale beach bums who favor boutique hotels or timeshare accommodations with kitchens and living areas.

In addition to these districts, Oranjestad offers luxurious accommodations near restaurants, casinos, shops, and nightclubs. Small hotels and private villas are spread out across the island – many right on the water or within walking distance of a beach.

Since resorts compete fiercely for your patronage, all the large establishments have on-site casinos, fitness centers with spas, several restaurants and bars, lush landscaping to make you forget the desert-like natural terrain, amazing swimming pools, and a selection of classy shops.

Activity-specific packages, all-inclusive prices, and air-car-tour-accommodation rates may save you money, but do the math before you book a vacation that may not meet your expectations and needs. Sometimes, you can put together your own package at a better cost.

The following listings are recommended as good choices within their class based on location, price, and facilities. Summer and shoulder-season rates will be lower, sometimes by as much as half, and you can get excellent last-minute bargains year-round. An 8% tax and an 11% service charge will be added to your bill; ask in advance if the hotel adds a daily energy charge.

SLEEPING WITH THE STARS

Our suggested list of lodgings has been slashed to the bare bones for this guide. You can browse the Internet and we encourage you to do so. Here you'll find only the most recommended possibilities to fit a variety of budgets. Properties marked with one star (★) are highly recommended. When a single feature or the overall allure is particularly impressive, you'll find two stars (★★). Three stars (★★★) means, simply, WOW!

Hotel Rate Guide

Use the prices given for accommodations as a guide to the average high-season rate per standard double room. If the review is for an all-inclusive or all-suites resort or a multi-room condo/villa property, the listed price is the average during high season for two people sharing the smallest available unit.

Large resorts on Aruba often have a complex rate structure with prices changing from day to day within a single month. Also, some hotels give different values to their rooms depending on size, location, or view. If you deal with the hotel directly, don't accept the first price quote without asking questions. You may save a substantial amount by giving up amenities or a view that you really don't care about.

Resorts & Hotels

Unless otherwise noted, all of the following resorts and hotels are air-conditioned and equipped with telephones, cable or satellite color TVs, at least one swimming pool, and free parking. Most have at least one on-site restaurant. Exceptional hotel restaurants are listed in the dining section. Every establishment will be adequately-to-superbly furnished with the usual amenities. Only outstanding or unusual features and services are noted in each description. Check with travel agents for color brochures or visit websites for online photos and video tours.

Oranjestad

★ RENAISSANCE ARUBA BEACH RESORT & CASINO
L.G. Smith Blvd 82, Oranjestad, at Seaport Village
☎ 888-236-2427 or 8000-228-9290 (in the US & Canada) or 297-583-6000 (Aruba); fax 582-5317
www.arubarenaissance.com
558 rooms & suites
$230-$270

This exquisite five-star resort is located on the main coastal road running through downtown Oranjestad, right in the midst of all the action. The resort has a 24-hour casino, an open-air shopping mall, and three restaurants. A water taxi picks up guests at the dock of the lobby lagoon and takes

Renaissance Aruba

them to a private-island beach across the channel from the mainland. The list of watersports available on the island is impressive; snorkeling, diving, kayaking, banana-boat rides, waterbikes, waterskiing, tube rides, and buga-boat rides. Rooms are not large, but are quite adequate and nicely furnished. This is the place for business travelers and those who want easy access to shopping, restaurants, and nightlife.

Palm Beach High-Rise Resorts

The following multi-story beachside resorts are the most elegant on the island. Each tries to outdo the other with dazzling décor and numerous amenities, including beach services, watersports, theme-night dinner parties, opulent lobbies, several classy restaurants and a choice of indoor and outdoor bars. They are listed as they line up north-to-south along Palm Beach.

MARRIOTT RESORT & STELLARIS CASINO
☎ 800-228-9290 or 888-236-2427 (in the US & Canada) or 297-586-9000 (on Aruba); fax 297-586-0649; www.marriott.com
413 rooms & suites
$400-$475

★★MARRIOTT'S ARUBA OCEAN CLUB (timeshare accommodations)
☎ 800-228-9290 or 888-236-2427 (in the US & Canada) or 297-586-9000 (on Aruba); fax 297-586-0649
www.vacation-rentals.vacationclub.com
311 units, with more under construction
$525-$600

The resort's new 500-room addition may be complete by the time you visit, which will make this complex the biggest resort on the island and one of the

Marriott's Aruba Ocean Club

top three in size in the Caribbean. Even without the addition, the eight-floor hotel is a mega-plex of oversized rooms complete with mini-bars, walk-in closets, balconies, and double-sinks in the bathrooms. The only thing you might miss is spaciousness on the over-equipped beach, but it stretches forever to the south, so you have only to turn left and walk to a piece of sand you can call your own – or escape under the waterfall in the free-form pool.

The Ocean Club is a six-level every-luxury timeshare development with one- and two-bedroom suites, each with full kitchen and living/dining areas. Guests have access to the long list of amenities at the next-door sister resort, including lighted tennis courts, the **Mandara Spa**, and **Stellaris Casino**.

HOLIDAY INN SUNSPREE BEACH RESORT & CASINO
☎ 800-934-6750 (direct to the hotel from the US & Canada) or 297-586-3600 (on Aruba); fax 297-586-5165
www.aruba.sunspreeresorts.com
600 rooms
$220-$280

SunSpree is the trademark of upscale Holiday Inn resorts in prime vacation locations. They feature extra amenities, such as watersports, kids' programs, and health spas. Rooms in this seven-story multi-tower resort are nicely decorated in upgraded SunSpree style. A recent multi-million dollar update added an activities center, game room, beach-side restaurant/ice cream bar, an entertainment deck around the large pool, a totally remodeled lobby and Inter-

Holiday Inn Sunspree

mezzo Day Spa. In addition, guests enjoy four lighted tennis courts, a beach volleyball court, a bocce court, and a fitness center. The location, between the giant Marriott complex and huge Playa Linda, is terrific, and the resort bustles with active families from dawn to late-night. Parents get a break by enrolling kids five to 12 years of age in the Little Rascals activities program. Quiet escape is found in hammocks hanging between tall palms on beautifully landscaped grounds. Be prepared for a line at check-in and for seating in the restaurants during meal times.

PLAYA LINDA BEACH RESORT

☎ 800-992-2015 (in the US & Canada) or 297-586-1000 (on Aruba); fax 297-586-3479; www.playalinda.com
209 studios & one- to two-bedroom units
$260-$280

Every unit in this nine-story timeshare resort has a balcony with an unobstructed view of the beach, thanks to the creative terraced design. Eight new one-bedroom lanai suites are located on the ground floor with direct

Playa Linda Beach Resort

access to the pool and beach. Other studio, one- and two-bedroom units have partial to full kitchens and living/dining areas with sleeper sofas. In addition to the usual long list of onsite amenities, including a large water-fall swimming pool, four jacuzzis and three lighted tennis courts, the resort has a new Indonesian-style spa.

★HYATT REGENCY ARUBA RESORT & CASINO
☎ 888-591-1284 (in the US & Canada) or 297-586-1234 (on Aruba); fax 297-586-1682; www.aruba.hyatt.com
360 rooms & suites
$390-$600

Standard rooms are small Hyatt-style – nice, but nothing special, and you must book a suite to get a balcony. The public areas, however, are spectacular. The best on the is-

Hyatt Regency

land. And, the suites range from excellent to incredible. If you go for the Governor's Suite on the restricted ninth floor, you'll get a whirlpool tub, fitness equipment, and large top-of-the-resort balconies on two sides, with views of both the white-sand beach and the multi-level pool. No money or imagination were spared on landscaping, and the lush grounds include towering cacti, blooming bougainvillea, and a fish-stocked lagoon. Camp Hyatt occupies kids three to 12 years of age with cooking lessons, storytelling, and outdoor activities.

OCCIDENTAL GRAND ARUBA RESORT & CASINO
☎ 800-858-2258 (in the US & Canada) or 297-586-4500 (on Aruba); fax 297-586-3191; www.occidentalhotels.com
391 rooms & suites (all-inclusive)
$225-$300 per person for a double

Humming activity surrounds this newly renovated resort catering to tour groups that book all-inclusive packages. Many guests never leave the property. They come for mindless sun, fun, and booze, and the Occidental gives them all they can handle. Rooms are nothing special, the bathrooms are small, and balconies are narrow. Ask for a ground floor room with a terrace, if you want more space. There's something going on at all times in the public areas, so singles, newly-weds, and families are never bored. Meals, snacks and beverages are available non-stop in six restaurants and five bars.

★★★RIU PALACE ARUBA

☎ 888-666-8816 (US & Canada) or 297-586-3900 (Aruba); fax 297-586-1941; www.riu.com/aruba
450 rooms and suites
$250-$350 per person double, all-inclusive

Riu Palace

The RIU hotel chain added this property (formerly the Aruba Grand Beach Reasort) to its prestigious "Palace" inventory in 2005. After two years of complete remodeling and modernization, the resort well deserves its five-star rating. Three buildings face a lovely stretch of Palm Beach, and the complex includes a casino, five theme restaurants, a selection of well-placed bars, a deluxe health spa, two pools and a wide selection of sports activities. The all-inclusive rates include everything from food to drinks, casino admission to watersports. Guests are rarely disappointed in any RIU-brand resort, and this one is especially fine.

★RADISSON ARUBA RESORT & CASINO

☎ 888-201-1718 (in the US) or 297-586-6555 (on Aruba); fax 297-586-3260; www.radisson.com/aruba
358 rooms & suites
$425-$575
Something about the Radisson gives guests a sense of spaciousness, even though it's located in the midst of busy Palm Beach and usually fully booked with vacationers. Its 14-acre grounds are set back quite a distance from the

white sand and sheltered from the outside world by gardens, Koi-stocked lagoons, waterfalls, and two large free-form swimming pools. Small to average-sized rooms are beautifully decorated in colonial-Caribbean style with louvered shutters and mahogany four-poster beds.

Pool at the Radisson Aruba

WESTIN ARUBA RESORT

☎ 800-996-3426 (in the US & Canada) or 297-586-4466 (on Aruba); fax 297-586-3403; www.starwoodhotels.com
480 rooms & suites
$425-$475 (all-inclusive); $230-$275 (room-only)

Room in the Westin Aruba

Could there be anything more decadent than lying pool-side on a cushy lounge chair in the warm Caribbean sun? Add to that being spritzed with cool water by a friendly attendant while nibbling fresh fruit from a wooden skewer. Life doesn't get any better than at the Westin. Large rooms in the 18-story tower are recently renovated, and views from upper-floor balconies are spectacular. Good restaurants, a children's program, and every imaginable amenity guarantee a perfect vacation. Choose either the all-inclusive program or room-only plan.

ARUBA PHOENIX BEACH RESORT

☎ 800-376-3484 (in the US & Canada) or 297-586-6066;
fax 297-586-1165; www.diviphoenix.com
101 units
$275-$300

As one of a dozen Divi Resorts on six Caribbean islands, including five on Aruba and one on Bonaire, this property offers studio, one- and two-bedroom apartments. The location, at the southern end of the

Aruba Phoenix Beach Resort

high-rise district, is excellent, except for occasionally strong winds, and guests have wonderful views from their large balconies. Ask for one of the 35 villas next to the 14-floor tower for extra-spacious rooms, an extended balcony, and a full kitchen. On-site facilities include two pools, a well-equipped fitness center, all watersports, and a mini-mart for stocking the kitchen.

Low-Rise Resorts

La Cabana All-Suite Beach Resort

The following resorts line up north-to-south along Eagle, Manchebo, and Druif Beaches, just south of Palm Beach. Each is no more than five floors high, and all feature most of the common amenities, while maintaining a relaxed ambiance. Casinos are nearby, rather than on-site, and watersports are limited to non-motorized choices. Many vacationers prefer the wider, quieter, less crowded beaches in this area, but singles and high-energy vacationers may find the activities list a bit sluggish, especially off-season.

★LA CABANA ALL-SUITE BEACH RESORT

☎ 800-835-7193; fax 212-476-9467 (in the US & Canada)
☎ 297-587-9000; fax 297-587-5474 (on Aruba)
www.lacabanaaruba.com
811 studios and one- , two- , and three-bedroom suites
$279

La Cabana differs from its low-rise neighbors by being across a narrow, low-traffic road from Eagle Beach, rather than opening directly onto the sand, and by having an on-site casino, the **Royal Cabana**. The huge, sprawling complex encompasses individually owned timeshare and rentable resort units, three swimming pools featuring water slides and waterfalls, five tennis courts, a fitness center, three restaurants, and five bars. Watersports equipment, lounge chairs, and shade cabanas are complimentary at the beach, and scuba diving, sailing, and sightseeing tours can be arranged through the activities center.

Honeymooners and singles will probably be happier staying somewhere else, but families will enjoy all the high-energy choices. Kids can sign up for the children's program through **Club Cabana Nana**, while teens chill out at the **Cabana Culture Club**. Adults can plan their own fun or check out the long list of scheduled activities posted in the lobby each day.

All the studios and suites have fully equipped kitchens or kitchenettes, a living area, and a private patio or balcony. The units have both air-conditioning and ceiling fans, and the bathrooms are outfitted with whirlpool tubs and hair dryers.

★★COSTA LINDA BEACH RESORT

☎ 800-992-2015 (in the US & Canada) or 297-583-8000; fax 297-583-6040; www.costalinda-aruba.com
155 suites
$550

Costa Linda

The name of this five-story resort means beautiful coast, and it perfectly describes the famous stretch of beach that it occupies. Eagle is Aruba's widest sugary-white sand beach and the resort takes advantage of the marvelous location. Each two- and three-bedroom unit has a large balcony looking out past the free-form pool, hot tubs, and landscaped grounds to the sweeping palm-studded beach and turquoise sea. Full kitchens, large living/dining areas with sleeper sofas, and two bathrooms mean you can spread out; the three-bedroom units have a mini-kitchen and an additional bathroom. The usual facilities and timeshare-type activities provide plenty to do, but many guests prefer to simply relax and enjoy the resort's peaceful charm. On-site restaurants and bars are run by the same restauranteurs who operate the Waterfront Crabhouse at Seaport Marketplace and La Gondola at Casa del Mar; the Alhambra Casino is next door.

★BUCUTI BEACH RESORT ARUBA
☎ 800-223-1108 (in the US & Canada) or 297-586-1100 (on Aruba); fax 297-586-5272; www.bucuti.com
63 rooms & suites
$200-$295

Honeymooners and roman-tics, listen up. This European-style boutique resort is fabulously quixotic and intent on your happiness. You may even request a private sunset dinner on the beach.

Suites have small kitchens. Kids are welcome, but not encouraged. If you bring little ones, they probably will have to play with kids next door at Costa Linda.

Bucuti Beach Resort

★★MANCHEBO BEACH RESORT
☎ 800-528-1234 (in the US & Canada) or 297-586-3444 (on Aruba); fax 297-586-2446; www.manchebo.com
71 units
$180-$200

Manchebo Beach resort

You'd never guess this small hotel is part of the Best Western chain. While it's not as glitzy as some of its neighbors, everything is clean and well maintained. The resort is popular with Europeans, but catching on with North Americans because the owners give guests friendly attention, the beach is fabulous, and rates are among the best value on the island. Couples may get married in the on-site seaside chapel, then spend their honeymoon tucked into one of the water-view rooms. The **French Steakhouse** serves marvelous meals, and some of the best steaks on Aruba, and two other restaurants offer delicious variety. The new outdoor spa features ocean-side service.

ARUBA BEACH CLUB
☎ 297-586-3000; fax 297-586-8191
www.arubabeachclub.net
131 studios & one-bedroom suites
$150-$250

If you're looking for room to spread out, this is the place. It's next door to the Casa del Mar, and guests may use the facilities of both time-share/hotels. Studios have a mini-kitchen; one-bedroom units have a full kitchen and extra living space. Plenty of activities keep the entire family busy.

CASA DEL MAR BEACH RESORT
☎ 297-586-7000; fax 297-582-9044
www.casadelmar-aruba.com
107 one- & two-bedroom units
$225-$450

As the more deluxe sister resort to the next-door Aruba Beach Club, Casa del Mar offers plenty of scheduled activities and a full slate of facilities. The one-bedroom units are an especially good value. All units have kitchens, living areas, and a balcony or patio. Alhambra Casino is nearby, and the beach is excellent. This is an ideal choice for families.

★DIVI ARUBA ALL-INCLUSIVE RESORT
☎ 800-554-2008 (in the US & Canada) or 297-525-5200 (on Aruba); fax 297-525-5203; www.diviaruba.com
203 rooms & suites
$210-$275 (all-inclusive)

Families with kids and newlyweds keep this popular resort booked most of the year. These are the people who want to know exactly how much to budget for their trip

Pool at Divi Aruba

and don't want any surprises when they pay the bill. Total costs are about what you would pay for a moderate-priced resort, plus meals. Divi is known for keeping their properties updated and offering a lot of activities. Food and service are good, Druif Beach is great, facilities are extensive, and you can pick and choose from five restaurants, three pools and six bars.

TAMARIJN ARUBA BEACH RESORT
☎ 800-554-2008 (in the US & Canada) or 297-525-5200 (on Aruba); fax 297-585-5203; www.tamarijnaruba.com
236 rooms
$190-$200 (all-inclusive)

Tamarijn Aruba Beach Resort

If you upgrade to the mega package, you'll get all the goodies offered at the Tamarijn, plus those available at sister resort, Divi Aruba All-Inclusive Resort. At about $20 per person per day, this is a good option because the beach at Divi is better. All rooms at Tamarijn have an ocean view, and the activity list will keep you busy from sunup until the wee hours of the morning. Comparing the mega all-inclusive costs to room-meals-drinks-activities elsewhere, Tamarijn is in the moderate price range.

Hotels off the Beach

TIERRA DEL SOL RESORT & COUNTRY CLUB

Located on the northern end of island, near the California Lighthouse

☎ 800-492-2015 (in the US & Canada), 297-586-7800; fax 297-586-4970; www.tierradelsol.com

114 villas and condos

$425

Tierra del Sol

Golfers consider these plush accommodations paradise. Well off the beach, but sometimes with a view of the water, the privately owned two-, three- and four-bedroom villas and condos have spacious living areas, well-equipped kitchens, extra bathrooms, and shaded patios. Most people who stay here take advantage of unlimited play on the Palm Springs-like championship golf course and take the complimentary shuttle to nearby Arashi Beach between tee times. Some of the villas have their own pool, and all guests may use the resort pool and lighted tennis courts. See *Where to Eat*, page 160, for information on the resort's impressive **Ventanas del Mar Restaurant**.

TALK OF THE TOWN BEACH RESORT

Located on the main coastal highway between the airport and Oranjestad

☎ 297-582-3380 (on Aruba); fax 297-582-0327

www.tottaruba.com

51 rooms & one- & two-bedroom suites

$159 per person, includes breakfast buffet

Compared to most other resorts on the island, this one looks a bit dull. However, it has everything you need, and the mostly young, mostly European crowd that stays here has a marvelous time – especially during Carnival, when they have a spectacular view of the parade route. Rooms are basic, but clean and well maintained. Guests get free admission to the **Havana Nightclub** (known for great happy hours) and the private **Havana Beach Club** (with a dive shop and snack bar/grill), across the street. Rooms surround an Olympic-sized, palm-shaded pool, and there is an on-site restaurant.

THE MILL RESORT & SUITES

Located across Irausquin Blvd from Palm Beach and the Wyndham Resort in the high-rise area

☎ 800-992-2015 (in the US & Canada) or 297-586-7700; fax 297-586-7271; www.millresort.com

200 rooms & suites

$180-$200

You can't miss this two-story resort for two reasons. First, it's the only low-rise in the high-rise area; second, it's right next to the landmark Dutch windmill. This is a

The Mill Resort & Suites

great place to save a little money. Everything is modern and clean, the units are spacious and well-equipped, and guests are within easy walking distance of all the glitz and glamour of the high-rise resorts. The resort even has a towel and lounge-chair hut on lively Palm Beach, but some guests prefer the party atmosphere around the resort pool.

ARUBA MILLENNIUM

Inland from Palm Beach off Highway 3 (Palm Beach Road) in Noord

☎ 297-586-3700; fax 297-586-2506

www.arubamillenniumresort.com

32 studio & one-bedroom units

$130-$172

Location and value are the big draws here. Less than a five-minute stroll inland from Palm Beach, the low-cost resort features a pool, sundeck, whirlpool tubs, and a mini-mart for stocking the fridge. Everything was updated recently, so expect clean, but basic, accommodations.

COCONUT INN

Inland from Palm Beach near Santa Anna Church in Noord

☎ 866-978-4952 (toll-free), 297-586-6288 (Aruba); fax 297-586-5433 ; www.coconutinn.com

40 studio & one-bedroom units

$80-$100

Coconut palms do indeed shade this tidy little motel located in a residential area. Breakfast is included in the room rate, and all units have either a full or mini-kitchen, so guests can save money on meals. The physically fit can easily manage the 20-minute hike to Palm Beach, but there's an on-site pool.

★CARIBBEAN PALM VILLAGE

Inland from Palm Beach near Santa Anna Church in Noord

☎ 297-586-2700; fax 297-586-2380; www.cpvr.com

228 studios & one- & two-bedroom units

$160-$225

Caribbean Palm Village

You can rent these spacious Mediterranean-style units from the resort, basically a timeshare property, when there's availability. Lush landscaping makes up for it being a mile from Palm Beach. There are two pools, and every unit has a full or mini-kitchen. You'll be tempted to skip cooking and dine at on-site **Valentinos** when you smell the luscious Italian aromas coming from the restaurant.

★AMSTERDAM MANOR BEACH RESORT

In the low-rise area across a narrow road from Eagle Beach
☎ 800-932-6509 or 297-527-1100; fax 297-527-1112
www.amsterdammanor.com
72 studios & one- & two-bedroom units
$232-$255

The name well describes this Hollandesque resort with multiple turrets and gables. Landscaped courtyards and a waterfall pool add to the quaint, lovely atmosphere. Guests enjoy a state-of-the-art outdoor cyberstation for accessing the Internet and e-mail, a garden

Amsterdam Manor

gazebo for quiet escapes, and an open-air bar for sunset happy hours. Free watersports, a children's playground, and planned weekly activities keep families, singles, and couples busy.

Rental Agencies

Contact one of the following for information about renting a condo, villa, apartment, or private home.

ARUBA SERVICES/THE MALMOK MANAGEMENT COMPANY

☎ 297-586-7569, 297-733-1773 (cell); www.arubaservices. com

ARUBA VILLA RENTALS
☎ 297-586-4290; fax 297-586-4490; www.aruba-villarentals.com

ARUBA LUXURY CONDOS
☎ 800-886-7822 (in the US), 866-875-2582 (in Canada); fax 401-989-5235; www.arubaluxurycondos.com

Where to Eat

 No need to dress for dinner. Restaurants on Aruba know you're on vacation, and probably sunburned, so they don't expect you to put on uncomfortable clothes. Chances are you'll be dining outdoors on a patio, perhaps overlooking the sea, and anything more than clean shorts or a colorful sun dress will appear pretentious.

For a small island, Aruba has a lot of places to eat, and most are good; a few are outstanding. The variety of cuisine is extensive, and you can find everything from Argentinian steaks to German Wienerschnitzel to Aruban fried funchi. Chefs are determined to wow you with their talent and become the topic of complimentary chatter around the resort swimming pool.

Unfortunately, if you plan to dine well and often, you will be spending heavily. Almost everything in the restaurants' kitchens is imported, and the cost is passed on to you. To ease the sting and allow visitors to try a variety of eateries, two programs are available: the Dine Around Program and the Visit Aruba Program.

DINE AROUND

The **Dine Around Program** is sponsored by the Aruba Gastronomic Association, www.arubadining.com. A long list of excellent restaurants belong to the program, which allows you to prepay for a package of three ($109), five ($177), or seven ($245) dinners that may be enjoyed at any of the member establishments. Each evening meal includes an appetizer, entrée, dessert, and coffee or tea. Another plan allows you to purchase five breakfasts or lunches plus four dinners for $214.

The **Visit Aruba Card** costs $12-$14 and allows cardholders to receive a discount at participating restaurants, as well as hotels, car rental agencies, and island attractions. Purchase the card before you leave home, and it will be delivered to your hotel. Contact Visit Aruba, www.visitaruba.com.

All-inclusive packages sometimes allow guests to dine at restaurants in other resorts, so ask when you make your reservation. Most resort restaurants serve wonderful meals, but you'll enjoy more variety if you try some of the independent establishments, as well.

Restaurants sometimes change their hours of operation during low season, and a few close for several weeks during the summer, so call ahead to avoid disappointment.

Dining With the Stars

Every restaurant listed in this guide is recommended, and you will find some marked with stars. One star (★) indicates that the restaurant is highly recommended, two stars (★★) mean you should make an extra effort to eat there, and three stars (★★★) promise an experience to remember. The rating may be for super value or an amazing view or, perhaps, simply the best "cheeseburgers in paradise."

Restaurant Price Guide

Use the prices given at the beginning of each restaurant listing as a guide to the average price of a mid-range meal per person, excluding drinks and tip.

Tipping

Some restaurants add a 10% to 15% service charge to your bill, so always review the charges before paying. The service charge is typically divided among all the employees of the restaurant, including the cooks, bus boys, and front-desk personnel. If you wish to reward your server with an extra tip, add it to your credit slip or hand cash directly to your waitress or waiter. An additional 5% seems right, if a service charge is automatically added. Otherwise, leave the usual 15% to 20% tip.

Oranjestad

MARANDI
L.G. Smith Blvd 1, next to Havana Beach Club
☎ 297-582-0157; www.marandiaruba.com
International/Caribbean
$2--$30
Daily 5:30-11pm
Reservations highly recommended.

Arrive early to secure a place on one of the cozy couches in the sand beside the water. This is the best place for sipping a cool drink while you watch the sun set. If you want to observe the chef at work, and it's an amazing experience, reserve a spot at "the kitchen table." Otherwise, ask to sit at one of the tables in the open-air thatched-roof palapa, where you will have an unimpeded view of the sky and sea. Fish is the specialty, but the menu includes chicken, beef and pork dishes. Everything is tweaked a bit with Caribbean spices and Euro-Asian-inspired sauces.

★★★CHEZ MATILDE
Havenstraat 23
☎ 297-583-9200; www.matildearuba.com
French & International
$30-$45 dinner, $20 lunch

Monday-Saturday, 11:30 am-2:30 pm and daily 6-11 pm
Reservations highly recommended

This is the swankiest place on the island, and if you're going to get dressed up and spend a lot of money, this is the place to do it. Even in the elegant atmosphere, the service is efficiently friendly. Ask for a table in  the back room, where you will be surrounded by greenery. Entreés include ostrich and wild boar, but you can get Châteaubriand or fish if you prefer. After dinner, indulge in crème brûlé and cognac.

DRIFTWOOD

Klipstraat 12
☎ 297-583-2515; www.driftwoodaruba.com
Aruban & seafood
$15-$30
Wednesday-Monday, 5:30-11 pm
Reservations highly recommended

Even with a reservation, you'll probably have to wait for a table during high season. The locally caught seafood includes octopus, squid, scallops, shrimp, and lobster. Many of the dishes are served Aruban-style, which means with a spicy tomato-based Creole sauce, but you can ask for something else. Since the fish is so fresh, you may want it lightly cooked and naked. Everything comes with side dishes and cornbread.

★ EL GAUCHO

Wilheminastraat 80
☎ 297-582-3677; www.elgaucho-aruba.com
Argentine
$20-$25
Monday-Saturday, 11:30 am-11 pm
Reservations highly recommended

This landmark restaurant gets booked up early, so call well in advance. The featured item is grilled Argentinian beef, and the large steaks and popular mixed-meat skewers are as tender and delicious as advertised. If you're not a meat eater, there are several fish choices, but strict vegetarians will be happier some place else.

IGUANA JOE'S

Royal Plaza Mall
☎ 297-583-9373; www.iguanajoesaruba.com
Aruban, Caribbean & Mexican
$8-$20
Monday-Saturday, 11 am-midnight; Sunday, 5 pm-midnight

Iguana Joe's

Original specialty drinks are the big draw here, but the food is surprisingly good as well. Large salads and thick burgers are recommended for lunch. Try the ribs or fajitas for dinner.

QUE PASA

Wilheminastraat 18
☎ 297-583-4888; www.quepasaaruba.com
International
Entrées $14-$25
Daily, 5 pm-12 am
Reservations recommended

Co-owners Addie and Marvin recently moved their popular restaurant to a new location at Wilhelminastraat 18, near City Hall. Customers now have a choice of eating in the colorful air conditioned dining room or on the breeze-cooled upstairs terrace. The menu has expanded and continues to change according to Chef Addie's whims, but expect international favorites among some creative dishes based on European, Caribbean, Mexican and Japanese recipes. Think fusion-gone-wild. Unfortunately, on a recent visit we were disappointed by the barbecued ribs, but everything else was excellent. We highly recommend the fried brie appetizer. The creamy French cheese is coated with nuts, topped with cranberries and perfectly complements drinks from the well-stocked bar. Entree choices range from fish, to chicken, to veal, lamb and beef. Most of the dishes are priced under $20, which allows you to indulge in dessert without blowing your budget. Go for the chocolate crème brûlée. You won't regret the calories.

Before you leave, take time to admire the art by local artists, which is hanging on the restaurant walls and is sold in the upstairs gallery.

★ CUBA'S COOKIN'

Wilhelminastraat 27
☎ 297-588-0627; www.cubascookin.com
Cuban
$10-$30
Monday-Saturday 11 am-midnight; Sunday, 6-11pm (closed Sundays during off-season)
Reservations recommended for dinner

Set in an 1877 colonial home across from the downtown police station, this cozy restaurant serves up authentic Cuban food. The atmosphere is fun and energetic, with colorful original art on the walls and a lively Cuban quartet playing jumpin' music. Try one of the icy specialty drinks to quench the fire of hot, hot, hot salsa served with yucca chips. The Churasco (a huge Cuban-style steak), and lobster enchiladas are a real treat. If you've never been to Havana, this is your chance.

THE WATERFRONT CRABHOUSE
Seaport Marketplace
☎ 297-583-5858
Caribbean, seafood & International
$8-$35
Daily, 8 am-11 pm
Reservations recommended

Waterfront Crabhouse

The menu is updated regularly, but if Chef Carlo is offering Scallops and Shrimp Florentine, order it. Open all day, the sea-theme restaurant is a great place to get breakfast or lunch after shopping the waterfront malls. Kids have a new menu featuring hamburgers, hot dogs and pasta.

SCANDALS
Seaport Marketplace
☎ 297-583-4488
Seafood & vegetarian
$10-$20
Monday-Saturday, 6 pm-1 am; Sunday, 5-11 pm
Reservations recommended for dinner

Chef Harmen and sous chef Pascal welcome special requests, but the menu is so varied, you will surely find several things to try. The grilled and garnished salmon is recommended. Happy hour on Fridays from 5 until 7 pm includes drink specials and snacks. Live music plays Saturdays beginning around 10 pm. On Sundays, the restaurant opens only for dinner, and those in the know drop in to enjoy the signature cheese fondue.

In the Resort Areas

FRENCH STEAKHOUSE
Manchebo Beach Resort
☎ 297-582-3444; www.manchebo.com/steakhouse
Steaks & seafood
$18-$25
Daily, 5:30-11 pm
Reservations recommended

Churrasco can mean different things in different countries, but at the French Steakhouse it means a thick cut of tenderloin from Argentina, marinated in red wine, olive oil and herbs, and grilled to order. Ooh-la-la! Now you know why the place is packed with hungry locals and visitors. The prices are right, too. Try the five-course Ambassador's meal for about $30. If you're not a meat lover, the seafood is just as good, and the wine list is one of the most extensive on the island. The adjoining Garden Terrace is open-air casual and serves breakfast daily 7 am-noon.

AQUA GRILL
Palm Beach, next to Amazonia Restaurant and across from the Hyatt
☎ 297-586-5900; www.aqua-grill.com
Seafood
$15-$30
Monday-Saturday 6-11 pm, Sunday 5-11 pm
Reservations recommended

Ignore the clamor of happy customers and focus on the superb seafood set before you at this

popular eatery. Noise ricochets off all the glass and metal in the wide-open spaces, but no one seems to mind, or even notice. Probably because of the marvelous selection of fresh seafood laid out on the raw bar and the fantastic aromas coming from the open kitchen. Stick to the grouper and snapper if you want fresh-off-the-boat local fish. Order lobster from Maine or king crab from Alaska if you prefer fresh-off-the-plane varieties from around the world. Either way, you won't be disappointed.

MOOMBA BEACH BAR & GRILL
Palm Beach
☎ 297-586-5365; www.moombabeach.com
International
$18-$35
Daily, 8 am-11 pm; bar stays open late

Look for lounge chairs and tables scattered around the sand on the beach between the Marriott Ocean Club and the Holiday Inn. This is MoomBa – part-restaurant, part-bar, all fun. You can spend the day and most of the night here playing pool, surfing the Internet, paddling a kayak along the shore, drinking icy beer and eating all your favorite foods. Breakfast, lunch and dinner are served seaside or in the shady palapa. Happy hour is 5-7 pm, with fruity frozen drinks the specialty. The menu is described as "Caribbean Chic," which means fun food, such as fajitas, pasta, and grilled meats. Once a month, MoomBa throws a full-moon party that draws a large crowd of locals and visitors who revel late into the night.

★TUSCANY

Aruba Marriott Resort, Palm Beach
☎ 297-586-9000
Italian
$20-$40
Daily, 6-11 pm
Reservations accepted

No explanations
needed. This northern
Italian restaurant is
just what you would
expect. Lovely atmo-
sphere. Excellent ser-
vice. Outstanding
cuisine. The menu
leans heavily toward
the popular recipes of
Florence: antipasti
starters;   meats

cooked with mushrooms and sun-dried tomatoes, served
with pesto-spiked vegetables; and Amaretto-laced gelato
for dessert. A piano plays in the background to add a bit of
grace to the rustic-touch setting.

★MADAME JEANETTE

Cunucu Abao 37
☎ 297-587-0184; www.madamejeanette.com
Caribbean & International
$23-$37
Wednesday-Monday, 6-10 pm
Reservations highly recommended

There's no one called Madame Jeanette here. In fact, the
name refers to a variety of pepper used by cooks all around
the island. Award-winning chefs Kasi and Boris oversee the
kitchen, which turns out a creative mix of Continental cuisine with an Austrian bent and a Caribbean twist. Prices are
amazingly reasonable. The garden seating is romantically
charming. The small diverse menu offers rotisserie beef,

sauced seafood, and pork Cordon Bleu. Madame is located a couple of miles inland, on the east/west road, across from the Amsterdam Beach Resort.

★★AMAZONIA CHURRASCARIA

Juan E. Irausquin Blvd 374, across from the Hyatt Hotel
☎ 297-586-4444; www.amazonia-aruba.com
Brazilian steakhouse & vegetarian
$22 (vegetarian) - $35 (meats)
Daily, 6-11 pm; Sundays 4-11 pm
Reservations recommended

Come hungry. It's all you can eat, and you'll want to eat a lot. First, you create a feast from the bountiful salad bar that features traditional goodies, plus delicacies such as portobello mushrooms, hearts of palm, and grilled red peppers. Cheese bread and a nice selection of cooked veggie dishes are brought to your table. Stop there if you're a light eater or vegetarian – otherwise, summon the strolling meat carvers. They cruise the dining room carrying a skewer of meat (beef, chicken, pork, and lamb) and a large carving knife. If you would like a serving of whatever they are carrying, simply signal, and they will slice off a generous portion for you to take onto your plate. If you'd like to try another selection, signal again. When you think you can't eat another bite, stop signaling. Pace yourself, and save room for one of the excellent desserts.

BUCCANEER

Gasparito 11C
☎ 297-586-6172
International & seafood
$10-$25
Monday-Saturday, 5:30-11 pm.
Reservations accepted

The big draw here is fish, alive and quite recently deceased. Huge saltwater aquariums are built into the walls of one dining room, and a large tropical fish tank dominates another. The menu features all kinds of seafood, from crabmeat cocktail to broiled lobster tail. Meat lovers have a choice of steak, pork chops, and broiled chicken.

★LE DOME

Juan E. Irausquin Blvd 224, across from Eagle Beach
☎ 297-587-1517; www.ledome-aruba.com
Belgian and French
$15-$45
Daily, noon-3 pm, 5-10:30 pm; Sunday brunch 11 am-3 pm
Reservations highly recommended

Make reservations early during high season. This fetching dome covers four dining areas, three indoor, and a terrific outdoor terrace with a view of the Caribbean. The menu changes frequently, but count on exquisite sauces over duck, lamb, seafood, and the best cuts of beef.

★PAPIAMENTO

Washington 61, Noord
☎ 297-586-4544; www.papiamentorestaurant.com
Caribbean, International & seafood
$20-$38
Tuesday-Sunday, 6-10:30 pm
Reservations highly recommended

This is your chance to get inside one of the island's well-preserved old manor houses. The Ellis family has fixed up their 150-year-old home, air-conditioned the indoor dining area, and set tables around the garden swimming pool. Award-winning family chefs prepare delicious seafood dishes, including the Clay Pot for two (seafood, veggies, and herbs steamed at 600° in a handmade pot). A few chicken and beef choices even out the menu. The food and atmosphere have earned the restaurant membership in the prestigious Chaine des Rotisseurs.

★★RUINAS DEL MAR

Hyatt Regency Aruba Resort
☎ 297-586-1234
Continental & seafood
$20-$40
Daily, 5:30-10:30 pm; Sunday brunch, 9 am-2 pm
Reservations requested during high season, recommended otherwise

Atmosphere is the main lure, but the food is as good (and as expensive) as you would expect it to be at a Hyatt. Ask to sit outside on the faux stone-ruin terrace overlooking the lagoon and sea. The breakfast buffet is extensive, and will keep you sufficiently full through most of the day. The dinner menu includes mixed seafood grill and a surf-and-turf with lobster. Sunday brunch is an island tradition that just got better with the arrival of Chef Miguel Garcia, who likes guests to linger over his decadent dishes and made-to-order creations.

SUNSET GRILLE

Radisson Aruba Resort
☎ 297-586-6555
Seafood & steakhouse
$25-$50
Daily, 6-11 pm; Sunday brunch, 11 am-2:30 pm
Reservations recommended

Among the resort restaurants, this one stands out because of its cosmopolitan cuisine, typical of that found in New York City or San Francisco. The steaks are huge, seafood is right from  the sea (try the pan-seared ruby red sushi-grade Ahi tuna), the wine list is impressive, and the fabulous desserts from the in-house bakery are large enough to share. More than 90 selections are listed on the wine list, which recently earned an "Award of Excellence" from *Wine Spectator* magazine.

North End

LA TRATTORIA EL FARO BLANCO
California Lighthouse
☎ 297-586-0787; www.aruba-latrattoria.com
Italian
$8-$13 (breakfast), $8-$15 (lunch), $20-$40 (dinner)
Daily 9 am-11 pm
Credit cards accepted
Reservations recommended for dinner

 The views are terrific from this hilltop location at the California Lighthouse on the island's northwest tip. You can get lunch, snacks, and drinks here when you tour this end of the island, but plan to return for dinner. Arrive in time to enjoy sunset from the terrace. It's spectacular. Ossobuco, filet mignon, and traditional Italian pasta dishes appear on the menu.

★VENTANAS DEL MAR

Tierra del Sol Aruba Resort
☎ 297-586-7800
International & seafood
$8-$12 (breakfast), $10-$18 (lunch), $20-$35 (dinner)
Daily 7:30 am-3 pm and 6:30-10 pm
Credit cards accepted
Reservations recommended

Oh, life is good when you have sea views, broken only by rolling golf-course greens and a historic lighthouse, and fresh food, improved by fine herbs and lightly seasoned sauces. Ask for an outdoor table. You won't find a more elegantly romantic spot on the island.

South End

★CHARLIE'S BAR

Zeppenveldstraat 56 (Main Street), San Nicolas
☎ 297-584-5086
Aruban and seafood
$12-$20
Monday-Saturday, noon-9:30 pm; bar stays open late

Don't miss this totally Aruban experience. More bar than restaurant, the funky interior is decorated with more than 60 years of memorabilia collected from customers by Charlie, the Dutch sailor who opened the hangout in 1941, and his son, Charles Brouns III (just call him Charlie), the current proprietor. The food is good, but not worth a special trip from the hotel district. Stop in for lunch or a snack and ice-cold beer when you tour the southern end of the island. Sit at the bar and chat with the bartenders, who will fill you in on all the latest gossip and tell you fantastic stories about Charlie's part in Aruba's wild past.

BRISAS DEL MAR

Savaneta 222A, Savaneta
☎ 297-584-7718; www.brisasdelmararuba.com
Seafood
$10-$25
Bar, daily, 3-11 pm; meals daily, noon-3 pm and 5-11 pm;
Sunday lunch, noon-3 pm
Reservations recommended

Recently renovated, this veteran seafood restaurant now
has new entrées at lunch and dinner. Sit on the open-air patio overlooking the Caribbean and enjoy a good fish dinner
with Aruban-style side dishes while you watch the sun set.
This family-owned restaurant is a longtime favorite of locals,
especially on Sunday afternoons, so call well in advance to
ensure getting a table. Consider having lunch here when
you tour the southern part of the island.

★★FLYING FISHBONE

Savaneta 344, Savaneta
☎ 297-584-2506
Seafood & International
$15-$30
Monday-Saturday, 5:30-10 pm
Reservations highly recommended

Put this enchanting
feet-in-the-sand res-
taurant on your list of
must-do places. The
food is excellent and
the wine selection is
good and affordable.
But, the secluded
beach setting in this
old fishing village is
what you come for.
Call well in advance to

Aerial view of the Flying Fishbone

request a table at the water's edge. Menu selections tend toward the nouveau; pesto sauce, fresh herbs, nuts, fruits, and

peppers are used in creative ways. You can't go wrong with the grilled seafood, but try something more adventurous for a real treat. Worth a special trip.

Nightlife

Aruba never sleeps. But, it does doze. After a long day on the beach, most tourists are ready to call it a night right after dinner. For those with more energy, a couple of the island's 11 casinos stay open 24/7, and many dance clubs start rolling about midnight and keep going as long as there are customers. Other nighttime activities include Vegas-style shows, current movies, local musical entertainment, and dinner/party cruises.

Pick up a free island publication to find out what's happening during the week. Most hotels and tourist spots have at least one of the local magazines: *Aruba Nights*, *K-Pasa*, or *Aruba Experience*. Also check the English-language newspapers: *Aruba Today* and *The News*. And don't ignore those colorful promotional pamphlets you'll see at your resort's activities desk. Many of them offer free drinks or discounts on admission.

You will fit perfectly into the night scene dressed in casual resort wear: a sundress or wrap skirt for the women; shorts or slacks and a polo shirt with sandals for either gender. Many of the young islanders like to dress up a bit, and you can't go wrong with summer-weight chic evening wear, especially if you plan to go to an upscale restaurant or trendy dance club.

Party Buses

You do the partying. They do the driving. What more could you ask for?

You must be 18 or older to join the fun, but there's no upward age limit, and many of the party-goers are well over 35.

BANANA BUS
☎ 297-993-0757; www.bananabusaruba.com
Tuesday-Thursday, 8 pm-1 am
Go bananas at this rolling party that takes place on a yellow-and-green open-air bus. Dance onboard as you travel from one bar to another. Five drinks and pick-up at your hotel are included in the $37 price.

KUKOO KUNUKU
☎ 297-586-2010; wwwkukookunuku.com
Monday-Saturday, 6 pm-midnight

Hop aboard the wildly painted 1957 Chevy Paranda bus for an open-air trip through the *cunucu* (countryside). The driver picks you up and delivers you back home, so all you have to do is party. The fun begins with a sunset cham-pagne toast, continues with an outdoor dinner, and

moves on to several bars. The first drink at each stop is free. Total cost for dinner, drinks, and delivery to and from your hotel is $59 per person. Book online for a $5 discount.

 *Check with the activities desk at your hotel or read through the free tourist publications to find out which resorts are hosting theme-night dinners during your stay. You don't have to be a guest of the hotel to attend, and the buffet dinner and live entertainment are usually well done. Try to attend at least one of these events. Some of the best include: the **Aruban Folkloric Show**, the **Carnival Extravaganza**, **Havana Night**, and the **Steel-band and Limbo Barbecue**.*

Dinner & Party Cruises

JOLLY PIRATES
☎ 297-586-8107; www.jollypirates.com
Thursday, 8:30-11:30 pm

Party cruise (Fernando Arroniz)

Get to the De Palm Pier (near the Aruba Grand Resort) at least a half-hour early so you can get settled, and bring your swimsuit and a towel, in case you have to walk the plank. Afterwards, swing pirate-style out on a rope and drop into the moonlit sea for a swim. Kids are welcome at $24.75 and adults pay $49.50.

TATTOO PARTY CRUISE
☎ 297-586-2010; www.arubaadventures.com/tattoo
Tuesday-Saturday, 8 pm-midnight

You must be 18 or older to join the festivities aboard this three-level catamaran. The bar serves $1 house drinks and $2 premium drinks on the second level, dancing takes place to a live band on the first level, and dinner is served under the stars on the top level. Bands and menus rotate on a nightly basis, so call early in the week to find out who's playing and what's for dinner each evening. The price is $44. Bring your swimsuit and a towel if you want to take a moonlight swim. The *Tattoo* departs De Palm Pier near the Aruba Grand Resort.

Casinos

At one time, gambling was the main reason some tourists came to Aruba. Now, there are many things to keep visitors busy, but the casinos remain popular centers of entertainment. Every one is a glitzy display of buzzing activity, humming conversations, and clanging bells.

The **Crystal Casino**, Renassance Resort (☎ 297-583-6000) across from the waterfront in Oranjestad, is open 24 hours a day, every day of the week. It's lavishly decorated with marble, brass, and gold leaf, all lighted by dripping-crystal chandeliers. Live entertainment is featured in the main room each evening, and a long-running Latin dance-and-music show is featured in the adjoining **Crystal Theatre**.

The only casino actually on the waterfront is the **Seaport Casino** (☎ 297-583-6000), which is about half the size of the Crystal and located across L.G. Smith Blvd at the Seaport Marketplace. It's a more casual place, with the usual tables and slot machines, plus bingo games on Tuesdays and Sundays. Live entertainment is featured Friday and Saturday nights.

The **Alhambra Casino and Aladdin Theatre** (☎ 297-583-5000), on Manchebo Beach in the low-rise resort area, is probably the most popular entertainment center on the island. The doorman, dressed as a genie, will shake your hand as you enter and welcome you to his world of Moorish fantasy. Inside, you'll find several bars and a restaurant, as well as more than 300 slot machines and the usual gaming tables. The theater features various acts, including singers, dancers, and impersonators. Shops out back are open until midnight, but the casino doesn't close until about 3 am.

The largest casino on the island is **Royal Cabana** at La Cabana Beach Resort (☎ 297-587-4665) in the low-rise hotel area. Its **Tropicana Showroom** has 600 seats and features a popular female impersonator show. The huge casino has the usual slots (more than 300) and gaming tables (more than 30), plus jewelry, cigar, and souvenir shops.

In the high-rise hotel district, all the big resorts have a casino. The **Westin Casablanca** (☎ 297-586-4466) has a bar and live music. Big-buck gamblers gather in the back and the Cabaret Royal Showroom features a review from Havana. **Copacabana** (☎ 297-586-1234) at the **Hyatt** has an impressive Rio theme. Stop in just to look around and put a few coins in the slots, even if you're not a gambler. A live band provides music every evening. The **Excelsior** (☎ 297-586-7777) at the **Holiday Inn** draws a crowd on Mondays, Wednesdays, and Fridays for 3:30 pm bingo games.

Live music sets a jovial mood at **Marriott's Stellaris** (☎ 297-586-9000). You can play the nickel slots or move up to high-rolling craps and blackjack. The **Royal Palm** (☎ 297-587-4665) at the **Occidental** hums with the sounds of roulette, Caribbean stud poker, and baccarat, but the pulse quickens nightly when the 10:30 bingo games begin.

Casino Hours & Etiquette

Aruba's 11 casinos open between 10 am and noon for slot-machine play, and late in the afternoon or early in the evening for game-table play. Call each casino for hours of operation and a schedule of entertainment; both may change seasonally. While dress is casual, most people wear resort-casual clothing to the casinos; swimsuits, short shorts, and beach shoes are out of place.

Clubs & Bars

You'll find great entertainment and cozy bars at all the high-rise resorts and many of the low-rise resorts. Trendy night spots and vivacious dance clubs line the waterfront and Mainstreet (Caya Betico Croes) in downtown Oranjestad. If you decide against taking one of the party buses, cab into town and bar hop along both roads. Friendly proprietors and locals welcome tourists and you'll feel right at home.

Don't make the mistake of thinking nightlife is dead when you pass deserted clubs at 11 pm. Wait an hour. The crowds start showing up about midnight; more pour in between 1 and 2 in the morning.

Hot spots change, but at publication, the following clubs and bars were the most popular. If you want up-to-the-minute info on where to find the best party, ask the young staff at your hotel or the restaurant waiters.

Club Time

Most bars open around noon and close at 2 am. Nightclubs open about 10 pm, really get going by midnight, and stay open until 3 am or when the last customer leaves. Call for specific hours and information about bands and special events.

First Class Karma Lounge (☎ 297-588-7928), in the Aventura Mall, draws a large well-dressed crowd with its Martini and Chivas Regal Bars. Near by, on the second level behind the Renaissance, **La Fiesta** (☎ 297-583-5896) has no real dance floor, but patrons dance on the wrap-around balcony and near the long bar.

Café Bahia (☎ 297-588-9982), on Weststraat across from the Royal Plaza Mall, opens its dance floor with disco music around 10 pm, after the main dinner service wraps up. Across the street, **Iguana Joe's** (☎ 297-583-9373), serves excellent drink specials in a wild and colorful space. Just down the street, **Carlos & Charlie's** (☎ 297-582-0355) is always packed with party-bus people, vacationers and locals who are drawn by the wide variety of music and the generous drink specials. Try a Mother Margarita, served in a 28-ounce souvenir glass.

A popular nightclub is in the Royal Plaza Mall on L.G. Smith Blvd – **Mambo Jambo** (☎ 297-583-3632), a laid-back open-air place with a Latin-Caribbean flavor and music. **Choose a Name** (☎ 297-588-6200), behind Royal Plaza Mall on Havenstraat, is famous for terrific live music and stiff specialty drinks. **Jimmy's Place** (☎ 297-582-2550), a block off Caya Betico Croes (Main Street) at the corner of Kuisweg and Digicel, is known for its delicious food and caters to business people during the early evening. Around midnight, the Place draws a mixed straight and gay crowd with creative drinks and live music.

Jazz lovers and cigar connoisseurs head to **Garufa** (☎ 297-582-3677), a swanky place with a classy humidor. It serves premium liquors and liqueurs. Located across the street from El Gaucho Restaurant at Wilhelminastraat 63.

Cuba's Cookin' (☎ 297-588-0627), at Weststraat 37, is the place to find hot, hot, hot salsa and meringue music. To cool down, ask for a mojita, which is made with mint, sugar and rum.

Out on Palm Beach, between the Radisson and Aruba Grand hotels, the **Kokoa Bar** (☎ 297-586-2050) is popular with sandy tourists looking for a party. Happy hour runs from 3-5pm, but the crowd lingers until around 10 pm. After that, everyone meanders over to the palapas at **MoomBa Beach Bar and Grill** (☎ 297-586-5365), where the action continues late into the night.

Elsewhere on the island, **Le Soleil Lounge** at Tierra del Sol Resort & Country Club (☎ 297-586-7800) is a relaxed and surprisingly casual place to enjoy drinks and quiet conversation. Bikers keep **Black Hog** filled to overflowing most evenings. It's located at Adventure Golf, across from La Cabana Resort (☎ 297-587-6625).

Island Facts & Contacts

AIRPORT: Queen Beatrix International Airport, ☎ 297-582-4800, www.airportaruba.com..

ATMs: Widely available at locations throughout the island, including the airport, shopping centers, hotels, and banks. Most dispense only Aruban florin. Machines are connected to the Cirrus network and accept Visa and MasterCard.

BANKS: Most banks are located in Oranjestad and Noord (near the high-rise hotels), and are open Monday-Friday, 8 am-noon and 1:30-3:45 pm. The Caribbean Mercantile Bank at the airport is open daily, 8 am-4 pm, Saturday-Sunday, 10 am-6 pm.

CAPITAL: Oranjestad.

COUNTRY CODE: 297.

DEPARTURE TAX: $37 for international flights (usually added to the cost of your airline ticket). The tax from Aruba to Bonaire is $10 and to Curaçao is $20.

DRIVING: Traffic travels on the right side of the road, as in the US, Canada, and most of Europe.

ELECTRICITY: The voltage is 110 AC (60 cycles), and the outlets accept the same plugs used in North America.

EMERGENCY: As of March 1, 2002, the emergency number for fire, police, and ambulance became ☎ 911.

GAS STATIONS: At publication, gas prices were in the range of 88¢ per liter, which is roughly equivalent to $3.25 per gallon. Stations are conveniently located near towns and the hotel district, and most accept major credit cards.

GOVERNMENT: Aruba is an autonomous part of the Kingdom of the Netherlands; the Dutch Government is responsible for defense and foreign affairs. Local government is based on a parliamentary democracy.

HOSPITAL: Horacio Oduber Hospital on L.G. Smith Blvd, ☎ 297-587-4300.

Aruba

LANGUAGE: The official language is Dutch, but locals speak Papiamento (spelled Papiamentu on Bonaire). Many are multilingual and also speak Spanish, English, and German.

LEGAL AGE: 18 for drinking and gambling.

MONEY: The official currency of Aruba is the Aruban Florin (AF or Afl), which is divided into 100 cents. US and Canadian dollars and most major credit cards are widely accepted. Current exchange rates are stable at 1.77 Afl to the US dollar and 1.34 Afl to the Canadian dollar. One of the most unusual coins in the world is the square Aruban 50-cent piece.

 The Central Bank of Aruba does not permit coin change to be given in any other than Aruban currency; an exception is in the casinos. You may drop your leftover coins in the charity box at the airport.

PHARMACY: Botica Eagle, near the hospital on L.G. Smith Blvd, ☎ 297-587-6103.

PHONES: To call Aruba from North America, dial 011-297 + the seven-digit local number. The international access code is 011; the country code for Aruba is 297; the local number has seven digits. To call Aruba from Europe or most other countries, dial 00 (the international access number) + 297 + the seven-digit number.

On Aruba, dial only the seven-digit local number to reach local numbers.

Buy a phone card at hotel shops to make long distance and local calls on public phones. AT&T long distance is available by dialing 800-8000. To call internationally from Aruba, dial 00 plus the country code. (The country code for the US & Canada is 1.)

International cell phones may be rented at many hotel reception desks. Your cell phone from home will not work on the island.

POPULATION: 90,506 (2000 Central Bureau of Statistics).

PUBLICATIONS: These English-language magazines are available free in hotel lobbies and at many tourist attractions: *Aruba Nights*, *Aruba Experience*, *Menu*, and *Aruba Food and Wine*. Island news and current events are listed in English-language newspapers, *The News* and *Aruba Today*.

SAFETY: Aruba is considered safe. Take common precautions to avoid theft, especially from cars parked at tourist attractions and beaches.

SHOPPING HOURS: If a cruise ship is in Oranjestad, many stores will open on Sundays. Otherwise, shop hours are Monday-Saturday, 8:30 am-6 pm. Some stores remain open until 8 pm on select days. Some close for lunch and siesta from noon to 2 pm.

TAXES: There is a new 3% sales tax. Hotels legally add a government tax and service charge of 17.66%. In addition, most hotels add an energy tax per room per day. Ask in advance about these additions to the room rate. Restaurants often add a 10-15% service charge. Departure tax to the US is $37, usually included in the price of your airline ticket.

TAXIS: ☎ 582-2116 or 582-1604.

TIME: Aruba is on Atlantic Standard Time (AST) year-round, which is one hour later than Eastern Standard Time and four hours earlier than Greenwich Mean Time. The island does not observe Daylight Savings Time, so Aruba's time corresponds to Eastern Daylight Savings Time.

TOURIST INFORMATION: ☎ 800-TO-ARUBA (in the US & Canada); www.aruba.com. **Aruba Tourism Authority**, L.G. Smith Blvd 172, Oranjestad, ☎ 297-582-3777.

TRANSFER FEE: Passengers transferring to non-US-bound flights in Aruba are charged a $3 fee.

WATER: Tap water is purified seawater and safe for drinking .

WEBSITES: Dozens of sites offer information about activities, accommodations, and travel. The best general information sites are **www.aruba-travelguide.com** and **www. aruba.com**.

Aruba

Bonaire

Boca Bartol

Boca Cocolishi

Playa Chiquito

Washington/
Slagbaai
Nat'l Park

Playa Grandi

Onima

Boca Olivia

Brasil

Dos Pos

Rincon

Karpata

Fontein

Tras di
Montania

Spel

Playa
Frans

Santa
Barbara

Bolivia

Lagun

Playa
Lechi

Klein
Bonaire

Kralendijk

Sabana

Nieuw
Amsterdam

Lima

Lac
Bay

N

Public
Beach

Flamingo
Int'l Airport

Bachelor's
Beach

Sorob

Pink
Beach

Flamingo
Sanctuary

Pekel Meer

Oranje Pan

Willemstoren
Lighthouse

Paved Roads

Unpaved Roads
& Cycling Tracks

25 KM

15.5 MILES

Bonaire
Overview

Divers and eco-tourists cherish this quiet, sun-drenched island for its superior underwater world and arid natural beauty. In 1979, the Bonaire government declared the entire coastline and all the surrounding waters a protected marine reserve. As a result, anchoring is banned around its coral reefs, divers must adhere to a series of nature-sustaining rules, and boats

cannot dump ballast water within 12 miles of the island's coast.

Over the years Bonaire has consistently ranked as one of the world's top snorkeling and scuba destinations and has won eco-tourism awards for its superb preservation of nature. Development is rigorously controlled and intentionally slow-paced. Although it's larger than Aruba, Bonaire has a smaller population (15,000± verses 89,000±) and entertains fewer visitors (60,000± compared to 600,000± annually).

There are no fast-food chains, golf courses, or high-rise hotels. Only sparse vegetation grows on the rain-starved land, but beautiful nature flourishes everywhere. Graceful pink flamingos feed near stunning salt pans, lazy iguanas sprawl atop oversized limestone boulders, and frisky wild donkeys

Bougainvillea (Susan Swygert)

graze on untamed patches of scrub brush. Some 190 species of birds live and breed in the 13,500-acre national park that covers the entire northwest end of the island. A half-mile off the western shore, turtles and various waterfowl nest undisturbed on Klein Bonaire, a little spit of flat, rocky, uninhabited land that is destined to become another Antilles National Park.

The 15,000 residents of Bonaire are committed to preserving the island's colorful Dutch heritage and intrinsic beauty. Most of the friendly inhabitants speak several languages, including the official Dutch and colloquial Papiamentu (Papiamento on Curaçao and Aruba). Visitors are warmly welcomed and offered a variety of accommodations, restaurants, and activities.

Kralendijk (krawl-in-dike), is the capital and only sizeable town. It's nestled into the sheltered western curve of the croissant-shaped island and features a scattering of colorful shops, open-air restaurants, a vendor's market, and the historical Fort Oranje. Elsewhere on the 112-square-mile island, visitors spend time on the coral-strewn beaches,

Facing page: Ocean kayaking (Susan Swyget)

discover underwater treasures in the vast **Marine Park**, windsurf at **Lac Bay**, and hike through **Washington-Slagbaai National Park**.

Eight Reasons to Visit

- Unsurpassed diving and snorkeling sites in the Bonaire Marine Park.
- The tiny satellite island of Klein Bonaire.
- Eco-friendly Washington-Slagbaai National Park.
- Colonies of pink flamingos at Goto Meer.
- Excellent windsurfing at Lac Bay.
- Historic slave huts near the salt works.
- The chance to spot a few of the island's 190 bird species.
- Friendly residents.

THE OBELISKS OF BONAIRE

Look for three surviving obelisks near the salt pans. Around 1837, the Dutch government built four of these large stone structures to mark the spot where ships could pick up loads of salt for exportation. Originally, one was painted orange in honor of the Royal House of Orange, and each of the others was painted a color of the Dutch flag (red, white, and blue).

Unique Celebrations

January 1, **Maskarada**, is a truly unique Bonaire celebration. Residents disguise themselves in masks and colorful outfits to parade through the streets. The holiday has a long history on the island, but residents disagree over its origins. Some claim the celebration was started by the Caiquetio Indians, but it's more likely that the tradition has African roots and was brought to the island by slaves. Originally only adult males were allowed to participate. Today, women join the fun. The Kabes (head)

Maskarada

wears a crown and is in charge of organizing activities that include music, pranks, and parade stops at homes to ask for a bit of refreshment, typically rum.

April is the traditional month for the **Simadan Festival**, which started when the island's plantation owners first allowed slaves to farm their own small parcel of land. Owners of the *kunuku* (farm) invited friends to a pancake breakfast, then asked them to help harvest the crops (mostly maize or sorghum). Afterward, everyone stayed on to feast, dance, and play music. Residents of Rincón, the oldest town on the island, are responsible for maintaining the tradition of Simadan as a symbol of Bonaireans' helpfulness and good-natured spirits.

April 30, **Rincón Day** and the **Queen's Birthday**, is one of the most popular holidays on the island. Residents celebrate with a song festival, entertainment by local bands, a folk arts display, and plenty of food and drink.

September 6 is **Bonaire Day**, a national holiday and island-wide celebration hosted each year by one of the island's six neighborhoods.

October sees the **Bonaire International Sailing Regatta**, with sailboats from the micro class, guided from shore, to huge yachts and trimarans. After the races, everyone heads

to happy hour, followed by nightly music and entertainment.
☎ 717-5555; www.bonaireregatta.org.

> **TOURIST INFO:** For exact dates and informa-
> tion about this year's festivals and special
> events, contact **Tourism Corporation Bonaire**,
> ☎ 800-266-2473 (in the US) or 717-8322 (on
> Bonaire); www.infobonaire.com.

TELEPHONING

To call Bonaire from North America, dial
011-599 + the seven-digit local number,
which begins with 7, the island code. To
call from Europe or most other countries, dial 00 +
599 and the seven-digit number. On Bonaire itself,
dial only the seven-digit local number.

Getting to Bonaire

By Air

If you arrive by air, you will land on **Flamingo International Airport's** 8,100-foot-long runway.
The small, modern airport (the airport code is
BON) is on the west coast, about five minutes by car from
the capital, Kralendijk. Contact the airport at ☎ 717-5600 or
www.flamingoairport.com.

You'll find an ATM and car rental offices at the arrival terminal. Maps and tourist information are available outside the
baggage claim area, and taxis meet all flights.

Several carriers serve the island, and the number and frequency of flights is increasing. In addition, charter flights are
sometimes available, so check with vacation wholesalers
and certified travel agents who specialize in the Caribbean,
then double-check their quotes with a bit of Internet re-

search before you decide how to travel. With some investigation, you can uncover great deals, especially during the off-season.

North American travelers can fly non-stop from Houston TX and Newark NJ, and European vacationers can fly non-stop from Amsterdam. Connection flights leave from gateway cities in the US, with brief stops in Jamaica, Puerto Rico, or Curaçao.

See Documentation on pages 30-32 for information on visas and acceptable identification required for visitors to Bonaire.

LOCAL AIRLINE CONTACT INFORMATION	
Air Jamaica	☎ 800-523-5585 (in N America and the Caribbean), 599-9-888-2300 (on Curaçao); www.airjamaica.com
American Airlines/ American Eagle	☎ 599-717-3668 (on Bonaire), 800-433-7300 (in N. America)
Continental Airlines	☎ 297-588-0019 (on Aruba), 800-523-3273 (in N. America)
Delta Airlines	☎ 297-588-6119 (on Aruba); www.delta.com
Divi Divi Air	☎ 599-9-888-1050 (on Curaçao); www.flydivi.com
Dutch Antilles Express	☎ 715-3471 or 717-0808; www.flydae.com
KLM	☎ 297-582-3546 (on Aruba); www.klm.com
United Airlines	☎ 297-582-9592; www.united.com
US Airways	☎ 297-800-1580 (on Aruba); www.usairways.com

Bonaire

See *Getting Here* on pages 39-41 for additional airline information.

By Cruise Ship

 Holland America, Seabourn, Clipper, and Windjammer are a few of the cruise lines that regularly dock in Kralendijk's harbor. Taxis meet passengers when they disembark, but you won't need one to tour the town. Even leisurely strollers can walk from one end of town to the other in 10 minutes.

Tourist information, an ATM, restaurants, shops, and a casino are within walking distance of the dock. If you don't sign up with your cruise line for a shore excursion, you can take a taxi to the beach or hire a driver for a private island tour.

Tour Operators and a selection of scheduled excursions are listed under *Touring the Island* on page 184.

Leaving Bonaire

The international departure tax is $32 per person, and is not usually included in the price of your airline ticket. Some tour companies add the tax to your package price, so be sure to ask before you pay. Passengers taking a domestic flight to another ABC island pay $6 or NAfl 10 (see page 34 for currency exchange rates).

Getting Around
By Taxi

 Bonaire is a small island and many taxi drivers hang around the airport or town waterfront most of the day. If you want to take a taxi from some other location, call the dispatch stand at the airport, ☎ 717-8100.

Taxi drivers are excellent tour guides because, for the most part, they grew up on the island and cover it by car every day. A private tour runs about $25 per hour.

The government sets legal rates for unmetered taxis on Bonaire. Ask to see a rate schedule or agree in advance on a fare before you get into the cab. Expect to pay about $8 for a ride from the airport into town or to nearby beach hotels. A trip from the airport to the popular dive hotels just north of Kralendijk will run about $11. The fare to or from the waterfront in town is set at $7-$10 for west coast beaches and hotels; approximately $20 to Lac Bay on the east coast.

Taxi drivers are allowed to add an additional 20% to the regular fare on official holidays, Sundays, between the hours of 7 pm and midnight, and any time your belongings prevent them from closing their trunk securely. Between midnight and 7 am, the fare is 50% higher.

By Car

Car Rentals

 Roads are good on Bonaire, except in isolated areas of the countryside. A regular car will take you most places, but it's helpful to have a four-wheel-drive vehicle if you plan to explore out-of-the-way areas – and you should. Most rental policies prohibit driving traditional cars off-road or in the national park.

Driving is on the right, as in the US, Canada, and most of Europe. Distances and speedometers are in kilometers. Road signs are in Dutch, with international symbols, and the car rental agencies hand out a flyer with explanations. Take a look at it before you start off.

To rent, you must be more than 21 years old (some companies rent only to those older than 25) and have a driver's license that has been valid for at least two years. If you plan to decline insurance offered by the rental company, check with your insurance agency and the credit card you intend to use for payment and security to be sure that you are covered. Some credit card companies do not cover you for rentals outside your home country, or when you are driving a jeep, truck, or other non-traditional vehicle. American Express and Visa Gold Card customers are not covered when they rent a sports car or four-wheel-drive vehicle.

Rental rates vary season-to-season, but they average about $35-$40 per day for a small car with manual transmission, air-conditioning, and unlimited mileage. Jeeps, trucks, and minivans are in the $65-per-day range. Weekly rates are available and may work out to be less per day. Insurance add-ons begin at $10 per day, but you may be responsible for $500 worth of damage anyway. Check before you sign up.

INTERNATIONAL COMPANIES	
Avis	☎ 717-5795; www.avis.com
Budget	☎ 717-4700; www.bonaire-budgetcar.com
Hertz	☎ 717-7221; www.hertz.com
Alamo/National	☎ 717-7940; www.alamonationalbonaire.com

For toll-free numbers and website information see Getting Around on page 45.

LOCAL COMPANIES	
AB	☎ 717-8980; www.abcarrental.com
Everts	☎ 717-8719; www.evertscarrental.com
Flamingo	☎ 717-5588
Island	☎ 717-2100; www.islandrentalsbonaire.com
Samara	☎ 717-8188
Total	☎ 717-8313; www.totalcarrentalbonaire.com
Trupial	☎ 717-8487

By Bicycle, Scooter & Motorcycle

 Bonaire is small and flat, with little traffic, so visitors sometimes use bikes or motorcycles for basic transportation. Others enjoy exploring the countryside on bicycles. Six marked bike trails are laid out along the coast and through the national park. Local bike shops conduct guided tours.

 See Biking, page 233, for trail information.

Rates are about $10 per day for a three-speed bike, $15-$20 for a 21-speed bike, $28 for a scooter, $50 for a motorcycle, and $100 for a Harley. Some resorts have bikes for the use of their guests, and you can rent motorized and peddle-powered two-wheelers from the following shops.

BIKE RENTAL SHOPS
Bonaire Motorcycle Shop Kaya Grandi 54, Kralendijk, ☎ 717-7790; also at the airport, ☎ 717-8420
Cycle Bonaire Den Laman Bldg, Kaya Gobernador Debrot, Kralendijk, ☎ 717-2229; www.cyclebonaire.com
De Freewieler Kaya Grandi 61, Kralendijk, ☎ 717-8545 ATVs also available.
Hot Shot & Rento Fun Drive Kaya Grandi 47, Kralendijk, ☎ 717-2408; www.rentofunbonaire.com Dune buggies also available.

Touring the Island

Diving is the activity of choice for most visitors to Bonaire, but the island has a beautiful countryside and several interesting attractions. Plan to devote a day or parts of several days to sightseeing.

Getting Oriented

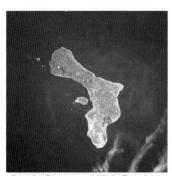

Bonaire from space (Klein Bonaire is the smaller island in the middle)

Locals give directions by landmarks, not street names. This can be a problem if you don't know the island well. However, Bonaire is only 24 miles long and three to seven miles wide, so you can't get very lost. The crescent-shaped island resembles a human bowing at the waist and floating in the Caribbean with feet pointing almost due south and head jutting toward the west. The wide middle thrusts a hip-like curve toward the east, and tiny Klein Bonaire is tucked into its western belly, directly across from the navel-level capital of **Kralendijk**.

In addition to Kralendijk, there is only one other sizable town, **Rincón**, and five small villages. Ninety-five percent of the land is undeveloped, and 100% of the surrounding water, including the outer island of Klein Bonaire, is protected as a Marine Park.

Bonaire's best features are underwater, and it has been a prime diving destination for more than two decades. However, if you enjoy undisturbed nature and simple pleasures, there's much to do above water.

Guided Tours

You can get a good overview of the island during a two- to three-hour excursion that stops at the top attractions and costs about $20 per person. Full-day tours that cover the Marine Park run about $55 per day and include lunch and a snorkeling break.

BONAIRE DIVE & ADVENTURE
Kaya Governador/ Debrot 77, Kralendijk
☎ 717-2229; www.bonairediveandadventure.com

BONAIRE TOURS AND VACATIONS
Kaya L.D. Gerharts 22, Kralendijk
☎ 717-8778; www.bonairetours.com

ARCHIE TOURS
Kaya Nikiboko Noord 33, Kralendijk
☎ 717-8630

OUTDOOR BONAIRE
☎ 791-6272; www.outdoorbonaire.com

TROPICAL TRAVEL
J.A. Abraham Blvd 80
☎ 567-0239; www.tropicaltravelbonaire.com

VOYAGER EVENTS
☎ 717-8190; www.voyagerevents.com

 See pages 199-200, for more information about transportation and guided tours on Klein Bonaire.

Self-Guided Tours

Walking Tour of Kralendijk

Bonaire's capital is Kralendijk (krawl-in-dike), which means coral dike, but most locals refer to the town as Playa, which means beach. It's a small, easily navigated town, bordered on the west by the Caribbean Sea. You can pick up a map at the cruise ship dock or the tourist office at Kaya Simon Bolivar 12.

Begin your stroll at **Fort Orange** on Kaya Charles E.B. Hellmund (coastal road) at the southern end of town. This

Kralendijk

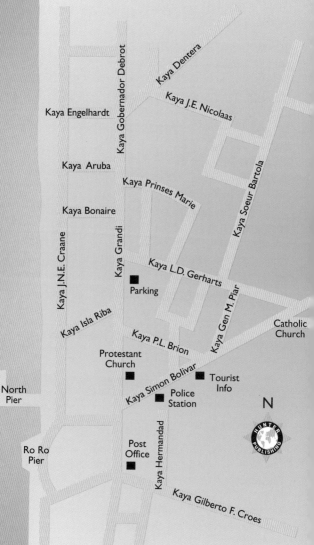

Kaya Dentera

Kaya J.E. Nicolaas

Kaya Engelhardt

Kaya Gobernador Debrot

Kaya Aruba

Kaya Prinses Marie

Kaya Soeur Bartola

Kaya Bonaire

Kaya Grandi

Kaya J.N.E. Craane

Kaya L.D. Gerharts

Parking

Kaya Gen M. Piar

Catholic
Church

Kaya Isla Riba

Kaya P.L. Brion

Protestant
Church

North
Pier

Kaya Simon Bolivar

Police
Station

Tourist
Info

N

Ro Ro
Pier

Post
Office

Kaya Hermandad

Kaya Gilberto F. Croes

© 2008 HUNTER PUBLISHING

Downrtown Kralendijk

miniature fortress was completed in 1639 and was allotted four cannon to protect the island, as well as the government offices within its walls. The cannon were never fired. In 1868, a wooden lighthouse was constructed beside the fort; it replaced by a stone tower in 1932. At one time, the island's commanding officer lived at the fort; later it held the fire and police departments. Today, it is used as the Haven Kantoor (Harbor Office) and City Hall.

The old **Bestuurskantoor** (government office) is adjacent to the fort. Offices are located elsewhere now, but the building's white-trimmed yellow exterior is a fine example of Dutch-Caribbean architecture, and its raised front porch is quite grand. The aqua-colored building next door is the restored **Customs Office**.

Heading north along the waterfront, you'll see dozens of sailboats in the harbor, and soon come to the open-air **Venezuelan Fruit Market**. The uninhabited offshore island of Klein Bonaire is directly out from the market. Grab a piece of fruit from the vendors or pick up a drink at Harborside Mall and move on to **Wilhelmina Park**, a fine place to rest up before you hike to the **Bonaire Museum** (Museo Boneriano).

Museo Boneriano is housed in a century-old building that has been restored to its former glory. Architecture fans will spend more time examining the mustard-colored plantation-style building than its contents. The museum features a fine shell collection, as well as photos, maps, and historic artifacts. There is an exhibit of Bonaire mythology titled "First

Bonaire

Bonaireans" by local artist Winfred Dania. It's on the northeast side of town, beyond the athletic stadium, near the Catholic church, at Kaya Sabana and Kaya J.C. van der Ree. Admission is about $2 and the doors are open Monday-Friday, 8 am-noon, and 1:30-5 pm, ☎ 717-8868.

South of Kralendijk

Near the airport, off the main coastal road leading out of Kralendijk, a sign points down a rutted dirt road to the ★**Donkey Sanctuary**. Take time to stop in for a visit. If she isn't busy with a sick or injured animal, founder Mariana Melis will show you around and let you pet and feed some of the sweet-natured orphaned and homeless burros she's taken in.

Save the Donkeys

Merina Melis at the Donkey Sanctuary (Martin DeWeger, Support Bonaire, Inc.)

The boarders at the Donkey Sanctuary are only a few of the 600 or more wild donkeys on Bonaire who descended from the beasts of burden that were once vital to the island's economy. The first animals were brought in during the mid-1800s to haul people, water, crops – anything that need to be carried from one place to another. They were especially useful in the salt flats because they had an amazing memory and, after a few trips up and down the same path, could be counted on to deliver their load of salt and return for another without a human attendant.

Once trucks and machinery made their jobs obsolete, the gentle beasts found themselves unemployed and unwanted. With nothing better to do, they roamed the countryside, feeding on scrub brush and private gardens, and reproducing at a rather rapid rate. Soon the island had herds of feral donkeys; a problem with no practical solution. To make matters worse, many of them wandered onto the roadways where they were hit by cars and seriously injured or killed. Many times a nursing mother died, leaving a newborn with no means of survival.

A few years ago, Merina Melis visited from Holland and noticed numerous donkeys running wild on the island. Being a true animal lover with a bold stubborn streak, she set up a non-profit foundation, Save the Donkeys, to ease the suffering of old, sick, and orphaned burros. Her campaign captured international attention and, with the help of the Bonaire government, she was able to obtain a 61-acre parcel of land for her rescued animals.

Merina is justifiably proud of the shelter she has created. The compound includes an observation deck, an iguana garden, gift shop, stables, feeding areas, shaded resting spots, and, best of all, a walk-up snack bar with a serving window where Mariana dispenses treats to her pets. The grounds are immaculately clean; the animals well groomed.

The Donkey Sanctuary is open 10 am-4 pm, Tuesday-Sunday, at no charge, but donations are greatly appreciated. ☎ 717-7233 or 560-7607 (cell); www.bonairenature.com/donkey.

Continuing south along the coast, notice the small yellow boulders with black lettering at the side of the road. These are markers for **dive sites**, and most areas are excellent for a swimming and snorkeling, as well.

Soon you'll see huge blinding white hills backed by giant turquoise and pink pools, proof that the salt industry is thriving, once again. In the distance, flocks of flamingos, osprey, heron, and other marine birds feed at **Pekelmeer Flamingo**

Sanctuary. A blue obelisk stands near the water's edge as a docking guide for transport ships. A bit farther on, a dirt road leads down to **Pink Beach**.

Read about The Obelisks of Bonaire on page 176 and Pink Beach on page 206.

At the side of the main road, in an area called ★**Witte Pan**, notice the small stone huts. These are a stunning reminder of the heartless treatment of slaves. Dutch companies depended on slave labor to process and export salt to Europe, and the workers were quartered, first in crude

Slave huts (V.C. Vulto)

stick-and-grass shanties, then in these stone huts. Stoop down and enter the windowless interior to get an idea of what it was like to sleep here after a long day of labor. Usually, five or six men shared the cramped space. There were no cooking or washing facilities, and the huts were used only for sleeping.

More slave huts and obelisks are on the coast at **Rode Pan**, just before Willemstoren Lighthouse, built in 1837 on the island's southern tip. As you round the curve of the island and look north up the east coast, notice how the sea changes from calm to choppy.

The east-coast road passes **Sorobon Beach** on Lac Bay. You can stop to watch the windsurfers in the sheltered, shallow-water cove as they sail over the turquoise sea powered by a steady onshore wind. The bay is now a protected recreation area, and the Bonaire Marine Park will not allow further development along the shore.

Mangroves growing on the north side of the cove make **Lac Bay** a favorite with nature lovers. Marine birds and sea animals breed in the undergrowth; birdwatchers should bring along a pair of binoculars. On the south shore, unclothed vacationers relax on the sand at the naturalist **Sorobon Beach Resort**.

A dirt road near the water mill on the main road leads to **Cai**, a small fishing village. Eco-tourists will appreciate the natural landscape that attracts marine birds such as egrets and cow-herons. This is also the location of the island's

Bonaire cactus (Chris Richards)

newest attraction, the **Bonaire Butterfly Farm**, a walk-through exhibit of the most colorful species of butterflies from South and Central America. Signs along the road leading to Cai point the way. Once there, you'll see butterflies that come from special rain forest projects in Costa Rica through a program designed to conserve the environment by making agreements with farmers to breed butterflies for profit instead of harvesting trees and plants from rain forests. Plans are in the works for Bonaire to begin a similar conservation program. The island is home to 80 species of butterflies, but due to the importation of non-native trees and plants, indigenous butterfly-hosting vegetation is now scarce. The Butterfly Farm will establish a garden containing host plants for Bonaire butterflies in cooperation with several local and international organizations. Visit the farm Monday-Saturday, 9 am-5 pm. The entrance fee is $12 for adults, and $8 for children up to 12 years old. ☎ 786-3040 or 701-3040.

Did You Know? *Conch is now protected by the Marine Park, so if you're served conch at a restaurant, it's imported.*

Back on the road, you round the north curve of the bay and see heaps of discarded conch shells at **Boca Cai**. If you stroll along the shore, enjoy the clean smell of the salt-scented breeze and watch the surf break over the windward reef. With a mask and snorkel, you can explore the water around the mangroves where hundreds of species of fish feed and breed. (See *Adventures on Water*,

Conch shells (Chris Richards)

pages 225-26, for information about renting a kayak at Jibe City, the best way to explore the mangroves.)

On Sundays, you will find plenty of company at Boca Cai, especially around the snack shack called **Lac Suit** (South Lake). Tour buses sometimes drop off a load of visitors, but mostly the crowd is made up of locals who come out to eat and party. The food is low on the gourmet scale, but you can get some fried fish, goat stew, and funchi, if you're hungry.

The real draw is music. Around mid-afternoon, a local musician or band (often the well-known Tipico Bonariano or Glen I Su Gang) begins to play and everyone starts dancing, including grandmothers and wet-from-the-sea kids. The action goes on as long as the cheap-rum punch lasts.

☆ Tour a Kunuku Home

Ellen Cochrane-Herrera, a lovely Bonaire native, invites visitors to tour her countryside home, **Kunuku Rooi Lamoenchi**, which has been in her family more than 100 years. She leads the two-hour walking tour herself every morning and afternoon, and tells interesting stories about life on the former plantation as she explains the antique tools, furniture, and household items, which are all original to the property. After touring the house, guests visit the grounds, an old slave wall, a dam built by hand in 1908, and aloe fields. The countryside is lovely, and it is quite possible to wander aimlessly for hours through the woodlands, discovering indigenous plants and breathtaking views of the ocean. The house is located in the countryside east of Kralendijk and not marked on most maps. You can easily become lost, so ask for a brochure with a map at the activities desk of your hotel or call Ellen for directions. Tour times vary, so call ahead to make reservations. The cost is $12 for adults and $6 for children between the ages of six and 12. ☎ 717-8489; www.webpagecur.com/rooilamoenchi.

North of Kralendijk

Follow the scenic coastal road out of the capital past several resorts and the water distillation plant to Kaya Karpata, just past the deserted landhuis. This road will take you to **Rincón** (Spanish for corner), the oldest town on the island, founded by the Spanish, and among the oldest in the Caribbean. At first glance, there is no reason to stop but, as you drive through, remember that this was once a slave community that became the birthplace of many of the island's political and business leaders. It is also the town that hosts the largest parade during Carnival and it's the place to be on April 30th, Rincón Day (Dia di Rincón) and the Queen's Birthday, one of the most popular holidays of the year.

Rincón

On the first Saturday of each month, dozens of stands are set up along the streets for **Marshe Rincón**, Market Day. If you're not busy elsewhere, stop to browse the displays of fresh fruit, crafts, homemade foods, and plants.

Rock painting at Boca Onima

Then follow the large road signs to **Boca Onima** off the eastern coastal road. This small water inlet is lined with cliffs carved by the crashing sea. A trail leads to ancient Indian inscriptions under the coral overhangs. Nearby, spring water pours into the recently opened **Fontein Cave** and feeds three freshwater pools, where you can take a cool dip. Fruit trees and tropical plants make this a shady oasis for a picnic or nap.

Take Kaya Onima back north until it curves inland and becomes Kaya Rincón, which will take you back to Rincón. From town you can pick up Kaya Paramira heading toward **Dos Pos** (Two Wells). This is an area of lush vegetation with large fruit trees and farmland.

At the **tower windmill**, you can stop and read about the well and its historical importance. In 1898, a stone edge was built around the open well to make it more convenient for residents to draw water into tin cans. In 1940, the windmill and reservoir were constructed, and in 1949, two water distribution systems were installed, with water for Rincón coming from Dos Pos to Subida di Para Mira, where it was piped into village homes.

*If you have time before leaving the Rincón area, stop at **Alta Mira Unjo**, a small park with a hilltop overlook that provides striking vistas of the island and distant sea. It's up a signed, shell-lined dirt road on the west side of town.*

Young flamingo (Susan Swygert)

★**Kaminda Goto** (the road to Goto) follows the shores of ★**Lake Goto** (Gotomeer) and offers superb views. Gotomeer is on the southwest border of the national park and is an ideal place to watch flocks of flamingos as they feed. Although most nest in Pekelmeer, some nest at Goto, and you have a good chance of a close-up view, if you sit quietly and wait. Benches at the paved and bricked **Salina Grandé** lookout provide an excellent place to rest and observe.

Tiny **Falcon Island**, in the middle of the lake, has been farmed by a Rincón family for several generations. As you walk or drive around the lake (walking is better), look for unusual geological structures and evidence of ancient Indian settlements. (Three archeological sites are located near the water.) Large iguanas roam the area and sun themselves on rocks. Various birds nest and feed in the trees, and you may spot one of the rare Bonaire loras. Only about 300 of the wild parrots survive on the island, even though they are a protected species.

To get back to Kralendijk, turn south when you reach the west-coast road near the BOPEC Oil Terminal.

★ ★ Washington-Slagbaai National Park

Washington-Slagbai National Park (Susan Swygert)

The national park covers the entire northwestern tip of Bonaire, approximately 13,500 acres, and encompasses dive sites, hiking trails, a driving tour, salt pans, a landlocked lake, and scenic hillsides. Before it became a park, the land was two privately owned plantations or farms (*kunuku* in Papiamento) called Washington and Slagbaai. Each *kunuku* grew divi-divi trees (the pods were processed into tannin for use in tanning animal hides) and aloe (used in laxatives and cosmetics), produced charcoal from mesquite trees, and raised cattle and goats.

In 1969, the Washington Plantation became a public park. Ten years later, the Slagbaai property was added. Today, visitors spend the day touring the preserve, climbing the rocky hills, picnicking, and swimming in calm water off the western shore.

Two driving routes wind through the park: **Yellow**, covering 21 miles along the northern coast; **Green**, covering the west and mid-sections. Pick up a map at the entrance and follow the dirt road that interests you most. If you have time, the yellow route is best, but it takes a full day to complete at a sightseeing pace. The terrain is natural, rugged, and wear covered in desert scrub and cactus. Be sure to have water, snacks and sunscreen, and closed-toe shoes with you so you can stop to hike in particularly interesting areas. Bring along a swimsuit and snorkel equipment so you can cool off with a dip in the sea.

HIGHLIGHTS OF THE PARK

- ★**Brandaris Hill** (Subi Brandaris), the highest point on the island at 784 feet. A trail leads from a parking lot up the ridge to the top (allow about two hours to make the round-trip), where there are fabulous views of the coast, countryside, and Caribbean Sea. On a particularly clear day, it's possible to see Curaçao to the west. Follow the rocks marked with yellow paint to stay on the trail.

  A wide cactus-lined cement road allows motorists and bikers to get to the top more quickly.

- **Salina Matijs**, a scenic viewing point just inside the park entrance. If there is water in the salt pan, birds will be congregating in the area.
- **Boca Chikitu**, a sand dune area around a sandy cove. Stick to the shore; a strong riptide makes swimming dangerous.
- **Seru Grandi**, a geographically interesting stretch of terraced land that reveals the island's formation through

several millennia. You can drive through the area or take a walking trail almost to the top, at 177 feet elevation.

- **Boca Cocolishi (Kokolishi)**, a broken-shell, gravel, and black-sand beach with a small, shallow pool for swimming.

- **Seru Bentana**, called Window Hill because of a window-shaped boulder at the top of the rise, has a splendid view of the sea.

- **Pos di Mangel**, a dependably good place to watch birds gather in the morning and late afternoon. The area always has water, which attracts a variety of tropical birds, including the green lora, Bonaire's yellow-winged Caribbean parrot.

- **Playa Funchi**, one of the island's prime snorkeling spots and a good place to see parrot fish. The beach is rocky, but has some shade. Watch for resident iguanas and lizards that have come to expect treats from visitors.

- **Boca Slagbaai**, reached by a scenic cliff road, is another prime snorkeling beach just outside the no-diving marine reserve. The beach is rocky in spots, but there's enough sand for a picnic on each end of the cove.

Boca Slagbaai (www.shorediving.com)

The park is open 8 am-5 pm daily, except on official holidays, but the last entry is at 2:45 pm. Entrance fees are $10 for adults and $6 for children younger than 15. No credit cards. ☎ 717-8444.

Klein Bonaire

Klein, or little, Bonaire is a deserted island about a half-mile off the western shore of the main island, opposite Kralendijk. It was privately owned until 1999, when the Bonaire government bought it for $5 million – financed by the government of the Netherlands and private donations. Plans are underway to make it a national park, and its land and surrounding waters already are under the protection of the Bonaire Marine Park.

At least 76 plant species and 55 animal species live on Klein, some rare or endangered. Hawksbill and loggerhead turtles nest on shore, and juveniles feed in the sea grass beds and the nearby coral reefs.

Seacow Watertaxi and **Skiffy Watertaxi** shuttle passengers across the narrow channel several times per day. The trip takes about 10 minutes and round-trip tickets are $14 for

Kralendijk with Klein Bonaire offshore (V.C. Vulto)

adults, $7 for children between the ages of four and 12 (free for kids under four). Reservations aren't necessary; just show up at the waterfront in Kralendijk Monday-Saturday at 10 am, noon, 2 or 4 pm. Return trips depart Klein at 12:30, 2:30 and 4:30 pm. On Sundays, the only departure from Kralendijk is at 10 am; the return from Klein is at 4:30 pm. Seacow's sailboat *Baka di Laman* (☎ 780-7126) leaves from Karel's Beach Bar. Skiffy's catamaran *Kantika di Amor* (☎ 790-5399) departs from the Nautico Marina.

See below for information about guided snorkeling tours and evening trips to Klein Bonaire.

Adventures on Water

Bonaire Marine Park, ☎ 717-8444, www.bmp.org, has safeguarded the island's coasts, reefs, sea life, and surrounding waters to a depth of 200 feet since 1971. Hundreds of identified species of marine creatures live on the reefs, and fishing, boating, diving, and snorkeling are strictly regulated to maintain the area's delicate ecology.

Due to these protective measures, excellent weather, and superb visibility, Bonaire is ranked the number one dive destination in the Caribbean and is an ecotourism award winner. There's plenty to see in the sea because it is against the law to remove anything, dead or alive, except recently dropped trash. The Netherlands Antilles National Parks Foundation (STINAPA) manages the park, maintains 70 public moorings,

Elephant-ear sponge (Susan Swygert)

Bonaire Marine Park

Boca Bartol

Washington-Slagbaai National Park

Rincon

Brasil

Indian Inscriptions

N

Boca Oliva

Fontein

Spelonk

Bolivia

RESERVE

Barcadera Caves

Klein Bonaire

Kralendijk

Punt Vierkant

Lac Bay

Sorobon

Akzo Salt Works

Pekel Meer

Willemstoren Lighthouse

MARINE RESERVES: Areas labeled "reserve" are used for scientific research. Diving, swimming and snorkeling are prohibited in these areas.

3.2 KM

2 MILES

© 2008 HUNTER PUBLISHING, INC

pays four rangers, monitors reef activity, and runs various educational programs, financed by charging more than 50,000 visiting divers an annual $25 nature fee.

Various conservation groups serve under the umbrella of the Bonaire Nature Alliance to ensure high standards for dive operators, promote ecotourism, and keep the island and its waters clean. Slide shows, workshops, and educational brochures keep up awareness of the groups' goals and inform visitors of regulations and proper conduct while on the island.

While diving is the number one tourist lure, other water activities come in a close second. Snorkeling is popular because of the abundant marine life living on the coral-covered ocean shelf that starts in shallow water at the shoreline. The calm leeward-side waters and east-side Lac Bay are excellent also for boating, kayaking, and windsurfing. Deep-sea fishing is possible beyond the reef.

 By the tourist bureau's count, snorkelers actually outnumber divers, but the figures are probably misleading because, while most divers also snorkel, not all snorkelers dive.

Best Beaches

Surprisingly, Bonaire is not known for excellent beaches. Most are narrow and rocky but, once you do the barefoot jig down to the sea, you'll be rewarded with warm, calm, crystal-clear water.

 Boka or boca means mouth, and indicates an inlet where the sea cuts into the shore. Playa means beach, but not necessarily sandy beach.

Facing page: Squirrelfish (Susan Swygert)

Four pleasant beaches are located inside the boundaries of Washington-Slagbaai National Park:

Playa Chikitu, the first beach on the east coast as you follow the yellow route through the park, is too dangerous for swimming because of a powerful undertow. However, the beach is perfect for strolling, and the limestone formations around the inlet contain fossilized shells and marine creatures.

★**Boca Cocolishi (Kokolishi)** offers fabulous views. The shallow pool carved into a limestone shelf above the sea is safe for swimming and snorkeling. The beach itself is mostly gravel and shells. This area's geological features are stunning.

Playa Funchi, on the calmer west coast, has a strong current farther out, but snorkelers can see lovely coral and fish along the shallow shelf close to shore. Don't expect a sandy beach, but there is some shade, and the iguanas and lizards will come right up to you looking for a bit of bread.

Playa Funchi (www.shorediving.com)

 Did You Know? *This bay was once the shipping dock for Washington Plantation, and the remains of a stone pier are left standing in the sea.*

Boca Slagbaai is a stretch of rocky white sand lined with mustard-colored buildings that were built in the mid-1800s, when the park was a private plantation. Today, the restored structures house offices for the park administrators, but at one time they were warehouses and offices for the plantation's export business.

Boca Slagbai South (www.shorediving.com)

Snorkeling is great just off the beach, and two cannon are in 10 feet of water off the south end of the bay. Divers can enter from the shore and swim out 40 feet to the drop-off, where turtles are sometimes spotted. Schools of fish, barracuda, and tarpon feed in the area.

East Coast Beaches

★★**Lac Cai**, on the northern curve of Lac Bay, and Sorobon, at the southern end, are two of the most popular beaches on the island, and the only safe places to swim on the east coast. Lac Cai has shallow water, and locals come here on weekends and holidays to picnic, listen to music, and swim. The beach is known for piles of old conch shells near the water's edge. (It is now illegal to catch or pick conch; what you get in restaurants is imported.)

Sorobon has a nudist area near the beach resort, but other parts of the sand are staked out by families, windsurfers, and tourists. The water is sheltered and calm enough for swimming and snorkeling. Mangroves along the coast draw birds and juvenile marine animals, and kayaks are available for guided or independent tours. Windsurfers rent equipment and catch the onshore breeze for a fast ride across the bay. A couple of snack shacks and a restaurant offer food and drinks.

Beaches South of Kralendijk

★**Pink Beach**, near the slave huts at Witte Pan, has been mentioned in *Caribbean Travel & Life Magazine* as one of the 10 most popular beaches in the Caribbean. These folks and their readers know beaches, so take their word for it. Short by most standards, this is the longest stretch of sand on the island. Bits of red coral cause the pink tinge, especially around sunset. There's no shade near the water and no facilities.

Playa Mangel or **Windsock**, at the end of the airport runway, has shade and a long expanse of sand. It's a favored snorkeling spot.

Bachelor Beach is a narrow strip of sand down a ladder off the main coast road south of the capital. The close-in reef is excellent for snorkeling.

Eighteen Palms is across from the governor's house, south of Kralendijk, inside the north entrance to the Plaza Resort, but open to the public. You can get snacks and drinks from the resort's beach bar.

Beaches North of Kralendijk

Nukove (www.shorediving.com)

Nukove is worth looking for. It's off a dirt road that runs beside the BOPEC Oil Terminal, near Lake Goto. Look for a sign pointing the way after the small saltwater pond called Salina Tern. Divers and snorkelers favor the spot because of the underwater sponges and colorful parrotfish. Lovers like the seclusion.

Thousand Steps actually has 67 stone steps leading from the main coast road to the little beach across from the Radio Netherlands transmitter towers. It offers good snorkeling

Thousand Steps (www.shorediving.com)

and shore diving, but watch out for sea urchins in the rocks. Enter the water at a sandy area or wear water shoes.

Beaches on Klein Bonaire

Klein's western coast is lined with white-sand beaches. Get to the island by rented kayak or water taxi, and watch out for turtle nests. There's elkhorn and staghorn coral in shallow water just off the northwest coast. Fish have been fed by divers, so some may approach people close to shore.

★**No Name** is especially popular with swimmers and sunbathers because of the palm-shaded sand. There's not much coral, but boat divers and snorkelers see plenty of fish at depths of 50 to 100 feet.

Just a Nice Dive pretty much says it all about this east coast spot. It's not a good beach, but coral is in very shallow water, so snorkeling is great. However, take care not to kick or stand on the reef. Impressive boulder coral is less than six feet down.

Jerry's Jam, also on the east side, is not a sunbathing spot, but snorkeling is terrific. A wide assortment of corals are found in shallow water, and there is an underwater cave where sea creatures hide out.

> **Warning:** It's against the law to catch turtles
> or disturb their nests. If you see a nesting tur-
> tle, report the sighting to the Bonaire Marine
> Park, ☎ 717-8444, or Sea Turtle Conserva-
> tion, ☎ 717-2225.

Diving & Snorkeling

 Snorkelers and divers who plan to do only a couple of dives with a guide during a multi-activity vacation will find sufficient information about the top
sites listed below.

The BMP publishes a *Dive and Tour Map* identifying 60
dive and snorkel sites on the main island and 23 on Klein
Bonaire. Most resorts have an on-site dive shop and offer
dive package vacations. Operators usually schedule morning, evening, and night dives by boat, and will arrange transportation to shore-dive locations.

 Since the Bonaire Marine Park (BMP) is too
extensive to be covered in a general travel
guide, serious divers, especially those who
enjoy independent shore dives, should pick
up a copy of *The Dive Sites of Aruba,
Bonaire and Curaçao* by Jack Jackson or
Diving Bonaire by George Lewbel and
Larry Martin. *Bonaire Diving Made Easy*
by Jessie Armacost is a helpful addition for
anyone planning independent shore dives.

Fifty-one of the marked dive sites can be reached from
shore, and several resort-based dive shops provide tanks
around the clock once you show your C-card and buy a $10
Marine Park admission tag. This means you're free to explore on your own any time of the day or night.

Because the island is an underwater preserve, certified divers can expect to have a buoyancy-control check before
they go out in order to limit fin damage on the reef. Park regulations prohibit touching (divers are not allowed to wear

gloves), collecting, or otherwise damaging anything living or dead under the water or on the shore. As a result of strict regulations, ongoing research, public education, and periodic closing of over-visited sites, Bonaire's Marine Park is a healthy, densely populated ecosystem.

The water temperature is between 78°F and 86°F year-round. Visibility ranges from 60 feet off the west coast of the main island, to 120 feet off Klein Bonaire. Most sites have a narrow, sloping shelf beginning in 10 to 30 feet of water near the shore. This reef terrace grows wider as it spreads south. Gorgonians and fire, staghorn, and elkhorn corals grow along this shelf and attract parrotfish, blue tangs, barracudas, damselfish, snappers, angelfish and many others.

Most of the shelves slope toward the sea beginning in about 30 feet of water. This drop-off zone ends in sand at 110 to 130 feet and is covered in colorful sponges and various corals (most notably mountainous star). Fish along the slopes include hamlets, spotted drums, blue and brown chromis, hogfish, and butterflyfish. Goatfish, stingrays, hermit crabs, and conch live on the sandy bottom along with well camouflaged peacock eye flounder, lizard fish, and scorpionfish. Lucky divers spot tarpon, turtles, and seahorses, and perhaps, in distant blue water, a passing shark or dolphin.

Experienced divers will appreciate Bonaire's special underwater features, such as the double reef separated by a sandy valley along the south coast, and the atypical spur-and-groove formations where coral grows perpendicular to the coast.

 Dive shops on Bonaire sell fish identification charts and books (a great one is *Reef Fish Identification: Florida, Caribbean, Bahamas* by Paul Humann and Ned DeLoach).

The Guided Snorkeling Program

The following operators participate in the Bonaire Guided Snorkel Experience Program with organized tours to specially selected reefs. Most of the trips take place from shore, rather than from a boat, and all begin with an informational briefing about the site. The guide leads participants along the reef, pointing out significant marine plants and fish. Equipment rental is included in the $25-$30 price, and programs are geared toward both experienced and novice snorkelers of all ages. Many dive shops organize snorkel trips and allow snorkelers to accompany divers on boat dives for around $12-$15, but the following are designated participants of the Bonaire Guided Snorkel (BGS) Experience.

BONAIRE GUIDED SNORKEL PARTICIPANTS	
Buddy Dive	Buddy Dive Resort, ☎ 717-5080; fax 717-8647; www.buddydive.com
Dive Inn Bonaire	Dive Inn Resort, ☎ 717-8761; fax 717-3563; www.diveinnbonaire.com
Bonaire Dive & Adventure	Sand Dollar Resort, ☎ 717-2229; fax 717-2227; www.diveandadventure.com
Wanna Dive Bonaire	Eden Beach Resort and City Café in Kralendijk, ☎ 717-8884; fax 717-6060; www.wannadive.com
Sea & Discover	Kaya Antonio Neuman #11, ☎ 717-5322; fax 717-5322; www.bonairenature.com

Dive Vacation Planners

If you plan to spend most of your time diving, or want to book a dives-included vacation, contact one of the following wholesalers with toll-free numbers in the US.

DIVE TOUR COMPANIES	
Caradonna Caribbean Tours	☎ 800-328-2288; www.caradonna.com
Caribbean Dive Tours	☎ 800-786-3483; www.cdtusa.com
Divi Holidays!	☎ 800-367-3484: www.diviresorts.com

Bonaire Pros	☎ 800-748-8733; www.bonairepros.com
Island Dreams	☎ 800-346-6116; www.islanddream.com
Maduro Dive Fanta-Seas	☎ 800-327-6709; www.maduro.com
Padi Travel Network	☎ 800-729-7234; www.padi.com
Ultimate Dive Travel, Ltd	☎ 800-737-3483: www.ultimatedivetravel.com

Top Dive Sites

Most of the following are also superb snorkeling sites. Those that are designated Bonaire Guided Snorkel Experience sites are indicated by (BGS) after the name. Expect to pay $12 to $15 to go along as a snorkeler on a dive-boat trip.

Pink Beach is known as a good easy-entry spot for snorkeling or shore diving. Currents are usually mild, but can become strong, so be cautious. The shelf is sandy, with gorgonian beds, staghorn coral, and sponges. Expect abundant fish, including peacock flounders, squirrelfish, and lizardfish.

Pink Beach (Susan Swygert)

Invisibles, just north of Pink Beach, is a two-reef site with sand between. It has great snorkeling on the shelf, which is covered in coral and gorgonians. The second reef, beyond the sand flat, is made up of narrow ridges separated by sand in about 70 feet of water. Angelfish, butterflyfish, hogfish and barracuda live along the reefs. Garden eels prefer the sandy spots.

Windsock (www.shorediving.com)

Windsock Steep, at the end of the runway opposite the airport, is popular because of mild currents and easy access. The sandy shelf has fire coral, elkhorn, staghorn, giant anemones, and gorgonians. Parrotfish live in the area. The slope is covered in sponges and coral, but patches of sand harbor garden eels. Divers often report seeing turtles and juvenile fish.

Calabas (www.shorediving.com)

Calabas, off the sandy beach or pier at the Divi Flamingo Resort (the on-site restaurant is also named Calabas), is an easy access dive and snorkel spot. The water is even lighted for night dives. Fish are the drawing card here, since the shelf is mostly sand with little coral. French angelfish, parrotfish, and blue tangs are plentiful; tarpon appear at night to feed, and barracuda hide under the pier. An anchor and lifeboat lie in 25 feet of water off the restaurant's pier. Spotted drums, eels, coneys, and grouper live along the slope.

The Lake, or Lake Bowker (named for Bruce Bowker, one of the island's original dive masters and owner of Carib Inn), can be accessed by boat or from shore. It features beautiful large sea fans, sea whips, and sea rods among purple tube sponges. Reef fish, such as parrotfish and damselfish, feed near shore, and divers can go to depths of 60 to 75 feet to explore a flat lake of sand between the landward and seaward reefs. The seaward reef has jumbo fish and huge coral formations. Look for the dive-site marker just south of the radio towers between the airport and the salt works.

Weber's Joy (www.shorediving.com)

Weber's Joy or **Witches Hut** is north of Kralendijk, just south of Thousand Steps. The water is usually calm and divers/ snorkelers can enter from shore or from a boat. Photography is great here because of the abundant fish along the shallow coral-covered shelf. At deeper levels, colorful sponges and manta rays make good photo subjects.

Thousand Steps (BGS), north of Weber's Joy and across from the southernmost radio tower, is reached by a stone staircase with 67 steep steps that seem like 1,000 when you climb them carrying a heavy bag of equipment after a dive. The water is normally calm, and the slope is covered with corals and sponges. Divers see giant star coral and sea whips in about 35 feet of water at the edge of the shelf. Snorkelers spot friendly queen angelfish and Spanish hogfish in shallow depths; divers often see turtles and rays at greater depths. Enter the water along the sandy patches to avoid stepping on sea urchins and swim to the right to find fish in underwater overhangs and small caves.

La Diana's Leap (www.shorediving.com)

La Dania's Leap, around the western curve of the island from Thousand Steps, is a marvelous drift dive/snorkel that can be done from shore, if you're brave enough to take the leap. You must have someone to pick you up at the other end – or a buddy willing to drive the car to the exit point (Karpata dive site, about 1.2 miles) and walk back. After you gear-up at the edge of the cliff, jump out and down into the sea, about five feet below. Turn north, toward your right, and drift along with the gentle current to Karpata, where you will see huge ship anchors and an old concrete pier – steps lead up the cliff to the parking area. Along the way, snorkelers pass over massive, pristine coral formations and a gorgonian thicket near the outer edge of the shallow shelf. Divers go to depths of 65-80 feet to explore a vertical wall with black corals and colorful sponges. You will know you've arrived at Karpata when you see research wires in about 35 feet of water.

Karpata, between La Dania's Leap and Gotomeer, is one of the island's favorite shore dives. Currents are light to moderate and photographers enjoy taking pictures of buddies posing beside one of the huge ship anchors embedded in the coral. This is a good spot for observing the unusual spur-and-groove coral formations at depths of 30 to 100 feet. The no-dive marine research area is to the west, but the drop-off to the east features staghorn coral, large gorgonians, and abundant fish, including wrasse, trunkfish, goatfish, and grouper. Occasionally, divers spot a hawksbill turtle in the area.

Playa Funchi, inside Washington-Slagbaai National Park, was once the harbor for Washington Plantation. Look for the foundation of the old stone pier. The

Karpata (www.shorediving.com)

water is so clear that you can see corals and fish from the cliffs above the bay. Snorkelers view abundant elkhorn and staghorn corals in shallow water as far as 130 feet from shore. Often, the current near the beach is gentle enough for young children, but it becomes moderate to strong at

Playa Funchi (www.shorediving.com)

greater depths, so divers must be experienced. Friendly spotted trunkfish approach divers in shallow water hoping for a treat. Deep-water fish include

horse-eye jacks, bar jacks, and buck-toothed wrasses.

Playa Bengè, just north of Playa Funchi, is a terrific snorkeling spot. Enter the water from the center of the beach and snorkel toward the north over a series of coral ridges separated by sandy furrows. Common fish in the area include snappers and large jewfish. Divers should be very experi-

Playa Bengè (www.shorediving.com)

enced to handle the strong currents at depths of 15-100 feet, where some of the island's most pristine corals found.

Boca Slagbaai, off a sheltered cove on the southwest side of the national park, features coral and sea fans in shallow water close to shore. Enter the water from the north side of the bay, where there is fine sand and no coral. Farther out, the current is moderate to strong, so divers should be very experienced. Two cannon lie in 10 feet of water at the south end of the cove, and six replicas from a movie set are farther out, where barracuda, tarpon, and rays congregate. Hawksbill turtles occasionally appear beyond the drop-off in about 40 feet of water. Buildings near the beach were built around 1868 and include the home of Slagbaai Plantation's manager, a Customs office, and a salt warehouse.

Leonora's Reef, off the northern shore of Klein Bonaire, is accessible only by boat. Currents are mild, so snorkelers and novice divers enjoy staghorn, elkhorn, fire, and star coral at shallow depths. Gorgonians are abundant in deeper water, where the slope descends sharply to sand at 120 feet. Large purple sponges and huge tiger grouper create great Kodak moments.

Sharon's Serenity, off the western shore of Klein Bonaire, near the lighthouse, is great for snorkelers, and the vertical walls hold interest for divers. Access is by boat, and the water is normally calm, but currents can become moderately strong on some days, so check with a dive operator before booking a trip. A shallow shelf extends about 145 feet from shore and features abundant tall gorgonians and a dense thicket of various corals. Fish in shallow depths include

French angelfish, damselfish, parrotfish, and trumpetfish. At the drop-off, mountainous star coral begins in about 25 feet of water, then slopes sharply in terraced layers to sand at 140 feet. Plate and wire corals grow in 80-100 feet of water, where divers see large jewfish, barracuda, and grouper.

Mi Dushi, off the northwestern coast of Klein Bonaire, has moderate currents and various corals at depths of 10-20 feet. Along the top of the drop-off, anemones and pencil coral are the highlight, while the slope is covered with a forest of wire corals, gorgonians, and huge sponges. Marine life includes snappers, jacks, and barracudas.

Just a Nice Dive (BGS), on Klein Bonaire, is a favorite, but accessible only by boat or kayak. Snorkelers can swim among the large brain coral and gorgonians in shallow water. Abundant marine life includes surgeonfish, butterflyfish, and parrotfish.

No Name (BGS), is about the only site on Klein Bonaire that is suitable for shore entry. Novice snorkelers will find calm water and schools of fish at shallow depths.

 A No-Dive Ecological Reserve Research & Area is designated on two acres of Bonaire Marine Park. It is along Playa Frans, on the leeward coast south of Washington-Slagbaai National Park between Boca Slagbaai and Karpata.

Dive Operators

You won't have a problem finding a dive shop. Most resorts have a facility on-site that is open to non-guests, and each offers a full slate of dive packages. Expect to pay around $35 to $40 for a single one-tank boat dive without equipment (tank, air, weights and belt are typically included in the price), $60 for an introductory resort course, and $350 for certification courses.

Most resorts and dive operators offer packages that represent big savings for divers who want to spend a lot of time in the water. If you have all of your own equipment, you can get a tank-and-unlimited-air package that will allow you to dive wherever you wish, as often as you wish, for $20-$25 per day. Most operators add a 15% service charge, and all add a 5% government tax to quoted prices. Be sure to ask if the service charge (tip) is added automatically before you book.

> *EMERGENCY INFO: San Francisco Hospital, in case you overdo it, is fully equipped to handle any emergency. Trained medical professionals are available at all times, and a recompression facility is located next to the hospital. San Francisco Hospital, Kaya Soeur Bartola 2, Kralendijk,* ☎ *717-8900. Recompression Chamber,* ☎ *717-7140. Ambulance/Police/Emergency,* ☎ *114.*

All dive shops on Bonaire are well equipped, have excellent safety records, comply with Marine Park regulations, and offer competitive prices. Most conduct certification courses, and many are staffed with multilingual guide/instructors. Differences among those listed include frequency of trips (especially night dives), type of boat, availability of shore-dive excursions, and staffing of the boat while divers are in the water.

BLACK DURGON SCUBA CENTER
Black Durgon Inn
Kaya Governador N. Debrot 145 (about two miles north of Kralendijk)
☎ 717-8846 (phone/fax); www.blackdurgon.com
Two dive sites, Small Wall and Black Durgon's Reef, are located just off shore from the inn and dive center. Staff speaks English, Dutch, German, and Spanish.

BLUE DIVERS
Kaya Norwega (Main Street), Kralendijk
☎ 717-6860; fax 717-6865; www.bluedivers-bonaire.com

Daniel Henggeler and Franklin Winklaar run this small dive shop and the adjacent accommodations, Palm Studios. Guided shore dives are available, as are small-group boat dives. Dive masters speak English, German, and Dutch.

BRUCE BOWKER'S CARIB INN

Julio A. Abraham Blvd, Carib Inn
☎ 717-8819; fax 717-5295; www.caribinn.com

Bruce Bowker is one of Bonaire's diving old-timers, a former student of legendary Captain Don. His scuba operation and small resort are considered a great value among divers. You get the best of everything you need, but few worldly distractions. Bruce opened the shop and resort in 1980, and most of the staff have been with him more than 10 years. In 2005, the Inn received a new dive boat and built a new beach hut at the water's edge.

BUDDY DIVE

Buddy Beach and Dive Resort
Kaya Gobernador Debrot
☎ 717-5080, 800-GO-BUDDY (in the US); fax 717-8647; www.buddydive.com

This PADI 5-star Gold Palm Resort operator has everything a diver could ask for, and the resort caters to underwater adventurers. Non-guests are welcome, and certification up to the assistant-instructor level is given. The amicable staff speaks English, French, German, and Dutch.

Sea Turtle Conservation Bonaire

STCB is a non-profit, non-governmental organization set up to help preserve sea turtles and their natural habitats through research and public awareness programs. They print and distribute educational materials, present public slide shows, and broadcast local media updates on a regular basis. Research projects include underwater surveys, beach patrols, resident-turtle counts, and monitoring of nesting activities. If you see a turtle in the water, report it on a sighting sheet in any dive shop. If you spot a nest on the beach, report it to STCB, ☎ 717-8399, or the Bonaire Marine Park, ☎ 717-8444.

CAPTAIN DON'S HABITAT
Captain Don's Habitat Resort
☎ 717-8290; fax 717-8240
www.habitatdiveresorts.com/bonaire

Wreck of the Hilma Hooker (Susan Swygert)

Bonaire's diving patriarch Don Stewart established this facility in the 1960s with the slogan "Diving Freedom" to signify the availability of tanks and air 24/365, with no reservations needed. Today, the no-stress tradition continues, with scheduled boat trips to more than 50 sites – or divers can simply take a giant stride off the onsite dock and descend to 30 feet, where wrasses and gobies glide past clusters of colorful coral. This everything-to-every-diver facility is a PADI 5-star Instructor Development Center, a NAUI

Dream Resort, an SSI Referral Facility, and a TDI Instruction Center, qualified to certify clients in everything from basic Open Water to Tri-Mix. The staff naturalist leads eco-tours, and mountain bikes and kayaks are available for rent. Instruction, tours, and assistance is given in Papiamento, English, Dutch, German, and Spanish. Captain Don Stewart is recognized as an "Honored Citizen of Bonaire" and a member of the Inter-

Longsnout seahorse & purple sea fan
(Susan Swygert)

national Scuba Diving Hall of Fame.

DEE SCARR'S TOUCH THE SEA
Kaya Governador Debrot 133
☎ 717-8529; www.touchthesea.com

Dee Scarr is a renowned environmentalist and naturalist who started the Touch the Sea project in 1982. Students of all ages have been instructed in the enjoyment of underwater recreation and exploration. Before each dive, she briefs participants on marine life so that divers recognize more life on the reef and take advantage of the opportunity to interact. Scarr is the author of three books, *Touch the Sea*, *Coral's Reef*, and *The Gentle Sea*. She personally leads each dive ($90 for a one-tank dive) and accepts non-certified divers up to advanced divers. If you want to meet Scarr before signing up, attend her slide presentation at Captain Don's Habitat on Monday evenings (see page 241). Call

Dee Scarr or Habitat (☎ 717-8290) for time and additional information.

DIVI DIVE BONAIRE

Divi Flamingo Beach Resort
☎ 717-8285; fax 717-8238; www.divibonaire.com

Grab a full tank and step off the pier at the Flamingo – you're off on a great dive anytime of day or night. Or, sign up for one of the all-day three-tank boat trips to sites off Washington-Slagbaai National Park or south around Margate Bay. Six customized boats provide shade, plenty of room to walk around, and wide swim platforms. The friendly professionals make diving fun and easy, whether you're just picking up a tank for a private shore dive or spending the day at a seldom-visited site.

DIVE INN BONAIRE

Kralendijk waterfront
☎ 717-8761; fax 717-8563; www.diveinnbonaire.com

This dive shop and adjacent seven-studio inn is across a narrow road from the waterfront and a private pier. Their boat leaves each day for personalized diving and snorkeling

Green moray (Susan Swygert)

trips off Klein Bonaire. Ask for lovely "Big Boss Babs," the owner and friendly director of this small laid-back operation. *Moonshadow*, the classic dive boat, has recently been over-hauled and given two new Yamaha engines.

DIVE FRIENDS (www.dive-friends-bonaire.com)

Both **Yellow Submarine** and **Photo Tours** operate under the umbrella name Dive Friends, with a total of four dive-shop locations and a retail store. Together they hold an im-pressive list of accreditations and awards and offer a stun-ning menu of services. Each of the four dive shops is equipped with top-quality rental gear, and their **Diver's Dis-count Store** (Kaya Grandi 18, Kralendijk, ☎ 717-5088) sells books, T-shirts and name-brand scuba equipment. Recognized as *National Geographic Family Dive Centers*, the operators specialize in all levels of certification, techni-cal diving, kids' programs and guided dives. Recently, the shops began offering Nitrox courses and installed a Nitrox filling station at their location at **Caribbean Court**, a resort on the west coast, north of town (☎ 717-7901). In addition to the two in-town shops and the Caribbean Court location, Dive Friends runs a small dive operation at **Hamlet Oasis**, a vacation rental complex just north of town (☎ 717-3988).

Yellow Submarine
Kaya Playa Lechi 24, Kralendijk
☎ 717-2929

Photo Tours Divers
Kaya Grandi 6, Kralendijk
☎ 717-3460

SEA & DISCOVER
Kaya A. Neuman 11, Kralendijk
☎ 717-5322; www.bonairenature.com/seaandiscover/
This half-day adventure includes a classroom presentation followed by a shore dive or snorkel. Only three divers or four snorkelers participate, so the instructor gives each person individual attention. Caren Eckrick, a marine biologist and certified PADI instructor, teaches students about life on the

reef so that they can better appreciate things they see while diving and snorkeling. The class and underwater tour cost $45 for divers and $40 for snorkelers.

TOUCAN DIVING

Plaza Resort
☎ 800-766-6016 (in the US), 717-2500
www.toucandiving.com

This PADI 5-star, NAUI, and IDD dive center offers filled tanks 24/365 for shore diving. In addition, their dive boats leave the resort's marina several times each day for underwater tours off the east coast and Washington-Slagbaai National Park. Nitrox is available, and photo/video equipment may be rented. Certification up to the instructor level is available in English, Papiamento, German, Dutch, and Spanish.

WANNA DIVE

Eden Beach Resort and City Café
☎ 717-8884; fax 717-3684; www.wannadive.com

This new shop has two locations, one at Eden Beach Resort (about a five-minute drive north of town), and the other at City Café (in Kralendijk). Owners Roeland "Bob" Labots and Bart Snelder explain that the two locations allow divers to experience different types of dive sites, right from shore, without hauling equipment around the island. Both locations are just a quick boat ride from Klein Bonaire, and both shops are fully equipped. Nitrox is available. Bob and Bart are from the Netherlands and both are fun-loving multilingual PADI instructors. Bart is also an SSI Platinum Pro. The two are committed to environmental issues, customer safety and satisfaction... and having a good time.

Windsurfing

The most popular watersport on Bonaire, after diving and snorkeling, is windsurfing. **Lac Bay**, on the east coast, has excellent conditions: shallow water, steady breezes, few or no choppy waves. Beginners stay close to shore where the water is smooth and protected. Experienced riders head farther out, where the sea provides challenging two- to four-foot swells. The bay is about three miles long and a mile and a half wide, with winds blowing directly onshore from the east at a steady 20-25 knots from January to August. September to December, the breeze drops to a constant 15-20 knots.

Windsurfer (Susan Swygert)

A coral barrier reef partially breaks up the long waves outside the bay, but the bay itself has no obstacles and fairly flat water.

Rental rates run about $20 per hour, $45 per half-day, and $60 per day to rent basic windsurfing equipment. Upgrades are an additional 10%-20%. Lessons start at around $45 per hour, including equipment.

Windsurfing Operators

JIBE CITY

☎ 717-5233; fax 717-4455; www.jibecity.com
Closed in September

Learn to windsurf or brush up on your techniques at this easy-going shop owned and operated by Ernst van Vliet. The staff includes Peter, a popular instructor who has been teaching windsurfing skills at Jibe City since 1997 and is known for his ability to quickly get beginners up and sailing. A well-stocked shop sells all the gear and some souvenirs, and the Hang Out Bar serves drinks and sandwiches. When you've had enough windsurfing, rent one of the sea kayaks ($10 for single seaters, $15 for doubles, per hour) and explore the bay.

BONAIRE WINDSURF PLACE

☎ 717-2288; fax 717-5279

www.bonairewindsurfplace.com

Champion windsurfers Patoen, Roger, and Elvis own and operate this shop and teach beginning through advanced techniques. Children five and older can sign up for a five-day clinic that was developed to train the Bonaire Kids, a group that competes in – and often wins – international events. The shop rents top-notch boards and sails and sells a variety of watersports basics. The beach bar offers drinks and sandwiches, and is a popular place for spectators as well as resting windsurfers. Open 10 am-6 pm daily, with a beach BBQ at 7 pm on Wednesdays.

Boating

Harbour Village Marina manages the 40 visiting-yacht moorings owned by the Bonaire Marine Park, and assigned by them in advance by VHF. Arriving vessels must check in at the arrival dock, clear Customs and Immigration, and receive information on Marine Park regulations before proceeding to their designated mooring.

Fishing boat under sail (Susan Swygert)

Each yacht is charged a mooring fee of $5.40 per night for vessels 60 feet (18 meters) or shorter, the same as the hotel tax for land-based visitors. The government now prohibits anchoring in Kralendijk Bay. The only exceptions to this regulation are for boats under nine feet in length using a stone anchor, and larger vessels with written advance authorization from the harbor master.

International Sailing Regatta

Bonaire hosts an annual regatta for sailboats of all sizes, from micro-boats to windsurfers to large yachts. For information about this year's event, contact **The Bonaire International Sailing Regatta Foundation**, Kaya Jan N.E. Cachi Craane 52, ☎ 717-5555; fax 717-0333; www.bonaireregatta.org.

Day Sails & Charters

There's no better way to spend a day or a week than cruising the waters around Bonaire and Klein Bonaire. If you don't have your own boat, join a scheduled group outing or charter a private boat. The following companies offer dinner cruises, half- and full-day snorkel tours, and long-distance trips to Venezuela, Curaçao and other islands. Snorkel/sightseeing sails run about $45 per person, sunset cruises are in the $35 range and dinner trips cost $75-$90 per person.

SAMUR SAILING CHARTERS
☎ 717-5592; fax 717-6677; www.infobonaire.com/samur
This genuine 56-foot Siamese junk was built in Bangkok, Thailand and is an elegant beauty. Reserve passage for the sunset Green Flash sailing, enjoy an authentic Thai dinner cruise, or take a morning trip to Klein Bonaire.

OSCARINA
Harbor Village Marina
☎ 790-7674; www.bonairesailing.com/oscarina

Captain Karen is in command of this Tayana 42 ocean-going yacht. You can learn to sail or simply sit back and relax on a half- or full-day-trip or a sunset cruise. Customized excursions include a No-frills Snorkel Trip, a Rich and Famous Charter, and everything in between.

WOODWIND CRUISES
Kralendijk Bay
☎ 786-7055; www.woodwindbonaire.com

Dedrie and Ulf Pedersen, from Trinidad, own the *Woodwind* and sail the classy trimaran around Bonaire on cruises lasting from three to five hours. Klein is a must-do stop but, depending on the day, the *Woodwind* usually stops at a second location to look for turtles and sea creatures. A buffet lunch, cold drinks and open bar are included in the slow-go trip.

MUSHI MUSHI
Natico Marina Pier, Kralendijk
☎ 786-5399 or 786-2474; fax 717-5397
www.bonairenauticomarina.com

You'll catch sight of this catamaran if you hang out around the marina for awhile, and for about $35 you can take a two-hour cruise – morning, afternoon or at sunset. Call for scheduled trips, which drift toward Klein and along the coast, or book a private trip and take her anywhere you wish.

For a ride over to Klein Bonaire, show up at the Nautico Marina across from City Café in Kralendijk Monday-Saturday, 10 am, noon, and 2 pm, or Sunday at 10 am. **Kantika di Amor**, *a luxurious watertaxi run by Skiffy, provides a quick ride for $14 per person round-trip.* ☎ 790-5399.

BAKA DI LAMAN (SEACOW)
Karel's Beach Bar Pier, Kralendijk
☎ 780-7126

Captain Patrick runs a daily shuttle from the main island to Klein Bonaire at 10 am, noon, 2 and 4 pm ($14), but you can call him a day in advance to book a two-hour snorkel trip with stops at two sites on Klein for $18 per person. He will also do shore tours, sunset cruises, and night-snorkeling trips. Check with him at the pier, or call his cell phone at the number above.

ANGEL SNORKEL & PHOTO SAFARIS

Town Pier

☎ 780-7838

The 45-foot *Angel* cruises to Klein Bonaire for snorkeling and photo opportunities.

PARASAIL BONAIRE

Kaya Kitara 25, Nikiboko Zuid – moored in Kralendijk

☎ 717-4998; cell 567-0940; fax 717-4998

www.parasailbonaire.com

You may spot this 28-foot custom-built boat leaving from Karel's Bear Bar Pier downtown or meeting up with passengers at one of the resort docks. Patrick, the PADI-certified dive master and parasail expert who drives this powerful speed machine, loves giving visitors a thrilling and safe bird's-eye view of the island. In addition to parasailing ($40), you can arrange snorkeling trips or zip over to Klein Bonaire for $25. Patrick and his boat are all yours for $125 an hour. Cruise, snooze, or try out every toy.

Parasail Bonaire

Fishing

Bonaire bonefishing (Susan Swygert)

Virgin fishing grounds lie just a half-mile off the coast, five minutes by boat beyond the reef. These unspoiled waters contain a great variety of game fish such as sailfish, marlin, tuna, wahoo, and swordfish. In addition, the island is rated one of the best bonefishing destinations in the world and offers excellent light-tackle fishing for species such as tarpon, permit and snook.

Most fishing by visitors is sport fishing, with a catch-and-release policy. However, if you have kitchen facilities, you may want to keep a fish from your bounty to prepare for friends or family. (Marlin is strictly catch-and-release due to the shrinking fish stocks.) Check with the captain when you book your reservation to be sure that he will allow you to keep some or all of your catch. Remember that fresh fish cannot be brought back into many countries, including Holland, Canada, and the US. It is also against Bonaire law for a non-resident to profit from fishing, so you are not allowed to sell your catch.

You may request that your catch be tagged with an official ID from the Bill Fish Foundation. Then, when your fish is caught again, you will be notified of the location of the catch and the size of the fish. It's interesting to see how much a fish grows from one catch to the next.

:*Fishing tournaments* *are held every couple of months on Bonaire, usually around holidays. Awards are given by weight and species. For dates and information on this year's events, check with Tourism Corporation Bonaire,* ☎ *717-8322; fax 717-8408; www. infobonaire.com/calendar.*

You can hire a boat and captain for either a full day or a half-day, with prices running $300 and up (depending on the length and distance of the trip), including tackle, bait and re-freshments. Fishing licenses are not required for non-commercial fishing; however, if you fish the waters of the Marine Park, you must purchase a $10 tag. Make your reservation early, especially during high season. The interest in fishing charters has increased tremendously over the last couple of years, and many visitors book more than one trip per week.

Fishing Operators

PISCATUR FISHING CHARTERS & TACKLE SHOP
Kaya J. Pop #4, Kralendijk
☎ 717-8774 or 780-0833 (cell); fax 717-2877
www.bonairefishing.com/piscatur

Captain Chris Morkos, a Bonaire native, runs a 42-foot customized Bertram-like boat that docks conveniently in the center of town. It's equipped with six Penn International reels, a 30-gallon live bait well, and top quality lures. The captain specializes in marlin. Rent the entire boat for a full day for $500, or call about joining an organized outing.

Catch of the day (Piscatur)

MULTIFISH CHARTERS (IGFA)

Kaya Krisolito #37, Kralendijk

☎ 717-3648 or 790-1228 (cell); www.bonairefishing.net

Captain Francis Verbinnen shares his enthusiasm with vacationers aboard M/V *Multifish*, a 32-foot Permacraft twin-diesel sportfishing boat. The custom-outfitted boat has a tuna tower, shaded deck, head, and a professional fighting chair. It's docked at the fishing pier on Playa Pabou, about a five-minute walk from Kralendijk. This outfitter also takes guests water-skiing and rents self-drive 20-foot powerboats by the full- or half-day.

BIG GAME SPORTSFISHING (IGFA)

Kaya Krisolito 6, Santa Barbara

☎ 717-6500; fax 717-7160

www.big-game-sport-fishing.com

Captain Cornelis and his son, Thomas, take guests bonefishing ($200), light-tackle reef fishing ($300), and night fishing for shark, grouper, and jacks ($400) aboard their 30-foot Hatteras named *Delfin*.

Adventures on Land

Visitors to Bonaire spend most of their time in the water, but there's plenty to do on land. Even if you think you're not a birdwatcher or nature lover, consider joining a group tour led by an expert who will point out fascinating creatures and plants.

Birdwatching & Nature Hikes

Parakeet

About 190 different bird species live or nest here, including parrots and flamingos. Local naturalist Jerry Ligon does a good job of showing you a vast assortment of the most interesting types during a trip through the Washington-Slagbaai National Park and other wilderness areas. Contact him at: **Bonaire Dive & Adventure**, Kaya

Governador N. Debrot #77, ☎ 717-2229; www.bonairedive
and adventure.com.

Biking

Sunset cycling (Susan Swygert)

Take a bike out to the desert, over to the coast, or up a mini-mountain to see Bonaire from a whole new angle. Most of the coastal roads are flat and have little traffic, so even inexperienced bikers can enjoy the ride. Advanced riders can go off-road for more adventure. Dutch road bikes and mountain bikes rent for about $15 per day. Guided tours are priced at around $40 for a half-day and $65 for a full day. Some of the resorts have bikes and you can also rent from these Kralendijk shops:

DE FREEWIELER
Kaya Grandi #61, Kralendijk
☎ 717-8545
ATVs also available.

HOT SHOT & RENTO FUN DRIVE
Kaya Grandi #47, Kralendijk
☎ 717-2408; www.rentofunbonaire.com
Dune buggies also available.

BONAIRE DIVE & ADVENTURE/CYCLE BONAIRE
Kaya Gobernador N. Debrot #77, Den Laman Bldg
☎ 717-2229; fax 717-2227

Shopping

Shopping is great fun on Bonaire. You won't find impressive bargains on luxury imports, but you can use up your $600 duty-free allowance on scuba gear, souvenir clothing, beachwear, marine-theme jewelry, and local arts. Most of the boutiques and jewelry stores are on KaKralendijk. Several shops are housed at Harbourside Shopping Mall, on Kaya Grandi. ☎ 717-5162.

Most in-town stores are open Monday-Saturday, 8 am-noon and 2-6 pm. US dollars or Antillean guilders may be used for all purchases, and credit cards are widely accepted.

 If you need cash, there's an ATM at the ABN-AMRO Bank at Harbourside Mall. Pick up a copy of Bonaire Affair or Bonaire Nights for discount coupons and information on new stores.

Sea-life jewelry is the featured item at **Atlantis** (☎ 717-7730) on Kaya Grandi 32B. Also, gold is sold by weight and there's a fine selection of silver jewelry, watches, and crystal. Marine subjects dominate the gift items, home decorations, and children's things at **Best Buddies** (☎ 717-7570), next door at Kaya Grandi 32. **Best Buddies at the Beach** (☎ 717-8285) is located on the grounds of the

Jewelry from Atlantis

Divi Flamingo Resort and carries tropical clothing for the whole family, sea-theme jewelry, and mini-market goodies. It's open every day.

 Valerie's Airport Shop (☎ 717-5324) *stocks T-shirts, chocolates, and souvenirs. This is the place to spend your remaining guilders before you board the plane for home.*

For island fashions, head to **Kaya Grandi**, behind City Café, where three brightly painted shops sell batik-fabric dresses, T-shirts, shorts, and hats. **Chez Claudette** (☎ 717-8571), at #14, has items hanging outside, and you will be tempted by colorful $18 dresses and $9 skirts. **Island Fashions** (☎ 717-7565), across the street at

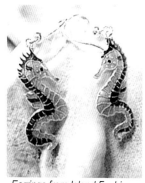

Earrings from Island Fashions

#5 in an historic house, has a large selection of locally made gift items, as well as batik clothing, T-shirts, unusual island jewelry. **Boutique Vita** (☎ 717-8438), at #16, has an adorable life-size island-woman doll sitting in a rocker on the porch. When you stop to admire her, you'll be drawn to the well-priced clothes hanging nearby. The wrap skirts are terrific swimsuit coverups.

Jodys Fashion, Music & Trends is a new shop in the Lagoen Hill section, east of Kralendijk, off Kaminda Lagoen. Owners Jo and Dymphie Bux have a colorful shop full of current European fashions (Replay, Armani, Diesel, and Bikkembergs), as well as a trendy mix of perfumes, gifts, and musical CDs. Open Tuesday-Saturday, 1-5 pm, ☎ 717-5215, www.jodysbonaire.com.

Bonaire

The best quality T-shirts are found at **Bonaire Gift Shop** (☎ 717-2201; www.bonairegiftshop.com), a blue building across from Banco di Carib at Kaya Grandi #13. They also carry a good selection of dive watches and underwater cameras, but they are best-known for having the largest selection of wines, beers and liquors.

The largest grocery store on Bonaire is ***Cultimara Supermarket*** *on the square at Kaya L.D. Gerharts 13, just inland from Kaya Grandi. Pick up picnic supplies, drinks for car trips, and condo supplies here. They stock a good supply of Dutch imports, such as cheese and chocolate. The in-store bakery makes fresh breads and desserts daily. ☎ 717-8278. Most supermarkets are open 8 am-6 pm, Monday-Saturday. Some mini-marts are open on Sundays.*

TIS (The Island Supplier) is a long-time wholesaler with a new retail outlet, offering fresh fruits, vegetables, meats, and other products, which come from the United States or Colombia. The best supply is available on Friday afternoons and Saturday mornings. The store is at Kaya Industria #28 on the northeast side of Kralendijk, open Monday-Friday, 7:30 am-12:30 pm and 2-5:30 pm; Saturday, 8 am-1 pm. ☎ 717-6446 or 717-6448.

Jan Art Gallery at Kaya Gloria 7, northeast of downtown, sells oil, watercolor, and acrylic paintings of Bonaire landscapes, island life, and underwater treasures by local artists. You can also pick up gift cards, prints, and crafts. Consider buying *The Nature of Bonaire*,

Print from Jan Art Gallery

a $20 video, as a souvenir. It's a 30-minute presentation of the island, both above and below the water. Call Janice, the owner, for detailed directions and the exact hours when the shop will be open. A good time to visit is during happy hour on Fridays, 5-7 pm. ☎ 717-5246, www.janartbonaire.com.

Cinnamon Art Gallery, on Kaya P.L. Brion, at Kaya Grandi directly behind Banco di Caribe, is well worth a visit. It's run by The Bonaire Artists Foundation, which is a non-profit group that runs on private donations and exhibits the work of local artists without pay or commission. When you buy through them, the entire purchase price goes directly to the artist. The gallery regularly shows

The Kikuluku Family
(Avy Benhamron, Cinnamon Art Gallery)

photography, jewelry, paintings and sculpture, with select artists featured on a rotating basis. Find out what's currently on exhibit at the website or visit the shop weekdays 10 am-noon and 2-5 pm; ☎ 786-9563; www.avybart.com/cinnamon.

Where to Stay

You can choose from super-luxurious to just-the-basics accommodations at eco-inns, full-service resorts, and vacation apartment complexes. The majority are on the water, but not necessarily on a sandy beach, and many have full-service on-site dive and watersports facilities, a couple of restaurants, and at least one freshwater swimming pool. Air-conditioning (sometimes only in the bedrooms), telephones, and televisions are standard, but ask when you make a reservation, because some of the best resorts take pride in avoiding noisy distractions in paradise.

If you're a diver, inquire about vacation packages that include daily boat dives and unlimited air for shore dives. Some also include meals, a rental car, and perhaps a few extras such as an island tour or spa services. These packaged deals usually offer a hefty savings, if you make use of everything that's included.

SLEEPING WITH THE STARS

Our suggested list of lodgings has been slashed to the bare bones for this guide. You can browse the Internet and we encourage you to do so. Here you'll find only the most recommended possibilities to fit a variety of budgets. Properties marked with one star (★) are highly recommended. When a single feature or the overall allure is particularly impressive, you'll find two stars (★★). Three stars (★★★) menas, simply, WOW!

Hotel Rate Guide

Use the prices given for accommodations as a guide to the average high-season rate per standard double room. If the review is for an all-inclusive or all-suites resort or a multi-room condo/villa property, the listed price is the average during high season for two people sharing the smallest available unit.

 The **area code** for Bonaire is 599. To phone from the US, dial 011-599, then the seven-digit number.

Resorts & Hotels

West Coast

★★HARBOUR VILLAGE BEACH CLUB
Kaya Gobernador N.Debrot No. 71
☎ 800-424-0004 or 717-7500; fax 717-7507
www.harbourvillage.com
70 rooms and suites
$330-$360

Recently accepted as a member of the prestigious Small Luxury Hotels of the World, this luxury resort is just a 15-minute walk from Kralendijk. It has its own beach, marina, dive shop, health club, tennis courts and restaurants. Standard rooms are small, but nicely decorated in tile and teak, have both ceiling fans and air-conditioning, and open into a well-

Harbour Village Beach Club

equipped bathroom with spa-quality amenities. You'll be well accommodated, even in these basic rooms. But upgrade to a suite and you get much more space, plus a beachfront location, private patio and a mini-bar with a small refrigerator. The landscaped grounds wrap around a private beach (with white sand, lounge chairs and hammocks) and a 60-slip full-service marina.

PLAZA RESORT BONAIRE

J.A. Abraham Boulevard #80

☎ 800-766-6016 (in the US & Canada) or 717-2500 (on Bonaire); www.plazaresortbonaire.com

198 suites and one- and two-bedroom villas

$250

Plaza has made this 12-acre retreat one of the prettiest spot on the island by adding thousands of plants and trees, and American divers have voted it one of the top 10 dive resorts in the world. The luxurious suites and apartments are clustered in nine two-story buildings scattered around a marina next to a sandy beach. Each unit has a mini- or full-size kitchen, oversized bathrooms, and a balcony or patio. On-site facilities include a full-service dive center (See *Toucan*

Plaza Resort Bonaire

Diving, page 224), three restaurants, a large freshwater swimming pool, a casino, four lighted tennis courts, a fitness center, and a watersports facility. Since the Plaza is beginning to show its age, don't expect five-star quality. However, it is still a fine resort, with excellent diving and a caring staff.

BUDDY DIVE RESORT

Kaya Governador Nicholaas Debrot

☎ 866-GO-BUDDY (in the US & Canada) or 717-5080; fax 717-8647; www.buddydive.com

46 rooms and one-, two-, or three-bedroom apartments

$120-$155

New owners, Martien and Ingrid Van der Valk, have taken over the property that was owned by Joop, Yvonne, and Debby Rauwers for more than 20 years. They

Buddy Dive Resort

are intent on keeping up the family atmosphere and superb diving facilities that have won Buddy many international awards. It was voted the number one Best Dive Resort in the Caribbean three years in a row by the German *Tauchen Dive Magazine*, and rated among the Top 20 Best Dive Resorts in the World by *Rodale's Scuba Diving Magazine USA*. Although the resort caters to divers, any guest will be content with the modern hotel rooms and spacious apartments that are just steps from two swimming pools, an outdoor Internet kiosk, and two restaurants, Bella Vista and Lion's Den. Check out the fabulous dive packages on their website. You can hardly stay home for less.

★ CAPTAIN DON'S HABITAT

Kaya Governador Nicholaas Debrot #103
☎ 800-327-6709 (Maduro Dive Fanta-Seas in the US) or 717-8290; fax 717-8240; www.habitatdiveresorts.com
93 rooms, villas, and cottages
$190

Diving Freedom is the slogan and concept Captain Don Stewart built a kingdom around. He's an international leader in the world-wide reef conservation movement and recognized as the father of diving on

Captain Don's Habitat

Bonaire. He opened Habitat in 1977, based on the easy-going idea that a diver should be able to grab a tank and hit the water at any time day or night. Both Americans and Europeans have supported his theory ever since. Cottage-style rooms and villas are surrounded by landscaped gardens and are just steps away from the sea. Almost every guest is a diver, and they gather on the sandy beach or at the oceanfront **Rum Runners Restaurant** to swap underwater stories. Dive packages are well-priced and the resort has a fleet of dive boats and ace guides who encourage few or no lead weights (buoyancy is emphasized and enthusiastically taught) to save the reef from diver damage. Up to six people can stay in a villa, and there are enough activities to keep non-divers busy.

★DIVI FLAMINGO BEACH RESORT & CASINO

Julio A. Abraham Blvd #40
☎ 800-367-3484 (in the US & Canada) or 717-8285; fax 717-8238; www.diviflamingo.com
145 rooms and studios
$150

Superior and deluxe rooms and larger studio units have balconies or patios overlooking landscaped gardens, a large swimming pool, and the sea. Standard rooms are small, but clean and comfortable, with window views of the garden. **Divi**

Divi Flamingo

Dive Bonaire (see page 222 for more information) is the on-site scuba center, and divers and snorkelers can enter the water from the Flamingo's pier or sign up for a boat dive. The resort is within walking distance of town, but there are bars, restaurants, shops, and a barefoot casino on the grounds. All-inclusive packages and dive packages are offered.

SOROBON BEACH RESORT

Lac Bay
☎ 717-8080; fax 717-6080; www.sorobonbeachresort.com
30 rooms
$270

This eco-inn on Lac Bay is a naturalist resort, so clothing is optional. Guests relax in total privacy behind palm tree shelters and lounge on the island's only nudist beach, without

Sorobon Beach Resort

TVs, radios, telephones or air-conditioning. Facilities include the **Sugarbird Restaurant** and a small shop selling necessities and souvenirs. Arrangements are made with outfitters on the island for dive trips and tours, and windsurfing centers are farther along the beach.

★★SAND DOLLAR

Kaya Governador N. Debrot #79
☎ 888-362-6043 or 717-8738; fax 717-8760
www.sanddollarbonaire.com
76 one- , two- , and three-bedroom condos
$155

Sand Dollar

Families come back again and again because the little kids love the **Sand Penny Club** and the big kids and parents love the **Dive and Adventure Center**. The condos are roomy and well-furnished. Each bedroom is air-conditioned and has its own bathroom. Lighted tennis courts, a swimming pool, and a couple of restaurants are on the property, and a long list of weekly activities keeps adventure travelers busy biking, kayaking and exploring.

EDEN BEACH RESORT

Kaya Governador N. Debrot

☎ 717-6720; fax 717-6710; www.edenbeach.com

32 one- and two-bedroom condos

$168

Eden Beach Resort

Guests love the beach, a 400-foot span of palm-studded sugar-white sand on the island's calm leeward coast. **Wannadive** is the on-site dive center, and kids can sign up for the Sea & Discover Program (see page 223). **Bongos Beach Bar** serves all meals and afternoon happy hours on tables set in the sand between the sea and a decked freshwater pool area.

Since Eden Beach was meant to be a complex of privately owned condos, each unit is home-like with spacious living/dining areas, practical cooking facilities. Lower-level one-bedroom units have a furnished patio, while those on the second floor have additional enclosed space. The larger units have a sleeper sofa downstairs in the living room and two bedrooms and two bathrooms upstairs.

East Coast & Inland

LAGOEN HILL

Lagoen Bay, east coast

☎ 717-2840 (on Bonaire); fax 31-252-34-17-80 (in the Netherlands); www.lagoenhill.com

30 studios, and one- , two- , or three-bedroom bungalows

$75

Located on the windward coast two miles east of Kralendijk, these privately owned bungalows are surrounded by a lovely garden. Onsite facilities include two swimming pools with attractive redbrick decking and a dive shop. Each unit has a shaded, furnished patio, ceiling

Lagoen Hill

fans, an equipped kitchen, and air-conditioned bedrooms.

COCO PALM GARDEN & CASA OLEANDER

Kaya van Eps #9
☎ 717-2108; fax 717-8193; www.cocopalmgarden.org
20 studios, apartments and houses
$60-$90

Coco Palm Garden

You can walk to beaches and dive sites on the southwest coast or quickly drive to Lac Bay (five minutes by car) from this tidy complex set in a quiet residential area. There's a small swimming pool with a private bar and restaurant on property, and each unit has a hammock and lounges in a landscaped garden. Next door, the two-bedroom Nos Kas vacation home offers extra living space, a full kitchen, and air-conditioned bedrooms. The furnished patio faces a landscaped garden. Other vacation homes and rental apartments are near or adjacent to the main complex and share the public areas. Call or check the website for a detailed description of each unit.

KON TIKI APARTMENTS & LAC BAY APARTMENTS/ VILLA

Kaminda Sorobon #64

☎ 717-5369; fax 717-5368; www.kontikibonaire.com

Five apartments

$85-$120 (including breakfast buffet)

Owners Miriam and Martin own and operate the popular Kon Tiki Beach Club Restaurant & Bar, near the windsurfing area on Lac Bay. They offer five choices of accommodations in their adjacent apartments and holiday villa. Visit the website to compare facilities and check out

Kon Tiki Apartments beach

their package deals.

SONRISA ROOMS & APARTMENTS

Kaya Finlandia

☎ 717-6633 or 786-3983 (cell); www.sonrisabonaire.com

12 rooms and one- or two-bedroom apartments

$110-$125

Sonrisa is a new complex south of Kralendijk, a short walk from a public beach and about five minutes by car from the airport. This is an ideal location for windsurfers because a shuttle runs guests to Bonaire Windsurf Place for a small fee each morning, and retrieves them each afternoon. All rooms have a private balcony or patio and are equipped with the modern touches: air conditioning, ceiling fans, room safes, a mini-fridge, coffee machines and cable TV. Rates include daily maid service, complimentary breakfast sandwich and coffee, and free wireless Internet. The accommodations are not fancy but, being new, everything is spotlessly clean and well organized. Dive centers, restaurants and shops are nearby.

Sonrisa Apartments

Rental Alternatives

SUNRENTALS BONAIRE
☎ 717-6130; fax 717-6136; www.sunrentals.an
Contact SunRentals for information about renting a condo, villa, apartment, or private home on the island. This agency also sets up dive packages and transportation.

BONAIRE LODGING; www.bonairelodging.com
Find a variety of budget-priced rooms, apartments, bungalows, and homes listed at this website. You will be directed to contact information after you click on accommodations that interest you.

BONAIRE STAYS
☎ 717-5134; fax 717-8534; www.bonairestays.com
Run by Bonaire Hotel and Tourism Association, this island-based group will hook you up with resorts, hotels and vacation rentals. The website also features activities, transportation and restaurants.

Where to Eat

Forget your opinion of hotel meals. Most of the restaurants attached to Bonaire's resorts are headed up by talented chefs who prepare a variety of international cuisines, including Indonesian, Asian,

Dutch, and good-ol'-American-style burgers. Independent restaurants compete for their share of customers by offering identical quality, a big splash of originality, and often some type of live entertainment.

If you want local fare, Antillean meals feature fresh-from-the-sea fish served with rice, beans, plantain (similar to cooked banana), and funchi (a cornmeal mush that appears on plates like a scoop of grainy yellow ice cream, but tastes much better than it looks). A small bowl or jar of pika sauce usually sits on each table and is used to flavor vegetables and meats. This local hot sauce is often homemade and varies in strength, so add it cautiously.

Many of the most popular restaurants are located right on the water, with fabulous views, especially during sunset happy hours, and after dark, when lights come on across the island. Plan to eat early. You'll be hungry anyway after a full day of diving or sightseeing, and most kitchens accept their last order around 10 pm.

During high season, make a reservation if you want to guarantee a table at a specific time and place. Otherwise, be more spontaneous, stroll Kralendijk's waterfront and allow the aromas, music, and views to draw you toward an empty table.

Dress casually, even for the best restaurants. Shorts are appropriate in all but the most elegant resorts, where men will want to wear long pants and a polo-type shirt, and women will be most comfortable in slacks or a sun dress.

Dining With the Stars

Every restaurant listed in this guide is recommended, and you will find some marked with stars. One star (★) indicates that the restaurant is highly recommended, two stars (★★) mean you should make an extra effort to eat there, and three stars (★★★) promise an experience to remember. The rating may be for super value or an amazing view or, perhaps, simply the best "cheeseburgers in paradise."

Restaurant Price Guide

Use the prices given at the beginning of each restaurant listing as a guide to the average price of a mid-range meal per person, excluding drinks and tip.

Unless noted otherwise, the establishments listed here accept credit cards. Some restaurants add a 10-15% service charge to your bill, so always review the charges before paying. The service charge is typically divided among all the employees of the restaurant. If you wish to reward your server with an extra tip, add it to your credit slip or hand cash directly to him/her. An additional 5% seems right, if a service charge is automatically added. Otherwise, leave the usual 15-20% tip.

In Kralendijk

★★RICHARD'S
J. A. Abraham Blvd. 60
☎ 717-5263
Seafood, International & vegetarian
$18-$25
Daily, 6-10 pm
Reservations recommended

Look for the little lights twinkling from the terrace entrance to this waterside restaurant south of town. Regulars begin gathering for happy hour at 5:30, and you'll feel right at home among the friendly crowd of residents and vacationers. Owners Richard, a native of Boston, and Mario, from Aruba, change the menu daily and keep the offerings limited, so everything is fresh and carefully prepared. The handwritten chalkboard menu typically offers a variety of grilled seafood and steaks, pasta and a vegetarian dishes. You can dine here several times during your vacation and always know you'll have a diverse choice of well-priced entrées.

ZEEZICHT SEASIDE
Kaya J.E. Craane 12
☎ 717-8434
International & seafood
$15-$22; prix fixe dinner, $35-$50
Daily, 8 am-11 pm
Reservations recommended

The name means "sea view" in Dutch, and it perfectly suits

this Bonaire landmark that overlooks the water in Kralendijk. Eat inside with air-conditioning, or sit outdoors and enjoy the breeze-cooled vista. Every meal comes with a trip to the salad bar, and regulars always start with the famous homemade soup. Sea-

Kon Tiki Apartments beach

food is served numerous ways, all delicious. No one should leave without dessert. Try the signature treat called Dead by Chocolate.

ZeeZicht Late Night Bar & Grill, adjacent to the main restaurant, offers a full dinner menu until 3 am, but many people just stop by for a late-night snack or to enjoy a specialty drink on the patio. (Closed Mondays.)

PIRATA NELLO
Kaya J.E. Craane 12
☎ 717-8434
Italian
$15-$20
Daily, 6-11:30 pm
Reservation recommended

Another spectacular place to watch the sunset. This gourmet Italian-style restaurant has an unequaled view of the sea from its second-floor location above ZeeZichts. For a real treat, try the lobster-stuffed pasta accompanied by a bottle of Chianti, followed by traditional tiramisu for dessert. The décor is nautical with a pirate theme, and if you ask directions from a resident, say you're looking for the pirate house.

★★CITY CAFÉ & CITY RESTAURANT

Kaya Grandi 7

☎ 717-8286; www.mainstreetbonaire.com

International

$8-$10 (breakfast), $12-$15 (lunch), $15-$20 (dinner)

Daily, 7-2 pm, breakfast, lunch & dinner

City Café has become a popular waterfront hangout right in the center of town (across from the fruit market). And for good reason. Locals say the bartenders make the best drinks on the island. Try

City Café

them during happy hour from 5:30 to 6:30 every afternoon. A live band plays on most weekends, drawing a crowd that often pours out into the street, andpatrons often stay until the place closes at 2 am.

City Restaurant serves meals all day and offers a lengthy international menu with choices for every taste. Seafood or vegetarian lasagna are good choices for dinner; French bread sandwiches make a filling lunch. If you like to start the day with a big meal, consider the three-egg breakfast.

*Need a fast-food fix? Head to **Wattaburger** on the Kaya Isla Riba next to City Café on the downtown waterfront. The "W" forms double arches in a takeoff on McDonald's. In addition to burgers and fries, there are Dutch favorites, and even cheese soufflé. Open Daily, 11 am- 11 pm. Friday and Saturday the doors stay open until 2 am.*

★CAPRICCIO

Kaya Isla Riba 1 (near Hotel Rochaline and City Café)
☎ 717-7230
Seafood & Italian specialties
$10-$20 (pizza), $22-$25 (main entrées)
Wednesday-Monday, 12-2 pm, 6:30-10:30 pm
Reservations recommended

Italian is done well at this cozy bistro. Whether it's pizza for lunch or home-made pasta for dinner, you won't be disap-pointed. If you're really hungry, go for the grand tour, a five-course gour-met meal you won't for-get. The wine selection is one of the best on the island, and the knowl-edgeable staff will help you choose the perfect bottle to complement your meal. Desserts and bread are homemade, so save room for one.

Capriccio

★MONA LISA
Kaya Grandi 15 (near City Café and Capriccio)
☎ 717-8718
French & international
$18-$30Monday-Friday, 6-10 pm
Reservations recommended

You never know what to expect at this old-world Dutch-style restaurant, because the chef creates the menu weekly around whatever is plentiful and delicious. Though the owners are Dutch, the meals tend toward French-influenced cuisine. If you sit in the bar, you may order a fixed-price dinner. Otherwise, ask your server what Chef Douwe suggests. The wine list is extensive. Some patrons come in only to enjoy a good bottle of wine and the European ambience, and the bar is open from 4 pm to 2 am weekdays.

DONNA & GIORGIO BAR RISTORANTI
Kaya Hellmund 25 (next to seaside entrance of Divi Flamingo Resort)
☎ 717-3799
Italian
$13-$25Bar open 5 pm-late
Dinner, 6:30-11 pm; closed Wednesday
Reservations recommended

Local art decorates this casual, lively bar and restaurant owned and operated by a husband-and-wife team. Home cooking Italian style is the theme and they carry it off well. Pizza and pasta are terrific, but try the seafood dishes, or the traditional osso bucco. Happy hour runs from 5:30 until 6:30 pm, and little snacks (*assagi*) are served at the bar all night.

★★IT RAINS FISHES
Kaya J.N.E Craane 24
☎ 717-8780
Seafood
$15-$22
Monday-Saturday, 6-11 pm
Reservations recommended

Salads are huge, enough to call a meal, and you may want to consider the Caesar- , Greek- , or Gyro-style for dinner so

Bonaire

that you can also manage one of the terrific chef-created desserts. In addition to good seafood, there are fabulous appetizers, and carefully prepared pasta, oriental chicken, pork ribs, and beef tenderloin. Located in the middle of town, the open-air seating allows nice views of the bay.

CASABLANCA

J. A. Abraham Boulevard 6
☎ 717 4433, www.restaurantcasablanca.com
Argentinian Grill
$ 10-$15 (lunch), $15-$30 (dinner)
Tuesday-Saturday 11:30 am-2:30 pm, 6-10:30pm, Sunday - Monday 6-10:30 pm
Reservations recommended

Plan to have dinner here on a Monday night, when the chefs prepare an all-you-can-eat Argentinean feast ($19) and photographer Albert Bianculli entertains with his underwater shots of local "mermaids" during the weekly event called Dushi Boneiru. On other evenings, order the signature meal, Mixed Grill for Two, which includes several pounds of the best cuts of beef and pork, plus sau-

sages, ribs, fish and chicken, all cooked over an open-to-view grill. If you don't have the appetite for such a filling repast, choose one of the smaller meals. You'll still have plenty to eat, since each plate is loaded with sides of French fries or rice and salad. Add a generous spoonful of Argentinean salsa or spicy Chimichurri sauce, and you have an authentic South American treat.

MAMBO JAMBO

Kaya L. D. Gerharts (next to Maduro & Curiels Bank)
☎ 701-8228
Thursday-Tuesday 8 am-2 am, breakfast (8-10 am), lunch (11 am-4 pm), dinner (4-10 pm), late-night menu (10 pm-midnight).
$5- $10 (breakfast), $8 - $12 (lunch), $12 - $18 (dinner)

Wilfried and Jolanda Schoof, prior owners of the Yachtclub Restaurant, recently opened this new eatery with seating on a pool-side patio or inside the air-conditioned dining room. The best thing on the  menu is the Rijsttafel, an Indonesian feast with small servings of many dishes including pork, chicken, fish and shrimp. If this doesn't appeal to you, try beef tenderloin, shrimp fried in beer batter or one of the pasta dishes. At lunch, the sandwiches are good, but try one of the Indonesian dishes for a real treat, and don't pass up pancakes for breakfast.

PAPAYA MOON CANTINA

Kaya Grandi #48
☎ 717-5025 , www.papayamooncantina.com
Tex/Mex
$14-$22
Wednesday-Monday 6-11pm, Happy Hour 6-7:30 pm
It's a bit unusual to find really good Mexican food in the Caribbean, but the Perpich family from Texas does the uncommon well. This newly opened cantina serves everything Tex/Mex and a few gourmet dishes (lobster enchiladas). We suggest you arrive during Happy Hour and start your meal

Bonaire

with a bowl of chips and salsa accompanied by one of the excellent Margaritas. The appetizers are creative and delicious, but don't fill up on them, because the entrée servings are generous. Finish the evening with an espresso and one of the distinctive desserts. We enjoyed crême brulée garnished with jalapeño jelly.

CHINA NOBO
Kaya Andres A. Emerenciana 4
☎ 717-8981
Chinese & Indonesian
$12-$20
Daily, 11 am-11 pm
Don't be put off by the pool tables, the food is sensational. Typical oriental dishes can be eaten at the casual air-conditioned restaurant or taken out. The Chan family serves large portions, so plan to share. Vegetarian dishes available.

Resort Restaurants

LA BALANDRA
Harbour Village Beach Resort
☎ 717-7500
Seafood & International
$8-$12 (breakfast), $10-$18 (lunch), $15-$25 (dinner)
Daily, breakfast 7:30-10:30 am, lunch noon-3 pm, dinner 7-10:30 pm
Credit cards accepted
Reservations recommended for dinner

Since its mention in *Travel + Leisure Magazine*, the wooden dock at La Balandra in Harbour Village has become **the** place to enjoy cocktails at sunset. Specialty nights are a good time to do this, then you can stay on for the candlelight theme dinner served on the beach.

BANANA TREE
Plaza Resort Bonaire
☎ 717-2500
International & Caribbean
$8-$12 (lunch), $15-$30 (dinner)
Daily, 11 am-11 pm

Everything at the Plaza is done well, but the Banana Tree goes the extra step with crisp white tablecloths and a garden setting. Try to go on a night when a local musician or band is playing (call ahead for the weekly schedule). With this gorgeous setting, you won't care what you're eating, but the salads and fresh fish are dependably good choices.

CARIBBEAN POINT
Plaza Resort Bonaire
☎ 717-2500
$10-$18 (breakfast), $12-20 (lunch), $25-$35 (dinner)
Reservations requested for dinner

Caribbean Point is the Plaza's charming indoor restaurant that serves an American-style buffet breakfast each morning. On Thursday nights, they hold a Caribbean Fiesta buffet featuring folkloric dancers and a local band. Make reservations well in advance during high season; this is one of the best shows on the island.

CHIBI CHIBI
Divi Flamingo Resort
☎ 717-8285
International
$8-$15 (lunch), $12-$25 (dinner)
Daily, 12-3 pm, 5-10 pm, beach service daily noon-5 pm
Reservations recommended for dinner

Ask for a waterside table above the sea at this two-level open-air restaurant. Lunch is salads, sandwiches, and such; dinner features a mix of fresh fish, steaks, and Asian specialties. The real highlight is the nightly underwater light show, which is simply fabulous. There's a large selection of wines available by the glass. After dinner, try your luck at the recently renovated barefoot casino.

Elsewhere on the Island

DEN LAMAN OCEANSIDE
Kaya Gob.N. Debrot 77 (between Sunset Beach Hotel and
Sand Dollar Beach Club)
☎ 717-4106
Seafood
$15 (vegetarian), $16-$20 (meats and seafood)
Wednesday-Monday, 5-10 pm
Reservations recommended
This popular restaurant makes good use of its ideal location
(between Sunset Beach Hotel and Sand Dollar Beach
Club), providing white-tablecloth-and-candlelight dining on
the seaside terrace. Start with pumpkin soup, then try the
fresh catch of the day, or choose one of the grilled-meat
combinations. Vegetarians will like the veggie lasagna, and
homemade cheesecake is the ideal end to dinner.

HILL TOP
Bonaire Caribbean Club, north of Captain Don's Habitat, off
the Coast Road
☎ 717-7901
International & Caribbean
$8-$12 (breakfast), $10-$15 (lunch), $18-$25 (dinner)
Daily, 7:30 am-10 pm
Reservations recommended

Call ahead to check
on theme dinners,
such as Churrasco
Night, featuring four
types of grilled meat
and all the trimmings.
The small pool-side
restaurant serves
breakfast, lunch, and
dinner; enjoy happy-
hour prices in the bar
from 6-7:30 pm daily.

Bonaire Caribbean Club aerial view

Nightlife

 Don't believe it when someone tells you there's nothing to do after dark on Bonaire. Those who say it most likely go to bed right after dinner so they can be up for the first dive trip the next morning.

Night Diving

Actually, Bonaire is quite active after sunset, and diving or snorkeling is one of the most popular nighttime activities. Almost all dive operators offer outings just as the sky darkens around sunset. Chemical lights are banned in the Marine Park, but four-cell flashlights put a whole new light on colorful coral formations and marine creatures that normally hide during daytime hours. Tarpon take advantage of the artificial beam to locate their dinner, so divers/snorkelers have a chance to watch the huge silvery fish chow down on smaller species that are attracted to the light like moths.

Slide Shows

As an alternative, many resorts host no-charge slide presentations by local underwater photographers. Even experienced divers are amazed at the variety of sea life and the vibrant colors captured on film. If you don't dive or snorkel, these shows offer a fabulous opportunity to see what all the excitement is about. If you have time for only one presentation, make it **Dee Scarr's Touch the Sea** (see page 221).

 *Pick up free copies of **Bonaire Holiday** or **Bonaire Nights** for current listings of island entertainment.*

In the unlikely event that you get bored with all things underwater, head to one of the bars, dance clubs, or casinos.

Bonaire

Some feature live entertainment, and all are casual places to meet new people and mingle with the locals.

Live Bands

Local musicians play regularly at bars and cafés, and for special theme-night parties at the resorts. Currently, one of the hottest entertainers is **Ralph Moogie Stewart**, a Floridian who has performed on Bonaire since 1990; first with Larry Sparky Thorne as the Kunuku Band, and more recently as a solo act. Look for him at **Captain Don's Habitat's Rum Runners Bar** (☎ 717-8290), **Buddy Dive**

Resort's Dock of the Bay Bar (☎ 717-5080), and **Plaza Resort's Tipsy Seashell Bar** (☎ 717-2500). If you like what you hear, take home his solo CD, *Fire*.

Captain Don's Rum Runners Bar

 *Find CDs by local musicians and bands at **Mundo Musical** in Lourdes Mall, Kralendijk, ☎ 717-8174.*

Popular bands include the 12-piece **Glen i Su Gang** (Glen and His Gang), a group of regular working guys who hold down day jobs, but get together to play folk-style music in the evening. They've been performing together since 1998. **Tipico Bonairiano** has been around many years, and the band is still popular for its use of standard and unusual instruments to produce original island music. It's a special treat to see them perform with the local **Kibrahacha Dancers** on Wednesday nights at the **Plaza Resort's Caribbean Point**, ☎ 717-2500.

Bars & Nightclubs

In addition to the resorts, which tend to sponsor rum-punch or theme-night parties on a rotating basis most nights of the week, the following hot spots often feature music, dancing, and live entertainment:

City Café, a casual hangout open nightly until 2 am with happy hour running from 5:30 until 6:30 pm, usually has live entertainment on weekends. It's on the waterfront side of Hotel Rochaline across from the Venezuelan fruit market in Kralendijk, ☎ 717-8286.

Mona Lisa is a Dutch bar located in a yellow island-style building with red doors on Kaya Grandi in the middle of town. This is a nice place to stop for a drink between 4 pm and 2 am, but don't plan to visit on Saturday or Sunday – it's closed. The highlight here is beer. They have a long international list, and Hans, the friendly bartender who is also one of the owners, will guide you to exactly the right brew. ☎ 717-8718.

Casinos

If you're feeling lucky, head for one of Bonaire's two casinos.

The **Plaza Resort Casino** sparkles with bright lights and buzzes with action. A hallway of slot machines leads to the gaming room, where guests try their hand at blackjack, roulette, and poker. Dress is smart casual; no shorts after sunset. Play begins at the slot machines at 4 pm, game tables open at 8 pm, and the bar closes at 4 am, ☎ 717-2450.

Divi Flamingo Casino is the recently renovated center-piece at the Flamingo Beach Resort. Known as the barefoot casino, the entire building has been redesigned with lovely landscaped grounds, an open-air bar, and an expanded gaming room with blackjack, roulette, poker, wheel of fortune, video games, and slot machines. The casual casino is open Monday through Saturday from 6 pm until 2 am, ☎ 717-8285.

Island Facts & Contacts

AIRPORT: Flamingo International Airport, ☎ 717-5600.

AREA CODE: 599 (for all of the Netherlands Antilles); 7 is the island code for Bonaire.

ATMs: Available at locations throughout the island, including the airport (Maduro & Curiel's Bank), Cultimara Supermarket in Kralendijk (MCB), large resorts, Harborside Mall, and banks in Kralendijk and Rincón.

BANKS: Most banks are in Kralendijk, but you will find branch offices in the villages of Hato (near the beach resorts) and Rincón. The main offices are open from 8:30 am until 3:30 pm, Monday through Friday. Branch offices close from noon until 1:15 pm. The airport bank (MCB) is open Monday, Wednesday, and Thursday, 8:30 am-noon and 1:15-3:30 pm; Tuesday and Friday, 8:30 am-noon and 1:15-5 pm; Saturday, 10 am-3 pm (☎ 715-5520).

CAPITAL: Kralendijk.

DEPARTURE TAX: $32 for international flights (sometimes added to the cost of your airline ticket).

DRIVING: Traffic travels on the right side of the road, as in the US, Canada, and most of Europe.

ELECTRICITY: The electrical voltage is 127/120 AC (50 cycles), and the outlets accept the same plugs used in North America. The voltage is higher than in North America and the cycles are lower, so some appliances overheat quickly. Most resorts provide hair dryers in the rooms. Both resorts and dive shops have charging converters for electronic equipment.

EMERGENCY: Police, ☎ 911. Ambulance and hospital, ☎ 114.

GAS STATIONS: Don't run out of gas on Sunday or late at night. The four stations (located in Kralendijk, and the village of Rincón) operate Monday-Saturday, 7 am-9 pm... usually.

GOVERNMENT: Bonaire is part of the Netherlands Antilles, which includes Curaçao, St. Maarten, St. Eustatius, and Saba. Curaçao is the capitol of the Netherlands Antilles, which is autonomous from the Kingdom of the Netherlands. However, the governor of the NA and the lieutenant governor of each island is appointed by the ruling monarch of the Kingdom. Each island's parliament is elected by popular vote, and citizens may vote at the age of 21.

HOSPITAL: San Francisco Hospital, Kaya Soeur Bartola #2, Kralendijk, ☎ 717-8900. A decompression chamber for divers is located next door, but you must go to the hospital first to be seen by an admitting doctor.

LANGUAGE: The official language is Dutch, but locals speak Papiamentu (spelled Papiamento on Aruba and Curaçao). Many residents are multilingual and also speak Spanish, English, and German.

LEGAL AGE: 18 for drinking and 21 for gambling. The island's drug laws are strict.

MONEY: The Netherlands Antillean florin (NAfl) is the official currency, and US $1 = NAfl 1.78 or NAfl 1 = 56¢, but the dollar is widely accepted. Plan to exchange only a small amount of money to pay for taxi fares, tips, and small purchases. Stores will convert prices for you at a good rate, about NAfl 1.75 = $1, but change is given in local currency. Major credit cards are accepted at large resorts and restaurants, and many stores, but smaller establishments may require cash.

PHARMACY: Botica Korona , Kaya Korona 180, ☎ 717-7552, and **Botica Bonaire**, Kaya Grandi 27, ☎ 717-8905.

Bonaire

PHONES: The international access code from North America is 011; the country code for the Netherlands Antilles is 599; the island code for Bonaire is 7. To call Bonaire from North America, dial 011-599+ the seven-digit local number, which begins with 7, the island code. If you are calling Bonaire from Europe or most of the rest of the world, you would dial 00 + 599 + the seven-digit local number.

On Bonaire, dial the local number, including the island code of 7.

Some cellular phone numbers are Curaçao numbers that begin with a number other than 7.

POPULATION: 14,400.

PUBLICATIONS: These magazines are available free in hotel lobbies and at many restaurants and tourist attractions: **Bonaire Holiday**, **Bonaire Nights**, **Bonaire Dining Guide**, and **Bonaire Affair**. Island news and current events are listed in the English-language newspaper **Bonaire Reporter**.

SAFETY: Bonaire is very safe. Take common-sense precautions to avoid theft, especially from cars parked at tourist attractions and beaches.

SHOPPING HOURS: Some stores open on Sunday when a cruise ship is in port. Otherwise, plan to shop Monday-Saturday, 8 am-noon, and 2-6 pm. A few shops may stay open during the lunch hours, especially when cruise-ship passengers are in town.

TAXES: A 5% sales tax is added to most purchases. In addition, hotels charge room tax of $6.50 per person, per day. A 10% service charge may be added to hotel and restaurant bills. Check before you include a tip.

TAXIS: ☎ 717-8100.

TIME: Bonaire is on Atlantic Standard Time (AST) year-round, which is one hour later than Eastern Standard Time and four hours earlier than Greenwich Mean Time. The island does not observe daylight savings time, so Bonaire's time is the same as Eastern Daylight Savings Time.

TOURIST INFORMATION: ☎ 800-266-2473; fax 212-956-5913 (in North America); www.infobonaire.com.

Tourism Corporation Bonaire (TCB), Kaya Grandi #2, Kralendijk, ☎ 717-8322; fax 717-8408.

WEBSITES: Dozens of sites offer information about activities, accommodations, and travel. The best general information sites are **www.infobonaire.com** and **www.bonaire.org**.

Curaçao

N

© 2008 HUNTER PUBLISHING, INC

9.6 KM
6 MILES

East Point

St. Joris Bay

Nieuwpoort

Spanish Water

St. Joris Bay

Santa Rosa

Caracas Bay

Curaçao Underwater Park

Brievengat

Boca Playa Canoa

Punda

Santa Maria

Schottegat

Hato Caves

Otrobanda

Willemstad

Hato Int'l Airport

Julianadorp

Bullenbaai

Boca Ascencion

Boca San Pedro

Bullen Bay

Playa Grandi

San Willibrordo

Bartol Bay

Caribbean Sea

Indian Inscription Caves

Barber

Boca Tabla

Soto

North Point

Mt. Christoffel National Park

Boca Sta. Cruz

Westpoint Bay

Lagún

Lagún Bay

Playa Kalki

Westpoint

Curaçao
Overview

Curaçao (say "cure-a-sow") is the largest and busiest of the island group and a multi-cultural leader in the southern Caribbean. More than 150,000 residents from 50 nations call the long, narrow island home. Its close proximity to the Venezuelan coast results in a mix of lusty Latin flair, easy-going Caribbean charm, venerable African heritage, and contemporary European sophistication. The local dialect, Papiamento, is a blend of languages, including Dutch, Spanish, English, Portuguese and several African idioms.

The United Nations Educational, Scientific, and Cultural Organization (UNESCO) honored the capital city, Willemstad, by designating it a World Heritage Site because of its striking Dutch colonial architecture. Among the most treasured buildings is the oldest continually operating synagogue in the Western Hemisphere, a centuries-old Protestant church, and a half-dozen early Dutch fortresses.

Upscale shops filled with fine European imports line pedestrian-only streets in colorful Willemstad. Shoppers look for bargains at the open-air markets, and discover great buys on locally made treasures in whimsical galleries. After dark, visitors join locals at restaurants featuring cuisine from a

Otrobanda & the Queen Emma Bridge (Paul Sullivan)

dozen countries, then try their luck at the elegant casinos or dance to live music at one of the many nightclubs.

The countryside draws travelers with historic plantation houses, a rugged national park, miles of picturesque beaches, and a new championship golf course. Divers and snorkelers spend time exploring the sea creatures that live on close-in underwater reefs and wrecks. Eco-tourists investigate caves, ride horseback through nature reserves, and hike along the craggy cliffs of the northwest coast.

A DOZEN REASONS TO VISIT

- **Pastel-painted buildings** along Willemstad's waterfront.
- The **Animal Encounters** habitat at the Sea Aquarium.
- The **Mushroom Forest** dive site.
- Water-carved cliffs and caverns at **Shete Boca Park**.
- Driving routes through **Christoffel National Park**.

- **Kurá Hulanda Museum** and restored historic village.
- The **Ostrich and Game Farm**.
- **Blue Bay Golf Course**.
- **Queen Emma pedestrian pontoon bridge**.
- The **Hato Caves**.
- Herbs and remedies at **Den Paradera**.
- The orchards and recreated slave village of **Hòfi Pachi Sprockel**.

Unique Celebrations

 Curaçao packs its yearly calendar with official holidays, flamboyant festivals, and internationally acclaimed events. Banks, post offices and most businesses close for many of the special days, and you can expect large crowds at the parks and beaches. Big events, such as Carnival, go on for several jubilant days or weeks, and you may want to schedule your trip to either avoid or coincide with the ecstacy.

 *Dates change somewhat from year to year for many holidays and events, so check with the **tourist bureau** for a current schedule before you make arrangements to visit the island.* ☎ 800-328-7222; www.Curaçao-tourism.com.

In addition to the traditional holidays celebrated on all three islands, Curaçao observes the following:

January 26, **Indian Republic Day**, is marked by the closing of Indian restaurants and shops.

April-May. The **Seú Folklore Festival** takes place the Monday after Easter Sunday. It is an official holiday, and a day for traditional celebrations that remind residents of the island's agricultural heritage. Even during the years of slavery, workers celebrated the end of the harvest, and once former slaves were free to farm their own land, the revelry increased with untamed enthusiasm. ☎ 599-9-737-3585 or 599-9-562-7036.

THE SEÚ BEAT

Seú is the name of the slaves' old trouble-and-toil music, which had a beat that was ideal for carting baskets of produce from fields to warehouses. Laborers moved from field to field, singing and swaying to the *seú* beat played on homemade drums and horns. Today, the celebration is continued by cultural groups, and *seú* musicians play instruments made from conch shells, cow horns, and hollow gourds. Parade marchers of all ages dress in muslin and sack cloth similar to the clothing worn by slaves and march through the streets of Punda and Otrobanda, districts of Willemstad.

April 30 is celebrated as the **Queen's Birthday** on all islands in the Netherlands Antilles, but on Curaçao the royal birth is commemorated with official ceremonies at Fort Amsterdam and festive decorations in the Punda section of Willemstad. Government offices, banks, and many stores are closed for the day.

May 1, **Labor Day**, is celebrated with sports competitions, dances, and picnics.

May 30, **The 1969 Commemoration**, is an unofficial holiday celebrated by trade unions in remembrance of the historic social uprising that gripped the island in 1969, when labor organizations demanded better working conditions. Most stores and businesses remain open, but trade unions organize public cultural activities, parades and pro-labor speeches.

July 2, **Flag Day**, is celebrated with morning festivities in Brionplein (Brion Plaza) in Otrobanda and in Parke Himnoy Bandera (Hymn and Flag Park) on the west end of the island.

July 26, Curaçao Day commemorates the discovery of the island in 1499.

Rosh Hashanah and **Yom Kippur** are celebrated by the Jews in **September** and **October**, and most Jewish-owned shops, banks, and businesses are closed.

Annual Events

January

During the annual four-day **Tumba Festival**, musicians from around the island compete to have their original music selected as the official Carnival Road March Song. The singer is

Tumba

named Tumba King or Queen. This crowd-drawing festival runs from Monday through Friday, with Thursday a welcome day of rest. (The date changes annually, depending on the beginning date of **Carnival**.) In addition to the musical competition, vendors sell beer and food, and spectators often dance late into the night. ☎ 599-9-738-3652, www.curacaocarnival.info/eng/index.php.

March

The **Annual International Blue Marlin Tournament** is a two-day conservation event featuring individual and team competition. Blue marlin is the priority catch. All billfish weighing less than 200 pounds are

Carnival

released. For dates and information, contact the Curaçao Yacht Club, ☎ 599-9-767-4627, www.curacaoyachtclub. com..

Spring

The **Curaçao Regatta** draws hundreds of sailors and colorful boats to the waters near the Sea Aquarium. The week-long regatta includes long- and short-distance competition for all types of sailors, including windsurfers, single-hulls, catamarans, and trimarans. For dates and information, ☎ 599-9-511-9292, www.curacaoregatta.com.

May

This is the traditional month for **The Curaçao International Jazz Festival**, which brings performers from around the world to the island for two days of concerts and jamming. Get a schedule and list of musicians for this year's event from the Curaçao Jazz Foundation, ☎ 599-9-515-JAZZ or 599-9-461-1866, www.curacaojazzfest.com.

June/July

The annual **Curaçao Salsa Festival** celebrates the Latin beat of salsa. Top South American and Caribbean musicians gather for an outdoor extravaganza each summer. Tickets and information are available through the Curaçao Tourist Board, ☎ 800-328-7226 and locally from the Curaçao Festival Center, ☎ 599-9-561-1268, www. curacaosalsatour.com.

The **area code** for Curaçao is 599+9. To phone from the US, dial 011-599-9, then the seven-digit number. On the island, dial only the seven-digit number.

Getting to Curaçao

By Air

 If you arrive by air, you will land at **Hato International Airport** (CUR, ☎ 599-9-839-1000), located on the north coast about six miles from the capital of Willemstad. Its runway is one of the longest in the Caribbean and accommodates jumbo jets from Europe and all of the Americas.

The airport is modern and passengers get through Customs quickly. There's a 24-hour automatic currency exchange machine and an ATM that disburses US dollars in the arrival area, along with a tourist information booth. Taxi stands are located just outside the terminal, and car rental offices are clustered together for easy rate comparisons.

American Airlines flies nonstop from Miami to Curaçao daily (2½ hours) and American Eagle has daily nonstop flights to the island from San Juan, Puerto Rico. KLM flies directly from Amsterdam several times a week. Avianca has service from Bogata; Aeropostal flies from Caracas.

LOCAL AIRLINE CONTACT INFORMATION	
Aeropostal	☎ 888-2808
American Airlines/American Eagle	☎ 869-5707
Avianca	☎ 868-0122
KLM	☎ 736-1422
Divi Divi	☎ 888-1050

 See the Travel Information *chapter, pages 39-41, for additional airline information. For flight information,* ☎ 868-1719.

Curaçao

By Cruise Ship

 Curaçao's cruise terminal in Otrobanda (a district within the capital city of Willemstad) is just steps from the island's charming Holland-like shopping district and UNESCO-designated World Heritage Sites. Large ships dock at the new Mega Pier, which is nearby. During peak season, it's not unusual to see two or more large passenger ships dock at the modern terminal, and approximately 200,000 visitors arrive by ship each year. Many find they don't have enough time on the island, and return as stay-over visitors.

Tourist information and an ATM are located on the dock; taxi drivers and tour operators meet arrivals to offer guided excursions of the capital and island. Bus and mini-bus service is available from Punda (across the Queen Emma Bridge) to several key tourist attractions, including the Seaquarium and beach.

 See Touring the Island, *page 279, for a listing of tour operators and information about sightseeing by bus or taxi.*

Leaving Curaçao

A departure tax (usually added to the cost of your airline ticket) is charged before passengers check in for their departing flight, and must be paid in US dollars or Netherlands Antilles guilders (NAfl). For international flights, the tax is $23 or NAfl 41. For flights within the Netherlands Antilles, the tax is $10 or NAfl 17.

Confirm your outgoing flight the day before your departure, and remember to arrive at the airport one-two hours before departure, in order to clear strict security checks.

Getting Around
Taxis

 Taxis are identified by a sign on the car and a TX on the license plate. They do not have meters, but fares to hotels are posted at the airport, and drivers are required to carry a government-approved rate sheet that you may ask to see if you suspect that you're not being quoted the correct fare. Most drivers are friendly, professional, and honest, so expect to be treated fairly.

 A 24-hour automatic currency exchange machine is located in the terminal. Get enough money here to pay for the taxi ride in guilders. It will be less confusing than trying to calculate the exchange rate, and drivers usually cannot make correct change in foreign currency.

Some hotels offer free shuttle service to and from the airport; a taxi will be about $15 to locations near Willemstad (a 15-minute ride). Expect to pay about $20 for the trip to Lions Dive Resort (on the opposite side of the city), and about $28 to Coral Cliff (on the west coast). If you have too much luggage to allow the trunk lid to close securely, you'll be charged a dollar or two extra. Rates legally increase by 25% after 11 pm, and a 10% tip is appropriate for good service, but not mandatory. If the driver helps you with your bags, or gives a mini-tour of the surroundings on the way to your destination, consider tipping more generously.

Taxis don't routinely cruise the island looking for passengers, so if you're leaving from someplace other than the airport, call the dispatcher to request transportation. If you need a ride early in the morning or late at night, make arrangements in advance.

Taxi Dispatch: ☎ 869-0747 or 868-1220 (airport).

Sightseeing tours by taxi should be arranged through your hotel to guarantee a comfortable cab and knowledgeable

Curaçao

driver. You'll pay about $25 per hour for up to four people, and establish the price before you get into the taxi. If you need a ride to a restaurant or attraction, ask if your hotel has a courtesy van. If not, request that someone at the front desk make arrangements for a taxi with a driver who speaks your language, drives a comfortable car (some are not air-conditioned), and knows the island well (even natives sometimes do not know all the restaurants and nightclubs).

 Note: *It's considered poor manners to get into the cab wearing a wet swimsuit or muddy shoes.*

Handelkadem Willemstad (Rodry 1)

By Car

Car Rentals

 Consider renting a car for at least a few days of your vacation so that you can explore all parts of the island. Curaçao has good roads, traffic travels on the right side, drivers are courteous, and international signs are posted.

Several car-rental offices are located at the airport and usually open daily from 8 am until 8 pm. Some off-site companies offer 24-hour pick-up and delivery or have offices at resorts. It's best to reserve a car before you leave on vacation to get the best rates and avoid sell-outs. If you want a car for only a few days, ask if your hotel has a rental company on-site or nearby.

Rental rates to vary season-to-season, but they average about $35 per day for a small car with manual transmission, air-conditioning and unlimited mileage. You will pay about $65 per day for a larger car , as well as for one with automatic transmission or four-wheel-drive. Weekly rates are available and usually work out to be less per day. Insurance add-ons begin at $10 per day, but you may be responsible for $500 worth of damage anyway. Check before you sign up. During high season, cars are reserved early, so you may find only larger cars with automatic transmission if you wait until the last minute. During low season, you can usually find special deals.

INTERNATIONAL CAR RENTAL COMPANIES	
Alamo	☎ 869-4433
Avis	☎ 461-1255 (main office), 868-1163 (airport)
Budget	☎ 868-3466 (main office), 868-3420 (airport)
Hertz	☎ 888-0088 (main office) or 888-0188 (airport)
National	☎ 869-4433 (airport)
Thrifty	☎ 461-3089

For toll-free numbers and website information see *Getting Around*, page 44.

LOCAL CAR RENTAL COMPANIES	
The car-rental offices are in Willemstad.	
Holiday	☎ 511-6068
Michel	☎ 888-8878 (www.michelrentacar.com)
Noordstar	☎ 737-5616 or 561-1763 (cell); www.noordstarrentalcar.com

Curaçao

By Bus

 Some hotels have complimentary or small-fee shuttle vans that take registered guests into town or to various beaches. In addition, a fleet of large yellow buses (called *konvoi* locally) run from Wilhelmina Plaza in Willemstad to many of the most traveled areas of the island, including beaches. Service is infrequent on Sundays, but on other days you can expect hourly departures from city bus stops for in-town routes and two-hour intervals for out-of-town routes.

Fares are given in guilders and based on direction/distance. A trip from the capital to the far northwest end of the island will cost about NAfl 1.50 (85¢); in-town and eastern destinations cost NAfl 1 (56¢). If you're serious about using public transportation, fill your pockets with guilders and pick up a copy of *Buki di Bus: Bus Schedules and Routes* at the Tourist Office, Pietermaai 19, ☎ 461-7182.

Touring the Island

Whether you see the capital of the Netherlands Antilles with a guide or on your own, you'll discover plenty of natural beauty (including more than 30 public beaches and a national park), interesting historical sites, and colorful architecture. The island is large compared to Aruba and Bonaire, but quite manageable, at about 182 square miles.

Getting Oriented

 Roads are in good condition and signs point the way to most attractions, so finding your way around is easy, whether you're driving in the countryside or walking through Willemstad. Pick up a free map at the front desk of your hotel, any car-rental office, information kiosks at the airport or cruise-ship terminal, or at the Tourism Development Bureau in Punda (Pietermaai 19, ☎ 434-8200).

The island is long (about 37 miles) and thin (no more than eight miles across), lying almost diagonal to due north-south. Little Klein Curaçao is about seven miles off the southeast coast.

Willemstad, the capital of both Curaçao and the Netherlands Antilles, is located a bit east of midpoint on the protected leeward coast of the island. **Hato Airport** is to the north, at about midpoint on the windward coast. The island extends northwest and southeast from the capital and airport, with the **Watamula Lighthouse** on the northwestern point, and the **Oostpunt Lighthouse** on the southeastern tip.

Guided Tours

Some of the island's attractions offer guided tours, but if you have only a few hours, or want a quick overview of the entire island before you head out to do your own exploring, contact one of the following tour operators:

▦ **Taber Tour** has a service desk in all the major hotels and offers a variety of tours on comfortable modern buses. ☎ 737-6637.

 Before signing up for a guided tour, ask if the guide speaks your language, and if the tour is conducted entirely or primarily in your language.

▦ **Peter Trips** features cultural and historical tours. The full-day outings cover the entire island; afternoon tours take in either the east or west ends; morning trips hit some of the top attractions. Groups must comprise two to 10 participants. ☎ 465-2703 or 561-5368 (cell).

▦ **Old City Tours-Anko vande Woude** takes a look at historical Otrobanda and Punda on Thursday afternoons at 5:15. Your guide will be a resident architect or art historian. ☎ 461-3554.

▦ **Atlantis Adventures** conducts the 1½-hour open-air trolley tours through Willemstad, starting at Fort Amsterdam. Call for exact departure times, ☎ 462-8833.

■ **Does Travel & Cadushi Tours** has scheduled excursions to many popular sites on the island, including Christoffel Park. Guides also lead visitors on walking tours of Otrobanda and bus tours of Punda. The all-day Great Tour goes into exclusive residential neighborhoods and out to the beaches. ☎ 461-1626.

■ **Curaçao Actief** specializes in eco-safari tours of the island with ample beach time. Other specialties include customized mountain-bike adventures, windsurfing, diving tours, and sailboat or canoe excursions. If you can dream it, they can arrange it. ☎ 433-8858; www. curacao-actief.com.

See *Adventures on Water*, pages 311 ff, for information on sightseeing by boat, snorkel/scuba trips, and party boats.

Self-Guided Tours

The capital city of Willemstad is the focal point of Curaçao, and you will want to spend at least a half-day seeing its colorful, historical sights. Along the way, hunt for bargains in the lively markets, stop for a snack at a waterside café, and rest in the shade of a palm tree in one of the lovely plazas. To get oriented, take the 90-minute trolley tour of the city, which leaves Fort Amsterdam at 10 am. Tickets are $20 for adults, $15 for children. Contact Atlantis Adventures for reservations, ☎ 461-0011, www.atlantisadventures.com.

★★★Willemstad-UNESCO World Heritage Site

First-time visitors to Curaçao, especially those who arrive by cruise ship, are amazed by the altogether un-Caribbean appearance of the capital city of Willemstad. The Dutch, never a people to leave home without their creature comforts, built a little Amsterdam for themselves when they came to colonize the island in 1634. Much of their creation remains, and UNESCO, the organization that takes worldwide heritage

Willemstad Area

Schout Bij Nacht Doorman Weg

Schottegateweg Oost

ZEELANDIA

Salina Weg

EMMASTAD

Blaauwbaai

Margriet laan

Pres Betancourt Blvd

PUNDA

Dr Martin Luther King Blvd

Pietermaai Weg

Schottegat

REFINERY

OTROBANDA

Schottegat Weg West

Roode Weg

Sint Anna Blvd

Weg Naar Welgelegen

Rector Zwijsendtraat

Franklin D Roosevelt Weg

Weg Naar Westpunt

Piscadera Weg

Caribbean Sea

N

NOT TO SCALE

Punda & Otrobanda (Ghettocash)

sites into its sheltering arms, has selected the city as a worthy spot to protect.

United Nations Educational, Scientific, and Cultural Organization (UNESCO) hands out its World Heritage titles sparingly and after intense scrutiny, so the designation is a true international honor. Once a cultural or natural site is selected for protection, UNESCO orchestrates its restoration and shields it from environmental threats to preserve it for future generations to enjoy.

Willemstad was selected because of its collection of European colonial structures that illustrate the evolution of a multi-cultural community over a period of 300 years. Each of the city's distinct districts has an individual history and culture that have entwined over the centuries to create a unique environment. The most interesting districts, historically and architecturally, are ★★**Punda** and ★**Otrobanda**, which face each other across Sint Annabaai (Saint Anna Bay), the entrance to Schottegat Harbor.

Waterfort and Fort Amsterdam, the oldest structures on the island, sit on the Punda (the point) side of the bay. The protective stone Waterfort went up soon after the Dutch West India Company (DWIC) arrived, and its arches now house seaside restaurants and shops. Fort Amsterdam was completed in 1648 and became the center point for the city's development. A church, government offices, and a residence for the island's administrator were built inside its walls.

The stunning arches of ★**Waterfort** are now an historic foundation for the Curaçao Plaza Hotel and several waterside restaurants and bars. The yellow fort complex is in excellent condition and now serves as the seat of government of the Netherlands Antilles. The Fort Church still has an active Dutch Protestant congregation, and the building also serves as a **museum** (☎ 461-1139) for old maps and artifacts. An English cannonball embedded in the church's southwest wall proves that the Dutch were not being paranoid when they fortified their city against attack.

Arch of Waterfort (Paul Sullivan)

The famous, or infamous, Vice Admiral **William Bligh**, made immortal by *Mutiny on the Bounty*, ordered the attack on Fort Amsterdam in 1804, during a 26-day siege of the city. Admission to the museum is $5 for adults and $3 for kids.

Protected by Waterfort and Fort Amsterdam, the Dutch went about their favorite pursuit, international trade. Schottegat Harbor hummed with activity, and warehouses went up along Punda's shore. Narrow streets were laid out beyond the waterfront for houses and shops. The enclosed town had more than 200 homes by the early 1700s, and there was limited space for new devel-

Buildings on Handelskade

opment, so people began building outside the fortress walls on a strip of land called **Pietermaai**.

Today, Pietermaai has been widened by landfill, but the original layout of perpendicular streets remains unchanged.

Handelskade, the street that runs along the waterfront of St. Anna Bay, is a showcase of 18th-century Dutch-Caribbean architecture. Many other original buildings have been restored in Punda's commercial section. Some of the large homes built in Pietermaai have been restored as well, and the Curaçao Tourism Development Bureau is located in a lovely yellow and white 18th-century mansion at Pietermaaiweg #19.

Otrobanda (Paul Sullivan)

Otrobanda (the other side) is, of course, on the opposite side of St. Anna Bay. Restricted building permits were given for the area as early as 1707, but regulations limited development to warehouses and small shops with living quarters on the second level. Citizens saw little merit in these stipulations since land was plentiful on the other side, so they ignored the laws and set about building large homes for themselves, similar to those built by wealthy landowners in the roomy countryside.

Unlike Punda, where city planning resulted in perpendicular streets and uniform architecture, Otrobanda became a village of narrow streets and tight alleyways twisting capriciously from the waterfront through the commercial areas and out to the residential neighborhoods. Within 70 years, 300 homes spread across the district, and it had as many shops, warehouses, and offices as Punda.

After emancipation, free slaves moved into the area and built houses and small businesses, some on property that was originally the garden of a large estate. Other ethnic groups were attracted to the other side as well, and soon the district was a thriving middle-class community of many nationalities and cultures. It remains so today.

★**Brionplein** (Brion Plaza) is the centerpiece of Otrobanda's waterfront. It is named for Pedro Luis Brión, a citizen of Curaçao, who fought with Simón Bolivar for Latin American independence. Many of Otrobanda's lovely restored homes are noted as childhood residences of the islands' honored politicians, lawyers, doctors, and entrepreneurs. Parts of the district are still rundown and waiting for renovation funds, but the breezy alleyways lead past magnificent examples of Dutch colonial architecture.

Unquestionably, the best restoration is ★★★**Kurá Hulanda** (Dutch yard). It's the imaginative work of Dutchman Jacob Gelt Dekker and his American business partner, John Padget. Their hands-on philanthropy has transformed an entire section of Otrabanda's dilapidated slum, known as the Iron Quarter, into a magnificently renovated historical

Kurá Hulanda

district – the best example of Dutch colonial architecture in the Caribbean.

★★**Museum Kurá Hulanda** is a lovely tribute to Africa and the citizens it lost to slavery. The circular central courtyard holds a double slap-in-the-face reminder of the cruelty inflicted on so many – two tall pillars supporting a crossbeam and an antique ship's bell. The bell

Kurá Hulanda, Surnamese House

was used to summon slaves to work; the crossbeam to tie them for beatings. Depressions worn into the wooden beam perfectly fit a man's wrists.

The thread that ties this African exhibit to Curaçao is the Dutch West India Company, whose most profitable merchandise was human beings. The museum stands on ground once used as a slave market – a Dutch yard – Kurá Hulanda. Open 10 am-5 pm daily; $6 adults. $3 kids. ☎ 434-7765.

Elsewhere in the reborn complex, 65 buildings have been refurbished according to strict UNESCO preservation guidelines. No outer walls or supporting interior structures have been removed, and everything has been painted or refinished to conform to the original design. Now shops, restaurants, and overnight villa accommodations occupy the colorful buildings. Narrow cobblestone streets wind among the former homes, warehouses, and small businesses that so closely resemble a 19th-century Dutch village, they might be found in Amsterdam – or Disney World.

Outside Kurá Hulanda's walls, Otrobanda is guarded on the Caribbean side by ★**Riffort**, built in 1828. Its restored ramparts now shelter Riffort Village, a shopping and entertainment center that offers panoramic views of Punda and the sea. At the other end of the waterfront road, just past the cruise ship terminal, is **Arawak Craft Products**, a small ceramics factory with an open workroom where artisans turn out miniature replicas of Curaçao's most noted mansions. ☎ 462-7249.

Inland, many streets are littered with construction projects as more buildings are being renovated. Conditioned walkers and devoted fans of architecture find many trea-

Belvedere

sures among the clutter. **Belvedere**, across from Leonard B. Smith Plaza (named for the US consul who built the floating Emma Bridge), is one of the most impressive. The grand white-trimmed yellow house was built in the mid-1800s and was once the governor's residence. Today, it hold the offices of a law firm, and the interior reception area is open to visitors during business hours. The Monument Foundation occupies the lovely mansion next door, and Leonard Smith's former home, Washington Villa, is behind a wooden fence across the plaza.

The **Curaçao Museum** is on the far western edge of Otrobanda, a fairly long walk from the waterfront, on Anthony van Leeuwenhoekstraat. The two-level landhuis-style building constructed in 1853 was once a hospital and now houses antique furniture, Indian artifacts, and local art. The lovely landscaped grounds are used for cultural events and concerts. Open Monday-Friday, 9 am-noon, 2-5 pm. ☎ 462-3873.

Otrobanda and Punda are connected across St. Anna Bay by the floating pontoon ★★★**Koningin Emmabrug (Queen Emma Bridge)**, named for Queen Emma of the Netherlands, who reigned from 1890 to 1898. The original bridge was designed by US Consul Leonard B. Smith in 1888 as a toll bridge and, until 1934, a small coin was collected from everyone who wished to cross. The current pedestrian structure, the third pontoon bridge to cross the bay, was built in 1939. Two powerful ship engines are required to move the 16 pontoons that support the 551-foot bridge – affectionately nicknamed "The Swinging Old Lady," because she's been swaying in the Caribbean breeze for more than a century.

The charming ★★**Koningin Wilhelminabrug (Queen Wilhelmina Bridge)** spans the Waaigat lagoon, and connects Punda with the district of **Scharloo**, once a flourishing Jewish community. The Scharloo area is interesting mostly to history hounds and architecture buffs, who enjoy its restored 19th-century mansions built with Italian and Spanish architectural features by Sephardic Jews who had been expelled from Europe. It is best discovered leisurely and with no direction (and only during daylight hours). The attractive yellow building near the end of the bridge is the **Office of Cultural Affairs**; on the waterfront just to the west is a renovated 18th-century mansion that houses the impressive **Maritime Museum**. ☎ 465-2327. Admission is $6 for adults and $4.80 for students and children. Open Tuesday-Sunday, 10 am-4 pm.

Wilhelminastraat leads to **Scharlooweg** and a white-trimmed rust-red building built in 1870 in the lovely landhuis style. Other former residences now house government agencies and private offices. Símon Bolivar Plein features a bust of the South American liberator; the **Sociedad Bolivariana**, a Venezuelan culture center, occupies the yellow building on one side of the plaza. On the opposite side is a magnificently renovated mansion with a spacious courtyard.

A white-trimmed green building at the far eastern end of Scharlooweg houses the **National Archives**. It has been meticulously restored and has a lovely fenced courtyard. Just beyond is **Julianaplein (Juliana Plaza)** and the light yellow refurbished mansion built in the late 1800s which is now the Radio Hoyer building.

 Punda means the point in Papiamento.

Punda's Famous Landmarks

If you have time only to hit the top spots, put the following places on your itinerary:

The ★**Floating Market**, located along the Waaigat waterfront on Sha Caprileskade, comes alive around 5 am every day, as it has for more than 150 years. Merchants from Venezuela and Colombia sell

Floating Market (Paul Sullivan)

fresh produce and fish from their small live-aboard boats docked in the harbor. It's a picturesque sight, so bring your

camera. Open Monday through Saturday, it closes at 6:30 pm. On Sundays, trading ends at 1 pm.

The ★**Old Market**, or Marshe, is housed in a distinctive round building

The Old Market (Paul Sullivan)

Punda

Waaigat

Speijk Straat

Kaya Junior Salas

Pietermaai Weg

Bus Station

Post Office

Central Market

De Ruyter Kade

Konnigin Wilhelminabrug

Prinsen Straat

Wolk Straat

Brandhofstraat

Kleine Werf

Floating Market

Sha Capriles Kade

Columbus Straat

Plaza JoJo Coreo

Maduro Straat

Kuiper Straat

Hendrik Plein

Wind Straat

Queen Wilhelmina Statue

Keuken Straat

Heeren Straat

Wilhelmina Plein

Handels Kade

Waterfort Straat

Sint Annabaai

Ferry Landing

Breede Straat Punda

Police Station

Tourist Bureau

Governor's Palace

Fort Amsterdam

Konigin Emmabrug

Government Plein

Plaza Piar

N

OTROBANDA

NOT TO SCALE

© 2008 HUNTER PUBLISHING,

beyond the Queen Wilhelmina footbridge, just down the street from the Floating Market. Time your visit for noon so you can sample local specialties in the company of residents on their lunch-hour break. It's noisy and bewildering, but dive right in as if you belong. The food is inexpensive and tasty, and vendors serve up generous portions. Hours are Monday through Friday from 11 am until 2 pm. ☎ 461-1170.

 There are 765 protected monuments and sites in the historic area of Willemstad.

The **Mikve Israel-Emanuel Synagogue** has the honor of being the oldest synagogue in continuous use in the New World. Construction began on the building at the corner of Columbusstraat and Hanchi di Snoa in 1651. It was dedicated in 1732 and still serves as a house of worship to an active congregation. The interior

The Mikve Israel Emanuel Synagogue

features mahogany furnishings, stained-glass windows, 18th-century brass chandeliers, and a sand floor (a reminder of the Jews' years of wandering in the desert, and also of the Jews' attempt to suppress the noises made by worshipers during secret services held throughout the Spanish Inquisition). Two buildings next door date from 1728 and house the precious collections of the **Jewish Cultural Historical Museum**. The old Torah scrolls are among the most interesting artifacts. Visitors are welcome at both the synagogue and museum, Monday through Friday from 9 until 11:45 am and again between 2:30 and 4:45 pm. Services are held Friday evenings at 6:30 and Saturday mornings at 10. When cruise ships are in port on a Sunday, the compound opens for tours. Admission to the museum is $3.50; admission to the synagogue is $2. ☎ 461-1067 (synagogue) and 461-1633 (museum).

Otrobanda's Best Attractions

The other side of the bay is known for the vibrant work-a-day life that takes place among striking 18th- and 19th-century Dutch colonial architecture. Those who have not visited recently will be awed by the sparkling renovations that have taken place. Wander aimlessly with your camera in hand, but don't miss:

★★**Museum Kurá Hulanda**, a privately-funded anthropological storehouse, has the largest African collection in the Caribbean. The compound itself is magnificent, and the exhibits are phenomenal. Visitors enter through a towering arched portal that is an exact replica of

Museum Kurá Hulanda (Paul Sullivan)

the city gate in Djenné, Mali. A huge bronze sculpture entitled "Africa" stands in the courtyard, resembling both the continent and a native man's head. Inside, artifacts, furniture, paintings, photographs, and books lay out the horrid story of slavery. Child-sized leg irons and a whipping post prepare visitors for the ultimate proof of man's capacity for cruelty – a full-scale replica of a dark oxygen-deprived hold of a ship, where Africans were imprisoned during the long voyage to the Americas. Admission is $6 for adults and $3

Otrobanda

Konigin Julianabrug

Cruise Ship Terminal

Kijkduin Straat

Gracia De noy Willems Blvd

PUNDA

Sint Annabaai

Ferry Landing

Emma Straat

Quinta Straat

Hoog Straat

Ijzer Straat

De Rouville Weg

Konigin Emmabrug

Aruba Straat

Klip Straat

Belvedere Straat

Sebastopol Straat

Police Station

Riffort

Frederik Straat

Rifwater Straat

Bus Station

Jan H Fergusson Str

Breede Straat Otrobanda

Baden Powell Weg

St. Thomas Weg

Pater Euwensweg

JHJ Hamelberg Weg

Governeur Van Slobbeweg

Rifhat

Z

HUNTER PUBLISHING

NOT TO SCALE

for children under 12; hours are 10 am until 5 pm daily.
☎ 434-7765; www.kurahulanda.com.

 Otrobanda means the other side in Papiamento.

The **Curaçao Museum** is housed in a restored government building that was constructed in 1853 and used as a hospital and quarantine center. Paintings, antique mahogany furniture displayed in replicas of traditional rooms, old maps, and artifacts trace the island's history from the Caiquetio Indians to the colonial period and on through the 20th century. The carillon on the roof is called The Four Royal Children, in honor of the daughters of Queen Juliana of the Netherlands. Take time to stroll around the shady yard, and admire the landhuis-style architecture. Admission is $5 for adults and $3 for children younger than 14. Hours are 9 am-noon and 2-5 pm, Monday through Friday, and 10 am-4 pm, Sunday; closed Saturday. On the far west side of Otrobanda on Van Leeuwenhoekstraat, ☎ 462-3873.

Basilica Santa Ana was built between 1734 and 1752, and dedicated as a basilica by Pope Paul VI in 1975. Its back entrance is tucked into a small walkway off breezy Conscientiesteeg, which is said to get its name (Conscience Street) from the repentant parishioners who came to the church to cleanse their conscience through confession. Peak inside the white-trimmed gray-stone building or sit for a moment on one of the wooden pews and enjoy the lovely side altars.

Scharloo

The district of Scharloo has beautiful brightly painted mansions and an intriguing maritime museum. Cross the Wilhelmina Bridge and stroll through the streets, then stop at:

The **Maritime Museum** opened in 1998 inside a renovated waterfront mansion built in 1729. The open wood-and-brass interior houses nautical artifacts from the island's past, as well as multimedia displays illustrating the importance the sea has played in Curaçao's development. Visitors are entertained and educated by a large display of relics, antique maps, and replicas of historic ships. Tour the harbor on the museum's ferry,

Scharloo mansion

have a snack at the waterside café, and pick up a souvenir in the gift shop. Open Tuesday-Sunday from 10 am until 4 pm, at the corner of Werfstraat and Van den Brandhofstraat on the harbor. Admission is $6 for adults and $4.50 for students and children younger than 12. ☎ 465-2327.

Sightseeing Southeast & North of Willemstad

★★★Curaçao Seaquarium

The Curaçao Seaquarium and its adjacent beach are the most popular tourist attractions on the island. A unique open-water design allows unfiltered plankton-rich sea water to continuously flow through the aquarium tanks so that hundreds of species of marine animals live in a habitat that is truly natural.

Outdoor lagoons, also openly joined with the sea, allow visitors to watch and interact with playful sea creatures such as turtles, rays, sea lions – even sharks. If you want to enjoy the fun without getting wet, you can watch divers in the lagoon through windows in the stationary semi-submerged Underwater Observatory.

Shark Feeding

 Hand-feeding a shark is one of the most talked about activities in the Animal Encounters dive. Participants are not required to be certified divers, and even novice swimmers can take part in the 10-feet-under adventure. Divers safely feed the sharks from behind a plexiglass barrier, while a photographer captures the event on film in such a way that friends back home won't suspect that there was a protective wall. While in the water, swimmers may also pet a stingray, play with a sea turtle, and frolic with schools of colorful fish. The cost for divers is $54; for snorkelers, $34.

 Reservations must be made 24 hours in advance for Animal Encounter. ☎ *461-6666 or 465-8900; www. curacao-sea-aquarium.com.*

Curaçao Seaquarium

Curaçao Eastern Driving Tour

To begin your driving tour, take the Queen Juliana Bridge east to Schottegat Weg. After Boca Plata Canoa (#8 on the map), retrace your route back to the traffic island and pick up the road to Caracasbaai.

1. Autonomy Monument
2. Landhuis Chobolobo (Curaçao Liquor Distillery)
3. Saninja (shopping/nightlife district)
4. Landhuis Brievengat
5. Hofi Pachi Sprockel (plantation museum)
6. Santa Rosa
7. Ronde Klip
8. Boca Playa Canoa
9. Caracasbaai
10. Fort Beekenberg
11. Spanish Water
12. Barbara Beach
13. Tafelberg

PAVED ROAD
.... DIRT ROAD

East Point

St. Joris Bay

N HUNTER PUBLISHING

Brievengat

Santa Rosa Weg

Weg Naar Montaña

Caracasbaai Weg

Schottegat Weg

Willemstad

Schottegat

Queen Juliana Bridge

St. Anna Bay

NOT TO SCALE

© 2008 HUNTER PUBLISHING, INC

Kid's Sea Camp

The Kid's Sea Camp is every child's fantasy and at the top of every parent's wish list. While the adults dive or pursue other grown-up activities, kids four and up have fun as they learn cool stuff. Even the youngest quickly discover ways to identify fish, find out how a reef grows and learn to love and feel safe in the ocean. The aim, in addition to introducing children to a life-long hobby and sport, is to encourage participants to conserve and protect the earth's oceans, reefs and marine animals. Children from four to eight years old learn to swim, snorkel and SASY (Supplied Air Snorkel for Youth) under the vigilant watch of experienced instructors. Older kids learn additional skills and can earn a Junior Open Water Diver certification. The week-long camps are held only during the summer and book up fast, so sign up early by phone or online, ☎ 800-433-3483; www.kidsseacamp. com.

Swim with Dolphins

At the Seaquarium lagoon, you can actually get into the water and play with gorgeous, graceful, fun-loving bottlenose dolphins. Trainers teach you how to interact with these amazing creatures, then send you out to swim and frolic on your own. Free educational presentations are held every day, and you can observe the dolphins from the shore of the saltwater lagoon while the park is open. If you really fall in love, sign up for the Dolphin Trainer Course, ☎ 465-8900; www.dolphin-academy.com.

The **Marine Awareness Center (MAC)** gives one-day courses that teach basic information about coral reefs and their importance to the ecosystem (Reef Impressions) and fascinating facts about marine animals (Ocean Encounters). Courses run about $70 for adults and $35 for children between the ages of six and 14. Call for information about the programs and enrollment, ☎ 461-6666.

Additional attractions inside the aquarium complex include a shell museum, video and 3-D slide show presentations, sea lion demonstrations, and educational displays. The open-air **Balau Restaurant** serves sandwiches, snacks, and drinks. Souvenirs and gifts featuring the aquarium's popular residents are for sale in the well-stocked shop.

The aquarium is open every day of the year from 8:30 am until 5:30 pm. Tickets are $15 for adults and $7.50 for children between the ages of two and 14. Watch for signs along the coast road southeast of Willemstad. ☎ 461-6666; www. curacao-sea-aquarium.com.

The Seaquarium Beach, adjacent to the aquarium, is one of the nicest on the island. Facilities include a dive shop, a watersports equipment rental hut, showers, restrooms, shops, and several waterfront restaurants and bars. The admission fee is $3 per person, per day.

Other Attractions

Locals call the eastern part of Curaçao **Banda Riba** or Band'ariba, which translates as "upwind." The far eastern tip of the island is privately owned and undeveloped, but the countryside north and near-east of Willemstad has lovely residential areas, yacht-filled harbors, and a few interesting attractions for tourists.

 Remember: Trade winds on the ABC Islands blow steadily from east to west.

The **Senior Curaçao Liqueur Distillery**, housed in the 17th-century Landhuis Chobolobo, still uses original 19th-century equipment to make a spicy cordial from the dried skins of lahara oranges. Lahara is the name given to a variety of local oranges that developed from Spanish orange

trees planted shortly after European colonization began. Curaçao's climate did not provide adequate moisture for the citrus trees, and the resulting fruit was too bitter to eat.

Curaçao

Resourceful islanders discovered that the peel of this orange produced an aromatic oil when it was dried in the sun. A family named Senior began making up a tasty alcoholic drink with the oil by adding exotic spices. In 1896, they began producing Curaçao Liqueur commercially at Landhuis Chobolobo.

You can take a free tour of the distillery (located off the Ring Road, east of the city), which still uses the original secret recipe to make the signature orange drink. Other flavors have been added, and you can sample rum-raisin, chocolate, coffee, and the startling Blue Curaçao. Imitations of the original are sold elsewhere, but an on-site gift shop sells the authentic original in quaint bottles. Visitors are welcome, Monday through Friday, 8 am-noon and 1-5 pm. A café sells snacks, and live bands perform. Call for information. ☎ 461-3526; www.curacaoliqueur.com.

The **Amstel Brewery** may be more to your liking if you're a beer drinker. Tours are given at the waterfront facility located at the Rijkseenheid Blvd exit off the Ring Road. Multilingual tours take place Tuesdays and Thursdays beginning at 9 am. Tickets cost $1 for adults, and tours are free for children between the ages of six and 12. Children younger than six are not allowed to enter the brewery. (All proceeds from ticket sales are donated to charity.) ☎ 434-1500.

 Amstel is the only beer made with distilled seawater.

Landhuizen

Landhuis Habaai

Landhuis is the Dutch word for villa and was used by colonists to describe the owner's house on a plantation. When Peter Stuyvesant was governor of the Netherlands Antilles, he divided Curaçao's countryside into estates. Slave labor was used to farm the arid land and mine salt. Some of these old homes now house restaurants or businesses, and some are open to the public for tours.

Curaçao has about 70 authentic landhuizen featuring Dutch architecture. Most are perched on top of a hill to symbolize the importance of the owner, offer the best views of the plantation, and catch cooling breezes. The hilltop position also allowed an owner to see the homes of other landholders so that he could signal them in case of an emergency. See page 309 for more about Curaçao's landhuizen.

Dinah's Botanic and Historic Garden, or **Den Paradera**, is indicated by signs on the roadway (Caracasbaaiweg – in the direction of Santa Barbara) and you will smell the herbs as you approach.

Entrance to Dinah's

The garden features dozens of varieties of local plants that have been used throughout history as folk medicines. If you're interested in herbal healing, gardening, or folklore, stop at the little yellow house surrounded by a cactus fence to ask owner Dinah Veeris about touring the grounds, which include a model historical village with a lodge built by Amazon Indians (ask Dinah to tell you the story). A shop sells cu-

Dinah herself

rative beverages (said to heal a variety of ailments) and perfumes made from herbs and flowers. Hours are 9 am until 6 pm daily and admission is $2.75 for adults, $1.

38 for children younger than 12. ☎ 767-5608; www.rootsandmedicine.com/curacao.

★**Spanish Water**, a sheltered bay on a picturesque stretch of coast, is filled with grand yachts and surrounded by upscale residential areas. From the top of the terraced cliffs, you have a panoramic view of the countryside and **Landhuis Brakkeput Mei Mei** (☎ 767-1500), which is now a restaurant. Plan to spend some time driving around this area, which will be fairly quiet during the week, but hopping with activity on weekends.

Caracasbaai

★**Caracasbaai**, on the southwest side of Spanish Water, was once dominated by the Shell Oil Terminal. Recently, the area has been transformed into one of the trendiest spots on the island, with an assortment of watersports equipment available at Baja Beach. Guides lead tours through Fort Beekenburg, built between 1701 and 1704 to defend Curaçao from pirates and foreign troops. Views from the tower are awesome.

The **Hato Caves**, near the airport, have an underground lake, waterfalls, and large chambers decorated with stalagmites and stalactites that are still growing and will eventually meet to form a single column. During hourly tours, guides point out shells and coral in the rock formations, which developed millions of years ago when Curaçao was under water. Shifts in the earth caused cracks in the cave walls and pieces fell from the top to create an opening. If you happen to be around at dusk, you'll see hundreds of bats flying out of this space to hunt for food.

The caves are part of an iguana-filled park with a patio snack bar. A walking trail leads to ancient Indian carvings that indicate the Caiquetios held religious ceremonies either inside or near the caves more than 1,500 years ago. Look for signs on the airport highway (Rooseveltweg) indicating the way to Hato Caves. The park is open daily from 10 am until 5 pm; admission is $6.50 for adults and $4.75 for children younger than 12. ☎ 868-0379.

Landhuis Brievengat, east of the airport on Bonhamweg, holds many musical shows and cultural events throughout the year. Experts think the house was built in the early 18th century for a plantation owner who grew aloe and raised cattle. A rare hurricane destroyed the property in 1877, and it was abandoned until Shell Oil bought it many years later in

Landhuis Brievengat

order to pump freshwater from the underground well. Shell donated the estate to the government of Curaçao in the mid-1950s, and the ruined mansion was restored to its original splendor. Notice the unusual towers at the sides of the house. They were once used as a prison for slaves who caused trouble. Visitors may tour Brievengat daily, 9:15 am-12:15 pm and 3-6 pm. Admission is $2 for adults and $1 for children younger than 12. Live bands and folklore groups often entertain (sometimes with dance lessons), but check *K-Pasa* for a listing of scheduled events, or call in advance for information, ☎ 691-4961.

Playa Kanoa, north from Brievengat on a paved road which becomes dirt, is a protected cove, and one of the only safe watersports areas on the rugged north coast. Local windsurfers frequent the bay, and you can swim in the placid water, but there's not much of a beach.

The **Ostrich and Game Farm**, near St. Joris Bay on the northeast coast, is the largest of its type outside Africa. You can visit by taking a guided tour in the black-and-white-striped Zebra Safari Jeep, which will pick you up at your hotel or cruise ship, or drive out to the secluded area on your own.

Did You Know? Ostriches are the largest birds in the world, and the fastest two-legged runners.

They are fascinating when seen in action. About 700 big birds live on the working ranch, and you will watch the ritual mating dance, observe the incubating jumbo eggs, hold a not-so-tiny chick, and feed a huge adult. Tours of the farm begin on the hour, Tuesday-Sunday, 9 am-4 pm. ☎ 747-2777; www.ostrichfarm.net.

The **African Art Shop**, located at the Ostrich Farm, features a spacious display of hand-crafted sculptures, wall hangings, and potato-print cloths from the southern parts of Africa. Ostrich-leather products make an unusual souvenir of your Caribbean trip. **Zambezi**, the attractive African-style stone-and-thatched-roof restaurant, is open for lunch and dinner. The menu highlights fresh hormone-free ostrich meat dishes and South African wines, but you also can order seafood and Zambezi beer. The shop is open Tuesday-Sunday, 9 am-5 pm. Lunch is served in the restaurant, Tuesday-Sunday, noon-4 pm; dinner hours are Wednesday-Sunday, 6-10 pm. Dinner reservations required. ☎ 747-2777; www.ostrichfarm.net.

Sightseeing West of Willemstad

The western part of the island is locally known as **Banda Abou** or Band'abou, which means "downwind." Christoffel National Park encompasses a large section of the west end, but the countryside is dotted with old fruit orchards and renovated plantation houses. Along the northern coast, jagged limestone bluffs tower over the raging sea.

★★★Christoffel National Park

This park showcases the island's desert-like terrain and protects a large variety of wildlife and plants. Four well-marked color-coded hiking trails wind through the 4,500-acre park, which was once three privately-owned plantations: Savonet, Zorgvlied,

Christoffelberg in the distance

and Zevenbergen. Driving routes lead out to the coasts and over lovely flower-strewn hills.

The small **Savonet Museum** at the entrance, is housed in one of the out buildings of the private Landhuis Savonet. It displays geological and archeological exhibits that illustrate the island's development and history. Visitors are welcome Monday-Saturday, 8 am-4 pm, and Sunday, 6 am-3 pm. ☎ 864-0363.

Christoffelberg, at 1,239 feet, is the highest point on the island and the focal point of the park. You can hike up in an hour or two, depending on the number of stops you make along the way (follow the red route). The trip isn't difficult, especially if you go early, while the sun is still low in the sky. At the top, you will have fabulous views of the western end of the island. (Bring snacks and plenty of water.)

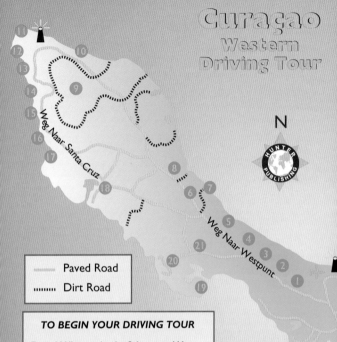

Curaçao
Western
Driving Tour

N

HUNTER PUBLISHING

Paved Road

.... Dirt Road

Willemstad

TO BEGIN YOUR DRIVING TOUR

From Willemstad, take Schottegat Weg to Roosevelt Weg to the intersection of Winston Churchill Weg. Turn right onto Jan Noorduynweg at the University of the Netherlands Antilles. Turn right onto Weg Naar Westpunt. Return to Willemstad via the Southern Cross.

1. Landhuis Papaya
2. Grote Berg
3. Kleine Berg
4. Landhuis Daniel
5. Tera Cora
6. Pos di San Pedro
7. Boca San Pedro
8. Landhuis Ascensión
9. Christoffel National Park & Christoffelberg
10. Boca Tabla
11. Watamula (western point)
12. Playa Kalki

13. Westpuntbaai
14. Knipbaai (beautiful beaches)
15. Playa Jeremi
16. Playa Lagún
17. Boca Santa Cruz
18. Soto/Groot Landhuis Santa Marta
19. Saliña Santa Marie (flamingos)
20. Willibrordus (village) & Cathedral of St. William Brothers
21. Landhuis Jan Kok
22. Hato Caves

NOT TO SCALE

© 2008 HUNTER PUBLISHING

Warning: *Watch for manchineel trees along the trails, and do not touch their leaves or fruit, which cause painful blisters on the skin. Recognize them by the shiny leaves and small apple-like fruit.*

Pick up maps, brochures, and guide books at the front entrance, then choose a drive (four-wheel-drive vehicles are suggested), hike, or tour to match your interests and allocated time, as well as your physical endurance. The guided walks at dawn and dusk are especially delightful because the small Curaçao deer and other wildlife are out looking for food at those times.

 Snakes: *Two types of snake live in the park – the whipsnake or meadow snake, and the minute silver snake. Both are harmless.*

The blue **Savonet route** leads out to the windward coast, where you can see Indian rock drawings that were made hundreds of years ago and explore a couple of caves carved into the cliffs. Follow the green route west from the Savonet Museum past the coral-and-rock ruins of the Zorgvlied plantation, where you can pick up the red hiking trail to the top of Christoffelberg.

The yellow **Zevenbergen route** is a lovely ride through the countryside, past orchid-studded hills with far-reaching vistas. It begins at Piedra de Monton (Mountain of Rocks). Former slaves believed that they could fly back to Africa if they deprived themselves of salted foods and stood at the top of Piedra de Monton. Stops along the route include Santa Martha Baai and the windy Seru Bientu. A short hiking path leads to the top of Bientu, where you will have striking vistas of the far western tip of the island.

The park is open to the public, Monday-Saturday, 8 am-4 pm, Sunday, 6 am-3 pm. Call for information about tours, special events, and park news. ☎ 864-0363; www.carmabi. org (click on park logo at bottom of page).

Rancho Alfin (☎ 864-0535) conducts tours by horseback and mountain bike. Jeep and walking tours of the park are available with park rangers by reservation (☎ 864-0363).

★Shete Boca National Park

West of Willemstad on the eastern side of the far north coast, this is a captivating part of the island. **Boca Tabla**, a cave washed out of the limestone cliffs, connects with seven inlets along a dirt trail.

Boca Tabla

Start by following the sign to Viewpoint Cave, then take the steps down into the wide cavern where waves echo loudly as they crash through the opening. Visitors often get soaked if they fail to anticipate the flash flood that occurs when huge waves wash into the cave. Topside, a path along the edge of the cliffs offers spectacular views, and you can hike to the other six inlets. **Boca Pistol** gets its name from the gunshot explosion of water that erupts from gaps in the rocks when the sea rams against the cliffs. The park is open daily, 9 am-5 pm; the entrance fee is $2 per person. Guided tours are available with a park ranger by reservation, ☎ 864-0444.

Landhuizen

The island has several notable old plantation mansions that have been restored to their natural beauty. Some now house restaurants or other businesses, but a few are open for special events and public visits. Many of the original homes have crumbed beyond repair due to the inferior building materials that were used during the colonial years.

Facing page: Shete Boka National Park

The ones that remain were built at the end of the 17th or beginning of the 18th century and feature architectural details that were popular in Holland much earlier. Often, pretentious land owners constructed their homes to appear years older than they were, so that it would seem that their family had inherited the estate from wealthy and prestigious ancestors.

A few to visit west of Willemstad:

Landhuis Ascención

Landhuis Ascención, off Weg Naar Westpunt south of the town of Barber, is now owned by the Royal Marines and is open free of charge the first Sunday of each month, 10 am-2 pm. ☎ 864-1950.

Landhuis Dokterstuin, just east of the Ascención estate, recently has been renovated in 17th-century country style with a thatched roof. **Restaurant Komedor Kriollo** serves spicy creole meals in the casual garden. Visitors are welcome daily, 9 am-7 pm, ☎ 864-2701.

Landhuis Daniel

Landhuis Daniel, on Weg Naar Westpunt south of the village of Tera Kora, is a romantic hotel with eight guest rooms, and a French/Caribbean restaurant. It's one of the oldest plantation houses on the island. You can drop by every day (except Tuesdays and Thursdays) between 9 am and 6 pm for a drink or snack served on the patio. Call in advance for room or dinner reservations, ☎ 864-8400.

Landhuis Knip (or Kenepa), on Weg Naar Santa Cruz near Playa Kenepa, is the site of a 1795 slave rebellion. Today, you can dress in island costumes to have your picture taken (this is a terrific souvenir), tour the collection of antique furniture and memorabilia, and enjoy refreshments in the café. The estate is open Tuesday-Friday, 11:30 am-4:50 pm, and Sunday, 10 am-4 pm. ☎ 864-0244.

For notable Landhuizen north and east of the capital, see Landhuis Brakkeput and Landhuis Brievengat, pages 361 and 303.

Adventures on Water

Curaçao has more than three dozen beaches, but those on the windward coast have strong currents and rough waves, making them dangerous for swimmers. Many on the leeward coast charge an entrance fee (between $3 and $6), but the sand is well groomed, and the beach bars, restrooms, showers, lockers, and rental equipment are well maintained. This guarantees a pleasant experience, and people usually stay most of the day.

Best Beaches

Most of the popular beaches are small coves with either sand or sand mixed with coral. Some of the resort and pay-per-visit beaches have been supplemented with powdery white sand. There are many spots to choose from, and you can usually find a secluded area with few or no other visitors, especially during the week. Most are accessible by regular car from the coastal road that runs along the leeward shore.

★**Mambo Beach** at the Seaquarium (see page 295) features a man-made stretch of sand, with lounge chairs, shade umbrellas, restaurants, bars, locker rooms, and a watersports center. Sea walls shelter the water and provide excellent conditions for snorkeling. Topless sunbathing is al-

Mambo Beach

lowed. Sunday afternoons are known as party time, with beach volleyball, watersports, and happy-hour prices at the Mambo Beach Bar. Admission is $3 and the beach is open daily, 8:30 am-5:30 pm. ☎ 461-8999.

★**Jan Thiel**, located near resorts east of Willemstad, has plenty of amenities, including a trendy restaurant, a dive center, and changing/restroom facilities. The snorkeling is especially good here. Beach hours are daily, 8 am-6 pm, and the charge is $3.50 per car on weekdays; $5 per car on weekends.

Barbara, at the southeast end of Spanish Waters Bay at Porta Blanku, is popular with families because of the placid water, which is ideal for young swimmers. Yachts often anchor offshore so that passengers can swim in to enjoy the beach and dine at the restaurant. Facilities include showers, toilets, and a bar; the beach is long enough for a leisurely stroll or an energetic jog. Understandably, this area gets crowded on weekends. The entrance fee is $2.25 per person; open 8 am-6 pm daily.

Baja on Caracas Bay Island, near the old Beekenburg Fort at Spanish Waters, has a sandy beach and a lot of watersports. The **Baja Beach Club** is a lively place after dark. No admission charge.

Blauwbaai (Blue Bay) is a large shady beach just northwest of Willemstad, near the village of Sint Michiel. It's popular with locals and visitors because of the soft white sand. Facilities include showers, toilets, and changing areas. No admission fee.

Daaibooibaai, at San Willibrordo, gets crowded on the weekends, so try to visit during the week, when you'll probably have the whole place to yourself. The beach is coral pebbles, and there are shade pergolas, but no other facilities. Admission is $3 per car, and hours are 8 am-5:30 pm.

Porto Marie is a long sandy man-made beach west of the capital. Shade is provided by rented umbrellas, and facilities include a bar, a watersports center, showers, and toilets. The sea floor slopes gently from the beach so children enjoy playing here. Admission is $2 per person on weekdays and $2.75 on weekends; the beach is open daily, 8 am-6 pm.

Turtle Beach at Kas Abou, west of Willemstad, has particularly beautiful water. Divers and snorkelers favor the offshore reef because of excellent visibility. There's plenty of shade and good facilities, including showers, toilets, and a small snack bar. Entrance fee is $5.75 per car on weekends and $4.50 per car on weekdays.

Boca Santa Martha, west of Willemstad, near the town of Soto, is the location of the Sunset Waters Beach Resort (formerly Coral Cliff Resort), and guests may use the lovely beach free of charge. Others must pay $4.50 per person.

Playa Kenepa and the nearby **Playa Abou**, a short distance south of Westpunt, and the sandy coves are gorgeous. Residents cook on the beaches on weekends, and things get pretty crowded, with families running in and out of the water. Try to visit on a weekday.

Playa Kenepa

Trees and thatch umbrellas provide some shade, and the

water is smooth and clear. Bring your snorkeling gear. A fee is charged at Aou Beach: $2.50 per car Monday-Saturday; $5 per car on Sunday.

Playa Lagun

Playa Lagun (also Lagoen) is a small cove surrounded by high cliffs south of Westpunt. Little caves on the southeast end are fun to explore, and the best entrance into the water is nearby. Concrete structures provide shelter for picnics and naps. No admission charge.

Playa Jeremi, near Landhuis Jeremi and the town of Lagun, has no facilities and little shade, but there's no entrance fee either, and the snorkeling is great. Watch your step going down the steps from the parking lot to the beautiful cove with picturesque rocks and calm water.

Playa Kalki is sheltered by the limestone Kadushi Cliffs near Westpunt and an excellent choice for a day on the beach. Bring your snorkeling gear. The sea floor slopes

Playa Kalki (Paul Sullivan)

gently and allows you to walk out quite a distance. The water is crystal clear and teeming with fish. No admission charge.

Playa Forti, at Westpunt on the far western end of the island, has black pebbly sand. You can look straight to the bottom of the sea through the clear-as-glass water. Little shade and no facilities, but you'll enjoy watching locals dive from the cliffs. No admission charge.

TRIPS TO KLEIN CURAÇAO

Dive operators and charter boats take passengers out to the oversized volcanic rock for beach parties, cookouts, and fantastic diving. The shore is covered in soft white sand, and the water is crystal clear, but there is no shade. The northeastern side tends to have rough seas, while the southeastern side routinely has calm water with gentle waves. If you want to go over to Klein, contact **Mermaid Boat Trips**, ☎ 560-1530; www.mermaidboattrips.com.

Diving & Snorkeling Sites

Experienced scuba divers have discovered the island's close-in reefs and abundant sea life. While Bonaire is still the most popular dive destination among the ABC Islands, Curaçao is gaining respect. Several wrecks provide interesting dives, and shore entrance is possible at a number of sites.

The fringe reefs have 55 identified species of hard corals and 35 varieties of gorgonians (often called soft corals), which draw a wide variety of fish, crabs, and shrimp. Rather than vertical walls, divers find gently sloping reefs at the western end of the island and steeply sloping reefs at the eastern end – all covered with a diverse variety of coral formations.

Curaçao

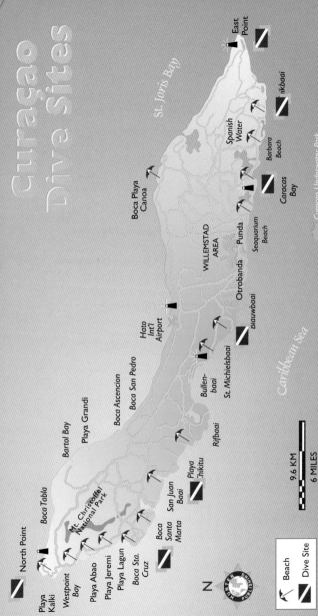

Curaçao Dive Sites

© 2008 HUNTER PUBLISHING, INC.

East Point

St. Joris Bay

iikbaai

Spanish Water

Boca Playa Canoa

Barbara Beach

Caracas Bay

Punda

Seaquarium Beach

WILLEMSTAD AREA

~ Curaçao Underwater Park

Otrobanda

Hato Int'l Airport

blauwbaai

Caribbean Sea

Bullen-baai

St. Michielsbaai

Boca San Pedro

Boca Ascencion

Rifbaai

Playa Grandi

Bartol Bay

Playa Jhikitu

San Juan Baai

Boca Tabla

Mt. Christoffel National Park

Boca Santa Marta

North Point

Playa Kalki

Westpoint Bay

Playa Abao

Playa Jeremi

Playa Lagun

Boca Sta. Cruz

9.6 KM

6 MILES

N

HUNTER PUBLISHING

Beach

Dive Site

★★★Curaçao Underwater Park (Onderwaterpark)

This runs from near the Seaquarium Beach (just south of St. Anna Bay and Willemstad) to the southern tip of the island, a distance of more

Bluestriped grunt (Susan Swygert)

than 12 miles. It was established in 1983 and is under the management of the Netherlands Antilles National Parks (STINAPA). Numbered buoys indicate dive sites inside the 1,483-acre park, and a marked snorkeling trail is laid out at buoy number three.

Tugboat is a marvelous wreck lying upright in 15 feet of calm water. It is surrounded by colorful corals that make a magnificent background for underwater photos. This old pilot boat is near a steep wall that drops to about 100 feet, where you'll see a sheet of corals.

Caracas Bay Lost Anchor features an anchor chain that seems to extend forever, just like the coral- and gorgonian-covered reef. Snorkelers can view a variety of colorful fish along the reef, beginning in about 20 feet of water.

West of Willemstad

Mushroom Forest, which is considered one of the top dives in the world, has an abundance of mushroom-shaped mountainous star corals that form a colorful forest. The corals look like mushrooms because their bases have eroded and formed narrow stalks topped by caps. Nearby, there's a shallow cave with a wide entrance. Schools of silversides swim beside divers, and a flashlight will illuminate brilliant

Curaçao

Tiger grouper (Susan Swygert)

colonies of orange cup corals. This is best as a boat dive because jagged cliffs at San Nicolas make entering the water difficult. Bring a compass to avoid becoming disoriented in the forest.

Sponge Forest, also off San Nicolas, is a good boat dive in calm water that features large sponges in about 50-60 feet of water. Stony corals and gorgonians are visible to snorkelers in more shallow water, and there's an abundance of French and queen angelfish, damselfish, and sergeant majors. Also, be on the lookout for cute pufferfish.

Porto Marie, near San Willibrordus, west of the capital, has two reefs running side-by-side, with a valley between them. Nurse sharks, giant groupers, spotted eagle rays, and turtles live in the valley, along with pairs of cornet fish. If you enter from the beach, you'll pay $2 per person admission fee. The entrance to the water has some coral, so wear your dive boots. Swim toward the mooring buoy in the center of the bay, where the water depth is about 30 feet. From here the reef slopes to the sandy valley at about 50 feet. The second reef is in 60 feet of water. Corals are healthy and along the reef you'll spot yellowtail snapper, triggerfish, parrotfish, and brown chromis.

Wet Suit City, or Harry's Hole, is off the beach at Santa Marta Bay near the Sunset Waters Beach Resort. As the name implies, it's best to wear a wet suit because of the profuse amount of fire coral. Juvenile brown chromis live among the fire coral, while eels and scorpionfish favor the sandy areas. A strong current at the drop-off makes this an intermediate dive, but novice divers and snorkelers enjoy the sights in shallow water near shore.

The Central Shore, from Bullen Bay to Jan Thiel

Bullen Bay, near the lighthouse southeast of the oil terminal, has protected shallow water close in. A steep drop-off begins in deeper water, where the current gets stronger. Look for crabs, lobster, peacock flounders, lizardfish, and goatfish.

Diver with hawksbill turtle (Susan Swygert)

Playa Largu, at Piscadera Bay, is a great boat dive that's suitable for snorkelers. A steep wall begins in fairly shallow water and descends to more than 135 feet. In about 60 feet of clear water, look for large groupers, snappers, and barracudas. Dolphins and turtles are also seen in the area. In September and October, divers often witness coral spawning here on nights following a full moon.

Sandy's Plateau is best reached by boat. It's out from Jan Thiel Beach, and snorkelers as well as divers can explore several areas of the plateau. Divers see healthy brain and star coral on the steep wall that drops from the plateau in about 30 feet of water. Fish seen along the plateau and wall include damselfish, chromis, wrasses, rock beauties, and trumpetfish.

Boca di Sorsaka, out from Jan Thiel Bay, can be done from shore or boat. A shelf in shallow water leads to a drop-off where a vertical wall descends more than 100 feet. Look for abundant gorgonians and sponges. Marine life includes angelfish, trunkfish, soldierfish and trumpetfish.

*See page 311 for additional shore-dive and
snorkeling sites off the island's beaches.*

CORAL & SPONGE SPAWNING

Yellow tube sponge (Susan Swygert)

A week after the full moon in September and October each year, Curaçao is the site of an amazing phenomenon called coral and sponge spawning. When conditions are just right, the corals and sponges simultaneously release a dense cloud of eggs and sperm in a colorful cloud. Divers from all over the world congregate to witness this night spectacle, which was first observed on Australia's Great Barrier Reef in 1981 and in the Caribbean in 1991. Various species spawn at different times on the same night. For information, or to volunteer to monitor the spawning, contact **Reef Care Curaçao**, ☎ 569-2099; www. reefcare.org.

Klein Curaçao, a tiny satellite island off the southeast coast, is almost two hours away by boat. Unlike the main island, it does have a unique wall, which bends to form caverns. There are no facilities on the island, but visitors go there to have parties, sunbathe, and dive.

Experienced divers can try the boat dive off the northern end, where a large cave in about 100 feet of water harbors nurse sharks. A wall above the cave is covered in corals.

Klein Curaçao

Turtles are often seen in the area. The main beach, on the western shore, has good dive sites at both the north and south end, which can be accessed from shore or by boat. Reef fish – including angels, soldierfish, banded butterflyfish, and parrotfish – are abundant, but coral formations are limited.

Dive Operators

Most dive shops are connected to resorts, hotels, or apartments. However, it is not necessary to be a registered guest in order to book a dive trip. Look for a shop near the area that you wish to explore to minimize the time it takes to reach the site. Package deals are the best way to go if you plan to spend a lot of time underwater. Take the time to call around for the best prices on the combination of dives that fit your needs.

Rates run $35 for a single-tank boat dive and $60 for a two-tank boat dive. Snorkelers can go along for about $20, including equipment. Guided shore dives are in the $25 range. Many packages include unlimited air for shore dives, a couple of boat dives per day, and perhaps a night dive. A 10% service charge may be added to quoted prices, so ask before you sign up and add an additional tip if necessary.

The **Seaquarium** offers a wide variety of diving and snorkeling activities. You can also get a great view of the underwater creatures without getting wet in the semi-submersible observatory. No certification is needed to join a group on an "Anumal Encounter," which is $34 for snorkelers and $54 for divers. Get into the park and take a one-tank shore dive for $26. For reservations and information on other activities, call the park, ☎ 461-6666; www.curacao-sea-aquarium. com.

The following centers are PADI certified, and instructors and guides speak English as well as other languages (usually Dutch, German, Spanish, and Papiamento). Other reputable shops operate on the island, so don't limit yourself to those below when you plan your trip.

The Curaçao Diving Operators Association (CDOA) has painted large rocks red and marked them with a white stripe to designate the dive sites that can be accessed from shore. The numbers and names of each site correspond to those marked on the **Drive & Dive Map,** *available for $6 at most dive shops and many retail stores and resorts.*

DIVING SCHOOL WEDERFOORT

Sint Michiel Bay
☎ 888-4414; fax 869-2062; www.divewederfoort.com
Eric and Yolanda Wederfoort run this shop at Boca Sami, west of Willemstad. They specialize in shore dives and training. Accommodations are available at nearby studios and apartments.

ATLANTIS DIVING

Drielstraat 6

☎ 465-8288, 560-3099 (cell); fax 461-2535; www.
atlantisdiving.com

A top center for almost 20 years, Atlantis offers a variety of
trips to less-visited sites, including Klein Curaçao. The dive
shop is well stocked and they service Suunto and Scubapro
gear. Owners, Jan Mooreland and Ingrid van den Bosch, will
impress you with their knowledge.

SCUBA DO

Jan Thiel Beach

☎ 767-9300, 560-8456 (cell); fax 767-9300; www.
divecenterscubado.com

Guests at Papagayo Beach Resort, Chogogo Beach Resort, and Livingstone Jan Thiel Resort can walk to this dive
center located directly on the beach within the Curaçao Underwater Park (see page 317).

OCEAN ENCOUNTERS

Lions Dive Hotel and Marina

☎ 461-8131; fax 461-8581; www.oceanencounters.com

Associated with Lions Dive and Superclubs Breezes, Lodge
Kurá Hulanda and Avila Beach Resort, the center is a PADI
5-Star Gold Palm facility. The custom-outfitted dive boats
are never overcrowded, ensuring personal attention and
comfort for each diver. The staff also assists with Animal Encounter at the adjacent Seaquarium.

HOLIDAY BEACH DIVE CENTER

Pater Euwensweg 31, Holiday Beach Hotel

☎ 462-5400; fax 462-4397; www.hol-beach.com

The in-town location makes this dive center convenient for
cruise passengers and those who want to combine sightseeing and shopping with diving. Their trips go to *Superior
Producer* wreck and nearby reefs.

AQUARIUS DIVE CENTER

Trupial Inn, Groot Davelaar 5

☎ 737-2248 or 524-6998 (cell)

www.divecenteraquarius.com

Curaçao

This center is run by Erik and Esther, who are from Holland, so many of the divers are Dutch, and some are going through their open-water certification. The staff is multilingual and speaks English. All-level courses are available, as well as guided boat dives.

TOUCAN DIVING
Kontiki Beach Club, Seaquarium Beach
☎ 465-3790; fax 465-3795
www.curacao-toucandiving.com
Located next to Mambo Beach. The highly experienced staff speaks several languages and organizes shore and boat dives to the top sites, including the reef directly out from the adjacent Seaquarium. A small, but well-stocked, shop carries snorkel and dive equipment.

THE DIVE BUS
Pierbaai, near Breezes Resort
☎ 693-8305 or 528-3263 (both cells)
www.the-dive-bus.com
If you like shore diving, hop on The Bus operated by PADI instructors Mark and Suzy Pinnell. These Brits have years of experience with big operators and now enjoy taking divers on relaxed dives right from Curacao's beaches. The Bus has a Hut next to Breezes Resort on Pierbaai, where training takes place and divers gear up for wreck and reef diving from the nearby shore. You can also sign up for an ATV-diving adventure, dive with the dolphins, sharks and rays at Seaquarium or take a guided snorkel tour.

Sailing

 Steady trade winds from the east provide power for sailors. Several sailing events take place on the island each year, including the **International Sailing Regatta** (January, www.curacaoregatta.com). The International Regatta has short-distance competition for windsurfers, Hobie Cats, and Sunfish; long-distance com-

petition for yachts; and a mid-distance open category for trimarans, catamarans, and other boats. If you've ever wanted to learn how to sail, take a few lessons on a catamaran. **Cat Sailing Curaçao**, at Jan Thiel Beach (☎ 527-5531 or 747-5830) offers beginner lessons for about $150 per person. After you know what you're doing, you can rent your own cat for around $34 per person per hour. You can also sign on for a captained tour along the coast.

The following operators organize sunset sails and full- or half-day trips, most including snorkeling and refreshments or lunch. Expect prices of $35 per person for a three- or four-hour sail to about $70 for a full day adventure.

Insulinde, a 120-foot steel ship, is operated by Captain Phil Jarman and staffed by an international crew, including chef Laara Fox. Day-trips, sunset cruises, and dinner sails are the specialty. Call for information and reservations, ☎ 560-1340; fax 461-1538; www.insulinde.com.

The Bounty

The *Bounty* is a nostalgic 90-foot multi-masted wooden schooner offering barefoot sailing adventures that include snorkel equipment, soft drinks, snacks, a salad buffet and an on-board barbeque.

Call for a schedule, ☎ 560-1887; www.bountyadventures.
com.

The *Mermaid* makes trips to Klein Curaçao three days a
week. Passengers are treated to a buffet lunch at a casual
beach house on the island, which has clean bathrooms and
a shaded patio. Contact Captain Cor for reservations and information about snorkeling or diving while you're on Klein.
☎ 560-1530; www.mermaidboattrips.com.

Miss Ann schedules all kinds of sailing activities, including
trips to Klein Curacao. Call to find out what's scheduled dur-

ing your visit, or ask
about arranging your
own group trip. ☎ 767-
1579, 560-1367 (cell);
fax 767-2685; www.
missannboattrips.com.

Carib Lady is a sleek
45-foot French cruis-
ing-racing yacht with a
teak deck. You can
take a sailing trip on
her by contacting the
proprietors of Carib-
bean Flower Apart-
ments, ☎ 869-5272;
www.caribflower.com.

Carib Lady

Windsurfing

Novices and experts enjoy the dependable winds and smooth water
surface at sheltered bays on
Curaçao. Rent a board and head to
secluded **Playa Konao** on the wind-
ward side, which is popular with local surfers on the weekend, but fairly deserted during the week. Beginners feel
safer in the sheltered bay at **Spanish Waters**. Another

choice is **Mambo Beach**, near the Seaquarium, where you'll have plenty of company. Board and sail rentals run around $15 per hour, and you'll need to leave a deposit of about $60.

Also try lessons and rentals from **Windsurfing Curaçao** on Caracas Bay Island, behind the gate at Baya Beach, east of Willemstad. ☎ 738-4555 or 524-4974 (cell); www.windsurfingcuracao.com.

Rental and lessons are available at the Seaquarium Beach from **Top Watersports Curaçao**, ☎ 461-7343. Rental prices run about $15 per hour, and you should expect to leave a deposit of $60.

Deep-Sea Fishing

 Anglers can fish for marlin, wahoo, kingfish, dolphin, and sailfish. Prices run $50 per person for a half-day and $75 for a full-day outing. All major resorts make arrangements at their activities desk, but if you want to make your own plans, call one of these operators:

Let's Fish, a 32-foot, fully-rigged fishing boat outfitted for serious fishermen and piloted by experienced captains, ☎ 561-1812 or 747-4489; www.letsfish.net.

Second Chance, operated by Miss Ann Boat Trips, is a 43-foot, fully-outfitted fishing boat with twin diesel engines. They'll pick you up at your hotel, if you reserve in advance. ☎ 767-1579, 560-1367 (cell); fax 767-2685; www.missannboattrips.com/fishing.htm.

Speedy's 40-foot cabin cruiser is equipped with twin diesel engines, GPS, and all the gear you need to catch the big ones. The crew will even prepare your fish at the end of the day. ☎ 560-4998 (cell) or 767-5195; www.speedyfishing.com.

In addition, you can contact **Pro Marine Yacht Services** to arrange private-charter and group fishing trips. ☎ 560-2081; www.curacaoboating.com.

Curaçao

Adventures on Land

Curaçao has plenty to occupy your time when you've tired of sightseeing and watersports.

Tennis

Lighted tennis courts are available for guests at several resorts, including the **Marriott**, **Breezes**, and **Holiday Beach**. Public courts are available at the **Santa Catharina Sports and Country Club**, ☎ 767-7030, and the **Curaçao Sports Club**, ☎ 737-9566. Call in advance for directions, hours, and court reservations. Court fees for non-guests of resorts and non-members of clubs range from $9 to $20 per hour.

Golf

Curaçao has a new 18-hole golf course in addition to an old nine-hole sand course. The new addition is part of a luxurious seaside residential and vacation complex at **Blue Bay Curaçao Golf and Beach Resort**. The AAA championship course is designed around the cliffs and sea on land

Blue Bay

that was formerly a plantation. Fees for 18 holes range from $65 to $105, depending on the season and time of day. Nine holes are half-price, and packages are available. For tee-time reservations and directions to the resort at Blauwbaai, a short distance west of the capital. ☎ 868-1755; www. bluebaygolf.com.

A more casual game of sand golf is possible at **Curaçao Golf and Squash Club** on Wilhelminalaan in Emmastad, on the north side of Schottegat Bay. Green fees are $15 to play 18 holes, and the club is open daily, 8 am-6 pm, ☎ 737-3590.

Hiking

 See pages 305-309 for details on hiking trails in **Christoffel National Park** and **Shete Boca National Park**.

Horseback Riding

 The national parks and Curaçao's arid countryside are ideal for sightseeing on horseback. Choose early morning or sunset rides for the coolest breezes and most active wildlife. Christoffel National Park has its own ranch with horses, and several other stables arrange group rides and individual outings along beaches, and over inland terrain that cannot be covered by car.

 Wear a hat, sunglasses, knee-length or longer pants, and sunscreen. If you want to ride in shorts or swimsuit, bring a thick beach towel to protect the front of your legs from sunburn, and the back of your legs from saddle sores.

Rates are $25 per hour, with ride-and-snorkel tours available at about $35. Your resort can make arrangements, or contact the following:

HORSEBACK RIDING OUTFITTERS	
Rancho Alfin (in Christoffel Park)	☎ 864-0535
Caracas Bay Horseback Riding Tours	☎ 747-0777
Rancho Allegre	☎ 868-1181
Ashari's Ranch	☎ 869-0315

Biking

 Experienced bikers will want to hit the dirt trails in the countryside or at Christoffel National Park, but others may prefer touring on paved roads outside the main traffic areas. Contact the following for information about rentals and guided tours that include a stop at one of the beaches for a swim:

BIKING OUTFITTERS	
Christoffel Park Rental Bike	☎ 864-0363
Dutch Dream	☎ 864-7377
Wannabike	☎ 527-3720
Curaçao Actief	☎ 433-8858; www.curacao-actief.com

Guided Adventure Tours

Curacao's outback is rugged and beautiful. The best way to see this area is off-road, and the following operators offer open-air guided tours.

Yellow Jeep Safari, ☎ 462-6262, www.jeep-safaris.com. Hop aboard a yellow Land Rover and let a driving pro show you the wild side of the island. Start on the north shore, drive through Christoffel National Park, cover the orchid route and cruise up to a 1,000-foot-high viewing point to see the island from a whole new slant.

Eric's ATV Adventures, ☎ 524-7418, www.curacao-atv.com. One of the friendliest guys on the island, Eric Raphaela, has a fleet of new ATVs just waiting for you to take on tour. You'll go places

Eric's ATV Adventures (Paul Sullivan)

you can't reach by car and see things most often cherished by hikers, mountain bikers and horseback riders. Plus, you'll have a terrific time driving your own all-terrain-vehicle.

Shopping

Punda Market (Paul Sullivan)

Curaçao offers some of the best shopping in the Caribbean. Pedestrian-only streets in Punda create a mall-like atmosphere with many shops conveniently located in one area. When cruise ships are docked in the harbor, merchants set up stalls along the waterfront in Punda and Otrobanda. Shopping centers on the outskirts of Willemstad add even more stores to the 200 or so located in the city.

Most shops are open Monday-Saturday, 8:30 am-12:30 pm and 2-6 pm, but some stay open continually throughout the day. Large stores accept credit cards and US dollars, as well as Netherlands Antilles guilders. Street vendors and small merchants usually accept US dollars, but most return change in guilders.

BEST BUYS

When shopping on Curaçao, look for Caribbean-made clothing, art, and jewelry, in addition to European imports, such as designer clothes, shoes, jewelry, perfume, linens, and electronics. Since the island is Dutch, Delft porcelain and hand-embroidered table linens are good buys. While Curaçao is not actually a duty-free island, the import taxes are low (about 3%), so prices are often better than in North America.

Punda shops (Paul Sullivan)

You may notice the **Free Trade Zone** located at the harbor. It's a regional distribution center for companies that buy merchandise in large quantities to sell in North America, Europe, Latin America, and Asia. This is not a duty-free shopping mall for tourists, but you may be able to buy here and ship directly back to your home. Ask, if you're interested..

The oldest and most interesting shops are located in a five-block area of Punda bordered by Handelskade and Sha Caprileskade on the waterfronts, Breedestraat to the south, and Columbusstraat to the east. Most of the stores are lined up along Heerenstraat and Breedestraat.

Penha & Sons (☎ 461-2266), at the corner of Heerenstraat and Breedestraat, was built in 1708 and is the oldest building in the city. The store has several branch locations and is known for high-end perfumes and clothing. **Boolchand's**, a camera and electronics company known widely throughout the Caribbean, is headquartered on Curaçao and has several stores in Punda,

Penha & Sons

including **Electronic World** on Heerenstraat across from Penha (☎ 461-6233).

Freeport Bargain Center at Heerenstraat 8 (☎ 461-5361) and **Freeport Jewelry** at Heerenstraat 25 (☎ 462-9706) have good deals on cameras, jewelry, watches, crystal, and porcelain. **The New Amsterdam Store**, Gomerzpein 14 (☎ 461-3239), opened in 1925 and is well known for hand-embroidered table linens and fine porcelain by Lladro, Hummel, and Delft. **Peltenburg Design**, on the Gomezplein #7 (☎ 465-2944), features unique inter-changeable jewelry crafted by Dutch designer Jan Peltenburg. One of the best art galleries on the island is **Gallery '86** (☎ 461-3417) at Scharlooweg 8.

The Yellow House, at Breedestraat 46 (☎ 461-3222), has been in business since 1887. It carries exquisite perfumes and cosmetics by companies such as Guerlain, Dior, and Elizabeth Arden. **Little Holland**, Braedestraat 37 (☎ 461-1768), sells a nice selection of shorts, shirts, ties, and prestigious cigars. Before you leave Punda, walk through the

Curaçao

small shops in the Waterfort Arches behind Fort Amsterdam.

On the Otrobanda side of town, look for unique shops, such as **Bamali**, at Breedestraat 2 (☎ 461-2258), which sells Indonesian-inspired clothes designed by the shop's owners, and **Curaçao Creations** (☎ 462-4516) on Schrijnwerkerstraat, off Breedestraat, a gallery of crafts made by local artists. **Riffort Village**, a shopping and entertainment center inside the seaside ramparts of Otrobanada's 19th-century fort, is now fully developed, and you will find a variety of shops inside the walls.

Where to Stay

 New and remodeled luxury resorts are conspicuous proof that tourism is thriving and growing on Curaçao. Big players such as Marriott, Hilton, and SuperClubs have sparkling new facilities, and independent owners are sinking millions of dollars into sumptuous resorts such as Kurá Hulanda and Avila Beach Resort.

If you prefer more modest accommodations, the **Curaçao Association of Apartments and Small Hotels** (CASHA) inspects member properties to guarantee consistent quality and traditional comforts. Most of these independently owned facilities are considerably less expensive and many have cooking facilities. Several suggestions are listed below, and you can check out others at the CASHA website, www.apartmentscuracao.com.

SLEEPING WITH THE STARS

Our suggested list of lodgings has been slashed to the bare bones for this guide. You can browse the Internet and we encourage you to do so. Here you'll find only the most recommended possibilities to fit a variety of budgets. Properties marked with one star (★) are highly recommended. When a single feature or the overall allure is particularly impressive, you'll find two stars (★★). Three stars (★★★) menas, simply, WOW!

Hotel Rate Guide

Use the prices given for accommodations as a guide to the average high-season rate per standard double room. If the review is for an all-inclusive or all-suites resort or a multi-room condo/villa property, the listed price is the average during high season for two people sharing the smallest available unit.

 The **area code** for Curaçao is 599+9. To phone from the US, dial 011-599-9, then the seven-digit number.

Resorts & Hotels

Unless otherwise noted, all of the following resorts and hotels are air-conditioned and equipped with telephones, cable or satellite color TVs, at least one swimming pool, and free parking. Most have at least one on-site restaurant. Exceptional hotel restaurants are listed in the dining section. Expect every listing to be adequately-to-superbly furnished with the usual amenities. Only outstanding or unusual features and services are noted in each description. Check with travel agents for color brochures or visit websites for online photos and video tours.

 When booking accommodations, ask if the 12% government tax is included. Also ask about additional energy and service fees.

In & Near Willemstad

★★★KURÁ HULANDA
De Rouvilleweg 47, Otrobanda
☎ 877-264-3106 (in North America), 434-7700; fax 434-7701; www.kurahulanda.com
120 rooms and suites
$280

Kurá Hulanda

This eight-block 65-building village is part-Disney, part old-world elegance and total indulgence. All the rooms and suites are 18th- and 19th-century Dutch colonial structures restored to UNESCO specifications for preserved historic buildings. Going a step beyond luxurious, the custom-crafted furnishings feature hand-carved mahogany beds and armoires, hand-woven linens, priceless antiques, and bet-you-can't-tell replicas. Bathrooms are spacious Indian marble hideaways with modern plumbing. Located in the heart of Otrobanda, a block from the bridge over St. Anna Bay into Punda, the ultra-secure compound offers quick access to the city. Two swimming pools, one an eco-pool with a waterfall formed from natural rocks, are ideal for relaxing after a day of shopping or sightseeing. The spa and fitness center are outfitted with state-of-the-art equipment and feature massage, personal training, and other services. Scheduled shuttle service is provided to the nearby beach club, and guests get preferential treatment at the Blue Bay Golf Course. If you're intent on working, all the machines and connections are provided in the business center, but your time can be better spent at the on-site African Museum (see the review on page 292). The two main restaurants (there are five total) are reviewed in the *Where to Eat* section, page 356-57.

You don't have to be newly wed to fall in love with the Indian Bridal Suite. The 900-square-foot open room is cleverly arranged into bedroom, living area, and bathroom to ensure complete togetherness and a bit of privacy. The furniture is silver – real silver. An oversized marriage bed is crafted of hammered sterling and covered in exquisite bridal linen. Other exquisite touches include white marble floors, a crystal chandelier, two TVs, a step-up whirlpool tub, and a separate shower with sterling silver walls.

HOWARD JOHNSON PLAZA HOTEL & CASINO

FD Rooseveltweg 524, Otrobanda
☎ 800-221-5333 (in North America) or 462-7800; fax 462-7803; www.hojo-curacao.com
100 rooms & suites
$110

HoJo Curaçao is not your father's Howard Johnson. This multi-colored complex on the Bionplein overlooking the harbor is cutting-edge chic and features a 1,500-square-foot casino, more than a dozen shops, and a

Howard Johnson Plaza

gourmet French restaurant. Guests are shuttled a short distance to the Bay Beach Club, an eco park with snorkeling, watersports, biking, horseback riding, and a full-service PADI dive center. The pool is small, but secluded in a peaceful area away from city noise.

OTROBANDA HOTEL & CASINO

Breedestraat, Otrobanda
☎ 462-7400; fax 462-7299; www.otrobandahotel.com
45 rooms
$115

You can't miss this bright blue hotel across the square from the new Howard Johnson, near the Queen Emma Bridge. There's a pool, casino, and restaurant, but no beach or

Otrobanda Hotel

beach shuttle. The Seaquarium Beach is 10 minutes away by car, but the hotel pool is lovely and a popular gathering spot. Most of the guests are European at this cozy, clean, and ideally located hotel.

VAN DER VALK PLAZA HOTEL AND CASINO

Plaza Piar, Punda

☎ 461-2500; fax 461-6543; www.plazahotelcuracao.com

254 rooms & suites

$100-$125

The high-rise Plaza offers a bit of the Netherlands in the Caribbean. It's right on the water above Fort Amsterdam, overlooking the Juliana Bridge and the bay.

Van Der Valk Plaza Hotel

There's no beach, but **Toucan Diving** is on-site and runs scuba, snorkeling and sightseeing boat trips from the hotel dock. The mostly-Dutch guests are a lively group who hang out at the pool, gather for happy hour, and dine at the openair **Waterfort Restaurant**. North Americans won't feel out of place. Staff and guests are friendly. The lobby is open-air, bright, and nicely furnished, but the rooms are small and just okay. Request a junior suite or luxury suite for more space.

★★ AVILA BEACH HOTEL

Penstraat 130, Pietermaai
☎ 800-747-8162 (in North America) or 461-4377; fax 461-1493; www.avilahotel.com
100 rooms & 10 suites
$140-$200

You're only a 10-minute walk from the center of town, when you stay at this land-mark hotel, which often hosts the royal family of the Netherlands. A shuttle bus runs guests into town. Two beaches

Avila Beach Hotel (Paul Sullivan)

and a small cove border the complex, which is made up of three buildings constructed at various times. **La Belle Alliance** is a restored 200-year-old mansion and an extension of deluxe rooms; the **Blues Wing** is the newer western section where all rooms have balconies or patios. Moderate rooms are in the **Classic Wing**. All accommodations are lovely, but the low-end rooms are small. Tall trees and carefully groomed landscaping add an air of elegance. The sandy man-made beaches have thatch umbrellas and trees for shade. Three restaurants, two bars, lighted tennis courts, and the ability to walk into town eliminate the need for a rental car. In 2006, the resort added a new swimming pool and fitness center.

HOLIDAY BEACH HOTEL AND CASINO

Pater Euwensweg, Otrobanda/Coconut Beach
☎ 462-5400; fax 462-4397; www.hol-beach.com
200 rooms
$135-$150

Sitting directly on Coconut Beach at the western edge of Otrobanda, the four-level Holiday gives plenty of value. The pool is large and actually nicer than the beach, which has thatched umbrellas and tall palms for shade, a calm lagoon for swimming, and a top-notch PADI dive center. Ask for an updated room with an ocean view. Some of the lower-end rooms are in need of new carpeting and paint. There are two restaurants, including a 24-hour **Denny's**, and a lot of activities, including a casino.

East of Willemstad

SUPERCLUBS BREEZES CURAÇAO

Dr. Martin Luther King Blvd 8, Seaquarium Beach
☎ 877-467-8737 (in North America) or 925-0925; fax 925-0334; www.breezescuracao.com
339 rooms & suites
$250-$300 (all-inclusive)

Superclubs Breezes

The price may seem high, but it includes everything. Literally, everything: room, meals, drinks, watersports, land activities, entertainment, airport transfers, taxes.... If you've never been to a super all-inclusive, this is a good one to try. The newly-opened $6 million resort shares a white-sand beach with the Seaquarium, and on-site facilities include three swimming pools, several Jacuzzis, a casino, a piano bar, a nightclub, a fitness center, and tennis courts. There is a selection of theme restaurants – **Pastafari** (Italian), **Jimmy'z Buffet** (continental and local dishes), **Munasan** (Japanese), plus a beach grill and a children's snack bar. Leave your wallet at home and just have fun at Superclubs.

LIONS DIVE & BEACH RESORT
Bapor Kibra
☎ 866-546-6734 (in North America) or 434-8888; fax 434-8889; www.lionsdive.com
72 rooms
$180-$200

Lions Dive & Beach Resort (www.usdivetravel.com)

Next door to the Seaquarium and Seaquarium Beach, just five miles east of Willemstad, Lions Dive enjoys a 15-year reputation as a serious scuba resort catering mostly to Dutch visitors. North Americans are discovering its attributes as Curaçao's tourism grows. Guests receive a card when they register that allows them free use of Seaquarium's long white-sand beach. The on-site **Ocen Encounters Dive Center** is an excellent five-star PADI facility run by a friendly multilingual staff. Ask for a room with a balcony overlooking the sea and, for more space, inquire about the new ocean-view cabanas and two-bedroom apartment. The lobby and **Rumors Restaurant** are open-air, casual, and nicely decorated. This is a family-friendly resort, so romantic couples and people who like a lot of quiet time may want to book elsewhere.

CHOGOGO RESORT

Jan Thiel Beach
☎ 747-2844; fax 747-2424; www.chogogo.com
60 bungalows, studios & apartments
$110 (per night; three-night minimum)

Room at Chogogo Resort

If you're staying three nights (the minimal rental), check out this resort community on rolling hills within walking distance of gorgeous Jan Thiel Baai. **Scuba Do Dive Center** (PADI five-star) offers diving and snorkeling trips from the beach, and the resort shuttle runs guests into town a few times each day. Or, just hang out in one of the comfy cloth lounge chairs beside the natural-rock swimming pool. You'll be out of the main tourist area, with mostly European (predominantly Dutch) neighbors. At meal time, wander over to the pool-side restaurant, which often features live music in the evenings.

PAPAGAYO BEACH RESORT

Jan Thiel Beach
☎ 800-652-2962 (in North America), 747-4333; fax 747-4322; www.papagayo-beach.com
75 villas
$215-$230
You may be tempted to settle into the hammock on your wrap-around veranda and never leave. Each of these lovely

villas is designed with fold-away shutter-walls that open to allow the fabulous Caribbean breezes to blow through the large lounge and kitchen areas. Kitchens have dishwashers and full refrigerators. Bedrooms are air-

Papagayo Beach Resort

conditioned. Each has a private bathroom. All the modern conveniences are provided, including Internet connections and remote-control TVs. The beach is within easy walking distance, and there's a large decked pool.

BON BINI SEASIDE RESORT

Seaquarium Beach
☎ 461-8000; fax 461-7500; www.bonbiniseasideresort.com
28 bungalows
$100

Bungalow at Bon Bini

Beautifully landscaped grounds surround these housekeeping cottages near the Seaquarium. Each has a fully-equipped kitchen, living area, one or two bedrooms, ceiling fans, air conditioning and cable TV. Guests have a choice of swimming and lounging at the swimming pool or on the white-sand beach. Willemstad is fewer than three miles away, and watersports are available at the nearby Seaquarium.

LIVINGSTONE RESORT

Jan Thiel Beach

☎ 800-221-5333 (in N. America), 747-0332; fax 767-9600; www.janthielresort.com

126 villas and apartments

$180-$225

Livingstone Resort

Jan Thiel Beach is about 10 minutes by car from downtown Willemstad, so this luxury resort is a good choice, if you want to be on the beach but near city amenities. Each of the lovely villas is designed in Mediterranean style, so you may feel as though you're vacationing in rural Italy. Deluxe features include a modern kitchens with dishwashers, living areas with cable/satellite TVs and large furnished patios. Guests share centrally-located facilities, such as a landscaped swimming pool, playground, minimart, open-air bar and full-service restaurant. On the nearby beach, you'll find a diving and watersports center, a beach club/disco, sand volleyball courts and additional restaurants.

★THE ROYAL SEA AQUARIUM RESORT

Seaquarium Beach

☎ 877-736-4554 (in N. America), 800-502-3838 (in Mexico), 465-6699; fax 465-6689; www.royalresorts.com

28 villas

$170-$190

Families love this resort at the Seaquarium. Each villa has two bedrooms and two baths, plus Murphy beds so they sleep up to six people. If your traveling group is smaller, the

units can be con-
figured into a
suite, sleeping up
to four, and a ho-
tel-sized room to
accommodate two
guests. You can
reserve the entire
villa, or just the
portion you need.
In the full-villa

Royal Seaquarium Resort

configuration, each unit has a full kitchen, a dining area, a
living room with an entertainment center and a patio. On-
site amenities include two pools, a hot tub, an activities center and a restaurant.

West of Willemstad

★FLORIS SUITE HOTEL
Piscadera Bay
☎ 800-781-1011 (in North America) or 462-6111; fax 462-
6211; www.florissuitehotel.com
72 suites
$160-$180

Beach at Floris Suite Hotel

Just three miles from the city
on lovely Piscadera Bay, this
luxurious, but surprisingly affordable, resort features junior
suites (with a king-size bed
and sofa) and one-bedroom
suites (with a king or two single beds and a queen-size
sleeper sofa in a separate living area). Each unit has a private patio or balcony
overlooking a lush garden and
free-form swimming pool. A
tennis court is on-site, and

Curaçao

guests may play golf at Blue Bay Golf Club (just 10 minutes by car), and enjoy Hook's Hut (the nearby private beach). The onsite restaurant is **Sjalotte**, an open-kitchen Mediterranean-style eatery located in a garden setting.

★MARRIOTT BEACH RESORT & EMERALD CASINO
Piscadera Bay
☎ 800-223-6388 (in North America) or 736-8800; fax 462-7502; www.marriotthotels.com/curmc
237 rooms & 10 suites
$220-$275

Marriott Beach Resort

Typical of Marriott, this three-level, five-star, four-diamond resort has all the luxurious amenities and elaborate styling to lure North American visitors. The private beach has a dive center with a custom-designed boat; the large dramatic pool features a swim-up bar; the fitness center is outfitted with state-of-the-art equipment; the 5,000-square-foot glitzy casino hosts live entertainment. Rooms won't disappoint you. They're fresh, bright, and outfitted with all the standard amenities and comforts.

★HILTON CURAÇAO RESORT
J.F. Kennedy Blvd, Piscadera Bay
☎ 877-464-4586 (in North America), 462-5000 (on Curaçao); fax 462-5846; www.hiltoncaribbean.com/curacao
197 room and suites
$180-$210
Overlook the typical mass-market rooms and enjoy the fabulous amenities at this anything-but-typical Hilton. The spa offers a great menu of services, the 5,000-square-foot casino features Las Vegas-style gaming, and three restaurants serve a variety of dining options. Twenty-five acres of

lush vegetation surround two pools, and the **Seascape Dive Center** offers scuba and snorkeling trips from the bay. The most unusual feature of the resort is the on-site **brewery**, which turns out two types of fresh beer every day. These house beers and a variety of international favorites are avail-

Hilton Curaçao Resort

able at the resort's restaurants and Captain Bligh's Bar.

HABITAT CURAÇAO

Boca Santa Maria
☎ 800-327-6709 (in North America) or 864-8304; fax 864-8464; www.habitatdiveresorts.com
56 rooms
$130

Habitat Curaçao

Like its sister resort on Bonaire, Habitat Curaçao is a diving paradise. Rooms are comfortable, nicely decorated, and have spectacular views of the sea and surrounding countryside. Visitors gather regularly at the open-air **Oceans Restaurant and Bar** to swap underwater adventure stories. When they aren't diving or talking about diving, guests hike or bike the nearby outback, swim in the large infinity pool, or take the complimentary shuttle into town. Check out the special deals on dive packages. The new art gallery has rotating shows with marine-theme works for sale.

★SUNSET WATERS BEACH HOTEL

Santa Marta Bay

☎ 866-578-6738 (in North America), 864-1233 (on Curaçao); fax 864-1237; www.sunsetwaters.com

70 rooms & one- , two- , or three-bedroom suites

$310-$325 all-inclusive

Sunset Waters

Standard rooms are basic and comfortable, with either one king-size or two double beds. Go for a deluxe room or suite to get more room and better views. The resort is located on a hill above a gorgeous crescent-shaped white-sand beach near the national park and popular dive sites. With the all-inclusive package, you get three meals daily, unlimited beverages, non-motorized watersports, nightly entertainment, complementary shuttle service to Willemstad, and all taxes and tips. Meals are served in two restaurants, both with great views of the sea, where the menu changes daily. There are three bars, including a swim-up pool bar, where guests enjoy a sunset happy hour every evening. Mike and Michelle Day operate the on-site dive shop, **Sunset Divers**. They make sure every diver has an excellent experience whether they dive the reef in calm waters off the beach or take the super-fast boat to other locations.

★★LODGE KURÁ HULANDA & BEACH CLUB

Playa Kalki/Westpunt

☎ 877-264-3106 (in N. America), 434-7700 or 864-0248, fax 434-7701; www.kurahulanda.com

80 rooms, suites and villas

$200-$225

Recently opened and already a hit with luxury-minded travelers, this beach-front property is the bucolic sister to the uptown Kurá Hulanda Resort in Willemstad. It offers all the comforts of an upscale resort, including high-quality Egyptian-cotton bedding, high-

Lodge Kurá Hulanda & Beach Club

speed Internet access and entertainment centers equipped with DVD players. But the real appeal to many vacationers is the secluded beachfront location. Colorful two-level buildings are scattered over 350 acres along the craggy cliffs at the island's remote western tip. Scuba diving and watersports are available at the private beach, and guests enjoy a freshwater swimming pool, tennis courts, bicycle rental, a fitness center and a full-service health spa. Food and beverages are available throughout the day and evening at the **Kalki Beach Bar and Grill**, the casual **Christoffel** pool-side bar and the international gourmet restaurant, **Watamula**. Complimentary shuttle service is provided into Willemstad.

Rental Agencies

Private vacation home rentals are becoming more common on Curaçao. The following agencies list a variety of villas, homes and apartments in diverse sizes and price ranges.

- **International Accommodations**, ☎ 800-490-0461, 736-2030, fax 736-6616; www.intac.an.
- **Great Rentals**, contact property owner directly; www.greatrentals.com.
- **Piscadera Bay Resort Rentals**, ☎ 462-6303, fax 462-5962; www.piscaderabayresort.com.

Where to Eat

Willemstad is home to dozens of ethnic groups and every imaginable mix of nationalities. So, it's not surprising that restaurants serve imported foods from around the world, which skillful chefs turn into imaginative dishes using local herbs and spices.

Local fare (*krioyo*) centers around fresh seafood and meats (particularly goat) accompanied by *funchi* (boiled cornmeal dish similar to polenta) and fried bananas or plantains. Other native favorites include *kabritu* (a goat stew with delicate spices), *aros moro* (rice and peas), *tutu* (a sweet cornmeal and bean dish), and *yuana* (stewed iguana). *Kadushi* (cactus) is served fried (tasty) and boiled into a slimy soup (not so tasty). The best place to try these dishes is at lunch in the covered market (*marshe*) on the Waaigat waterfront in Punda. Sample the *karkó* (conch) and *pastechi* (fried meat pie) or *lumpia* (fried vegetable pie).

For a sit-down lunch or dinner, all the major hotels have good-to-excellent restaurants and outdoor cafés. In Willemstad, the waterfront is lined with sidewalk eateries, and restaurants are tucked into the **Waterfort Arches** (behind Fort Amsterdam) on the Punda side and the newly renovated **Riffort** on the Otrobanda side.

If you get homesick, duck into a McDonald's, Denny's, Subway, or Pizza Hut for a fast-food fix. (But, don't admit this to anyone.)

A more exotic choice is the popular *rijsttafel* (rice table), a terrific Indonesian custom of presenting small plates of 10 to 30 or 40 different foods. Dutch favorites, such as stuffed cheese (*keshi yená*), and Latin dishes, such as paella, are two types of cuisine you should not miss while on Curaçao.

Make dinner reservations, especially during high season, especially if you really want to eat at a specific restaurant. Most restaurants accept credit cards and US dollars (those that don't are indicated below), as well as Netherlands Antilles guilders. Your bill will include a 5% government tax, and a 10-15% service charge is often added. Service charge fees are usually split among the staff, so give a small tip directly to your server if you think it's deserved.

 Dress Code: Residents dress up for dinner in the city or at a fine hotel, but slacks and a collared shirt for men and a casual sun dress, skirt or slacks for women is all that's required in most places. Bring a light sweater if you get cold easily, since indoor restaurants turn the air-conditioning down low and night air is cool if you dine outdoors near the water.

Dining With the Stars

Every restaurant listed in this guide is recommended, and you will find some marked with stars. One star (★) indicates that the restaurant is highly recommended, two stars (★★) mean you should make an extra effort to eat there, and three stars (★★★) promise an experience to remember. The rating may be for super value or an amazing view or, perhaps, simply the best "cheeseburgers in paradise."

Restaurant Price Guide

Use the prices given at the beginning of each restaurant listing as a guide to the average price of a mid-range meal per person, excluding drinks and tip.

Waterfort Terrace

One of the most outstanding structures on Willemstad's UNESCO World Heritage List is the Waterfort Arches. The 17th-century barrel-vaulted stone arches are a quarter-mile long and 30 feet tall – built to store munitions, food, and medical supplies for the military stationed at Fort Amsterdam. The thick walls and fortified roof protected Allied forces, who were here during World War II to protect the island's oil refinery from Nazi submarine attacks.

Today, the graceful old arches have been restored with modern facilities to house several restaurants, bars, and shops. The original flagstone walkway borders a narrow road on the land side, and a breezy esplanade borders the sea on the other side. Stop at one of the following restaurants for an outdoor lunch, a sunset drink, or a romantic dinner. All are grouped together on a terrace overlooking the harbor.

SCAMPI'S
☎ 465-0769
Seafood
$15-$25
Daily, 11 am-11 pm
Reservations recommended

Call to ask about theme nights. The menu features seafood with a creative twist. Try octopus salad or grilled conch in garlic sauce.

GRILL KING
☎ 461-6870
Steaks, ribs, chicken
$12-$18 (lunch), $16-$22 (dinner)
Monday-Saturday, 11 am-11 pm, Sunday, 5-11 pm
Reservations recommended

The dining room is open to the sea under a thatched roof, creating a magnificent ambiance. Service is friendly, and the menu is quite extensive. If you're really hungry, order the Mixed Grill (chicken, pork, sirloin, ribs, and sausage) or the Mixed Seafood (fish, shrimp, conch, calamari, and mussels). Salads and burgers are good at lunch.

LA PERGOLA
☎ 461-3482
Italian
$10-$20 (lunch), $15-$28 (dinner)
Monday-Saturday, 11 am-11 pm, Sunday, 5-11 pm
Reservations recommended

Menu offerings at this breezy restaurant include traditional Italian dishes, but most have an island touch. The ravioli is stuffed with local fresh seafood, pastas are flavored with olive oil and Caribbean herbs, fish comes sauced with garlicky tomatoes. Delicious. Service is friendly, and the setting is magnificent.

SMALL WORLD
☎ 465-5575
International
$12-$22
Monday-Saturday, 11 am-11 pm, Sunday, 5-11 pm
Reservations recommended

When this restaurant says international, they mean literally worldwide. The soup menu alone includes French onion, oriental vegetarian, and sopa de mariscos a la Catalana. Main courses go from Texas prime rib to Japanese shrimp sakura. Unfortunately, the wine and beer lists are not so broad. The view from the restaurant's deck built out over the water is stunning.

In & Near Willemstad

THE WINE CELLAR
Concordaistraat at Kaya Jonge Wacht, Scharloo
☎ 461-2178
International, seafood & prime beef
$15-$40
Monday-Friday, noon-2:30 pm; Monday-Saturday, 6-11:30 pm
Reservations required

With only eight tables, reservations are a must at this little bistro in an old house at the eastern edge of town. The food is terrific. Order something grilled. Ostrich, maybe? Other choices include poached salmon and veal in a red wine sauce. Of course, the wine list is lengthy and includes a variety of vintages from France, Italy, California, Australia, and Chile.

★★ BISTRO LE CLOCHARD

Riffort, on the waterfront in Otrobanda
☎ 462-5666
Swiss & French
$15-$20 (lunch), $20-$35 (dinner)
Daily, 12-2:30 pm and 6:30-11 pm (terrace open non-stop)
Credit cards accepted
Reservations highly recommended

Le Clochard

The Riffort on the Otrobanda waterfront is currently being developed into a world-class shopping and dining mall. Bistro Le Clochard has been on the lower level of the old fort for more than 20 years. It's a popular upscale place with a creative menu that features monthly surprises. The seafood and meat courses are outstanding, but for something different, try the fondue. The wine list and desserts meet all expectations.

When the Riffort development is complete, a casual coffee bar, and a daiquiri bar will join Bistro Le Clochard on the first level. On the third and fourth levels, plans call for several international restaurants, a piano bar, and a nightclub. Some, or all, may be open by the time you visit.

★★ RESTAURANT FORT NASSAU

Fort Nassau, near Point Juliana
☎ 461-3450
International & seafood
$18-$25 (lunch), $20-$30 (dinner)
Monday-Friday, 12-3 pm, daily, 6-11 pm
Credit cards accepted
Reservations highly recommended.

Built in 1797 by the Dutch to protect Curaçao from foreign attack, Fort Nassau is now recognized as a national monument and one of the best restaurants on the island. It sits on a hilltop overlooking the city and harbor (the harbor master still signals ships from here) and presents visitors with dazzling 360° vistas of the island and sea. Main courses focus on grilled meats and fish with innovative sauces. The appetizers, soups, and desserts are amazing. Complement your choices with one of the fine wines.

THE YELLOW BIRD

Hilton Curaçao Resort
☎ 462-5000
International and Antillean
$16 (breakfast), $12-$15 (lunch), $16-$25 (dinner)
Daily, 7 am-11 pm
Reservations recommended for dinner

This patio restaurant at the Hilton is a good place to get dependably tasty food all day. An American-style buffet is popular at breakfast. Try to come for one of the theme-night dinners when Asian, Mexican, and Caribbean specialties are served up with some type of entertainment. The resort's other restaurants include **La**

The Yellow Bird

Piazetta, serving gourmet Italian cuisine Tuesday-Saturday, 7-11 pm, and a casual **Beach Grill**, serving burgers, snacks, and drinks, 11 am-7 pm daily.

BAY SIGHT TERRACE

Otrobanda Hotel
☎ 462-7400
International
$12-$16 (breakfast), $12-$18 (lunch, $16-$25 (dinner)
Daily, 7 am-10 pm
Reservations accepted

If you want to get into town early, stop by the Bay Sight for an American-style breakfast on the terrace above the casino of

Otrobanda Hotel & Bay Sight Terrace

the Otrobanda Hotel. It's the blue building on the corner, across from the Queen Emma Bridge. This is a great place to people-watch. In the evening, try the steaks or seafood before you hit the casino. Happy Hour runs Friday from 7 to 10 pm, and there's live entertainment on Sunday nights.

★★JAIPUR
Hotel Kurá Hulanda
☎ 434-7700
Asian
$22-$30
Daily, 6-11 pm
Reservations highly recommended

Amid the colorful Dutch colonial buildings in the Kurá Hulanda compound, the outdoor Jaipur overlooks a waterfall in the natural-rock eco-swimming pool. For extra romance, ask for one of the ta-

Dining at Jaipur

bles perched on the rocks. You can watch your meal being prepared in the open kitchen by chefs wearing crisp white hats and jackets. Try the grilled fresh fish or Indian tandoori specialties at dinner. Snacks are served pool-side from noon until 6 pm.

JACOB'S BAR & TERRACE
Hotel Kurá Hulanda
☎ 434-7700
Snacks and drinks
$3-$12
Daily, 5 pm-midnight

Frequented by local business people and hotel guests, this elegantly appointed yet casual bar serves indoors or on the terrace in the shady courtyard. Spanish-style tapas accompany good wines, beers, and premium-liquor drinks. Happy hour, daily 5-7 pm, includes complimentary snacks.

★★★ASTROLAB OBSERVATORY RESTAURANT
Hotel Kurá Hulanda
☎ 434-7700
International
$30-$40
Monday-Saturday, 7-11 pm
Reservations highly recommended for dinner

Located adjacent to the Indian Marble Garden of this village complex, the restaurant gets its name from the collection of astrolabs (also spelled astrolabes) displayed there. An astrolabe was an early astronomical instrument used by scientists to observe the heavens and calculate time as it relates to the planets and stars. Dine indoors or al fresco on perfectly prepared beef and seafood specialties. The wine cellar holds a wide range of international vintages.

 The News Café, off the main courtyard inside the Kurá Huland village, is open daily, 6:30 am-10:30 pm for pick-up snacks and drinks to enjoy with your daily newspaper. The cappuccino is excellent, and all the pastries are freshly baked.

Curaçao

RESTAURANT KURÁ HULANDA
Hotel Kurá Hulanda
☎ 434-7700
International
$12-$22
Daily, noon-11:30 pm
Reservations recommended for dinner

Restaurant Kurá Hulanda

This garden restaurant, located beside the Kurá Hulanda African Museum, draws an artsy crowd with its eclectic ever-changing menu. Drop in before or after you tour the magnificent museum.

TASCA DON FRANCISCO
Julianaplein 39, Pietermaai
☎ 461-4515
Steaks and seafood
$12-$18 (lunch), $16-$25 (dinner)
Tuesday-Sunday, noon-3 pm and 6-11 pm
Reservations recommended

Make a reservation for prime dinner-hour seating because this restaurant is popular with residents. Try the paella, their signature dish. Other choices include fresh, boneless fish fillets and excellent steaks. Kids are welcome and they love the rock-walled interior décor.

★★BELLE TERRACE
Avila Beach Hotel
☎ 461-4377
Danish, BBQ & Antillean
$12-$20 (lunch), $15-$28 (dinner)
Daily, 7-10 am, noon-2:30 pm and 7-10 pm
Reservations at dinner required

The Avila Beach is where the Dutch royal family stays on visits to the island, so expect the best at the hotel's main restaurant. Lunch is casual, but don't show up for dinner in shorts and flip flops. While the staff is friendly and puts everyone at ease, you'll be out of place in anything other than island chic attire after sunset. The chef is Scandinavian, so Danish specialties appear on the menu, along with Continental and Caribbean favorites.

★BLUES

Avila Beach Hotel
☎ 461-4377
International & seafood
$15-$30
Tuesday-Sunday, 7-11 pm (bar is open daily 5 pm-1 am)
Reservations recommended

This restaurant, built out over the water at the end of a pier, is named for music, not the color of the sea. Live jazz plays here Thursdays, 6:30-9:30 pm and Saturdays, 10 pm-1 am. Drop by in time for happy hour on these nights (6-7 pm) and watch the sun slip into the Caribbean as you sip an icy drink. Then stay on for a lobster dinner and cool jazz.

In addition to Belle Terrace and Blues, Avila Beach has a casual patio café (buffet breakfast, 7-10 am, snacks and drinks, 2:30-7 pm) and a sail-shaded beach bar that's open daily from noon until late in the evening.

★PORTOFINO

Curaçao Marriott Resort
☎ 736-8800
Steaks, Italian
$20-$40
Daily, 6-11 pm
Reservations recommended

All of the restaurants at this Marriott serve superb cuisine. The Emerald Grill is known for great steaks; Palm Café serves breakfast and lunch outdoors on the garden patio. But Portofino really stands out, with its authentic Italian cuisine. On Sundays, make reservations for the popular Champagne brunch.

MAMBO BEACH BAR & RESTAURANT
Seaquarium Beach, Bapor Kibra
☎ 461-8999
International
$12-$25
Daily 10 am-10 pm, Friday-Saturday open until 11 pm
Reservations recommended for dinner

In the busy Seaquarium area, this restaurant is popular for casual lunches, nightly theme specials and live music during happy hour on Sundays from 5 to 6pm. The fresh catch of the day is always a good choice, and on Tuesday and Wednesday nights you can't go wrong with the tapas. Call or drop in to ask about scheduled theme dinners, and linger to enjoy the ocean views.

East of Willemstad

RIJSTTAFEL RESTAURANT
Mercuriusstraat 13, Salina
☎ 461-2606
Indonesian
$15-$30; buffet $22-$50
Monday-Saturday, noon-2 pm and 6-9:30 pm, Sunday, 6-9:30 pm
Reservations recommended

One of the best meals on the island is an Indonesian rice table, *rijsttafel*, and this is an excellent place to try it. Come for dinner when the selection is more extensive, about 20 dishes. Vegetarians can eat well here. It's best if you come with a group, so you can try a bit of everything. You do your own seasoning, so the dishes are spicy only if you make them so.

ROTI MAHAL
Kaya Max F. Henriquez, Salina
☎ 461-8300
Surinam and vegetarian
$10-$12 (lunch), $12-$18 (dinner)
Tuesday-Sunday, 11 am-2 pm and 5-8 pm

Drop in for a quick lunch or take-out dinner when you're in this area, just east of the city. (It's next door to the Maduro & Curiel Bank in the center of Salina.) The burrito-like rotis are excellent, and made from fresh chicken or shrimp. The curry is also tasty and you have a selection of vegetarian dishes.

THE RIBS FACTORY
Oude Caracasbaaiweg 54, Salina
☎ 461-0440
Tex-Mex and ribs
$8-$20

Barbecued ribs, French fries, and corn on the cob. You might as well be in the southern USA. Unless you're in Texas, where Mexican food includes cheesy enchiladas and spicy-hot quesadillas. You can get all these treats and super desserts at The Ribs Factory. If you plan a cozy evening at home, most dishes can be prepared for take-out.

LANDHUIS BRAKKEPUT MEI-MEI
Near Spanish Water, east of Willemstad
☎ 767-1500; www.brakkeputmeimei.com
Steaks & seafood
$16-$30
Daily, 6-11 pm
Reservations recommended

Set in a renovated caramel-colored *landhuis*, this restaurant is also a popular night spot. Locals and tourist gather on the breezy terrace to enjoy drinks and music, but the kitchen turns out great steaks. Vegetarians can fill their plate from the salad bar. Call ahead to ask about scheduled entertainment.

Curaçao

Elsewhere on the Island

★JAANCHI
Westpunt 15, near the western tip of the island
☎ 864-0126
Caribbean
$28-$35
Daily, 11:30 am-7 pm
There's no written menu. Jaanchi, the friendly owner, or one of his staff simply come to your table and tell you what the cook is preparing that day. Don't be surprised if its iguana or snake. Other options usually include some type of fresh fish, chicken, and goat or beef. Portions are large and come with a couple of Antillean side dishes. Jaanchi's father started the colorful little open-air restaurant in the 1930s, and the place has grown to be a legend and landmark on the far west end of the island. Ask to sit beside a window so you can watch the birds feeding on the patio or building a nest under the roof. On Sundays, local musicians provide entertainment.

★ZAMBEZI
Ostrich and Game Farm, near St. Joris Bay, northeast coast
☎ 747-2777
South African
$28-$35
Tuesday-Sunday, 12-5 pm, Wednesday-Sunday, 6-10 pm
Try an ostrich steak or some other exotic treat when you visit this sprawling ranch. The restaurant is open-air and covered by a thatch roof, so you feel as if you're actually on safari when you stop in for a cool drink or meal. South African wines are a specialty.

Nightlife

 Nightlife is hopping on Curaçao. New hot spots open regularly and old favorites feature live entertainment, happy hours, and theme-night parties to lure locals and visitors. Pick up a copy of the free weekly **K-Pasa** to find out what's happening while you're on the island. You can also check the free magazines – **Curaçao Visitor's Guide**, **Curaçao Holiday**, and **Curaçao Nights**.

Start your evening at one of the many happy hours held at bars, casinos, and restaurants throughout Willemstad. Then move on to dinner at one of more than 100 restaurants. (Make a reservation to insure a table during prime dinner hours.) Most kitchens close around 10 pm, even if the restaurant stays open later, so don't count on eating fashionably late.

Casinos

Casinos open at around 2 pm and go strong until early morning. The largest are located at major resorts, such as the **Howard Johnson Plaza** (☎ 462-7800), the **Marriott** (☎ 736-8800), **Holiday Beach** (☎ 462-

Casino at the Hilton

5400), and the **Hilton** (☎ 462-5000). All have slot and video machines, as well as poker, black jack, and roulette tables. Some, such as the Holiday Beach (☎ 462-5400), take bets on sports events. Kurá Hulanda has a new European-style casino on the street side (☎ 434-7700).

Resort Bars & Music

Resorts also offer a variety of bars, lounges, and dance clubs. Locals tend to hang out at beach bars with live bands or DJs, such as **Rumours** at Lions Dive Inn (☎ 461-7555) and **Blues** at Avila Beach Hotel (☎ 461-4377). Locals like to party on the beach at such places as **Mambo** (☎ 461-8999), and the adjoining **Wet & Wild** on Seaquarium Beach (☎ 465-3464) and **Baya Beach Club** on Caracas Bay (☎ 747-0777).

Other Nightspots

Salina, just east of Willemstad, is a trendy area right now. Top clubs include **The Living Room** (☎ 461-4443), a cozy restaurant and lounge with a dance floor; **Facade** (☎ 461-4640), a place to dress up and mix with upscale residents of all ages; **Olé Olé** (☎ 461-7707), a bar that often features live music; **The Music Factory** (TMF), the can't-be-missed purple building that features some type of music every night except Sunday (☎ 461-0631).

 Call the clubs and bars for exact directions.

If you want to get inside one of the old plantation houses, make reservations for dinner at **Landhuis Granbeeuw** (☎ 747-0614) on Cascoraweg in Santa Rosa, northeast of Willemstad. The three-course meal is well priced and served on the patio. Afterwards, stay on for live music and dancing until one in the morning.

Landhuis Chobolobo (☎ 461-3526) is the 17th-century estate that houses Senior Curaçao Liqueur Distillery. On weekends, the landhuis hosts local merenge and salsa bands, 10 pm-3 am. Call for current information and to be sure the house isn't closed for a private party.

In Willemstad, **Blues Beach Bar** (☎ 461-4377), on the pier at the Avila Hotel, is the place for fans of jazz. A nice variety of cocktails accompany the live music, which plays most nights. Both Riffort Village and Waterfort Terrace are well lighted and popular after dark. **The Daiquiri Bar** (☎ 462-5666) , a hut on the lower level of the Riffort with a few tables and chairs scattered nearby, is open until 11:30 pm, serving all types of specialty cocktails. The bar tender will mix up just about any concoction you can think of. **The Anchor Bar** (☎ 462-2982) closes around 11 pm, so plan to stop in early in the evening to enjoy the harbor views. At the **Waterfort, Terrace**, you can catch live Flamenco dancing at **Flamenco Restaurant and Tapas Bar** (☎ 465-9965) every Saturday evening. While you watch, enjoy tapas and sangria. Flamenco is open daily until midnight for drinks and snacks.

In the Seaquarium area of Bapor Kibra, meet-greet-'n-party time takes place inside and outside **Mambo Beach** (☎ 461-8999), **Kontiki** (☎ 465-1589), and **Wet & Wild** (☎ 561-2477). Most people show up for sunset cocktails, stay on for dinner, then listen to live music and dance until 3 or four in the morning.

Out on Piscadera Bay, south of Willemstad, the IN spot is **Hook's Hut** (☎ 462-6575) at Floris Suite Hotel. The food is great, and you can eat as late as 10 pm, but linger to enjoy the live music, which continues late into the night. Bands vary from jazz to reggae. Call for a schedule of entertainers.

Movies

Current films are shown at **The Movies Curaçao**, a six-screen theater at Plaza Mundo Merced. Call for a listing of times and titles. ☎ 465-1000; www.themoviescuracao.com.

Island Facts & Contacts

AIRPORT: Curaçao (Hato) International Airport and flight information, ☎ 868-1719.

AREA CODE: 599-9.

ATMs: Widely available at locations throughout the island, including the airport, which also has a 24-hour currency exchange machine. Most machines at hotels, shopping centers, and banks dispense only Netherlands Antillean guilders, but machines at select banks dispense US dollars.

BANKS: Most banks are open Monday-Friday, 8 am-3:30 pm. Maduro & Curiel's Bank at the airport is open Monday-Saturday, 8 am-8 pm, and Sunday, 9 am-4 pm. Maduro & Curiel's Bank at Zuikertuintje Supermarket (☎ 466-0777 or 466-1100, call for directions) is open Monday-Friday, 8 am-6 pm, and Saturdays, 8:30 am-6 pm.

CAPITAL: Willemstad

DEPARTURE TAX: US $20 for international departures (usually added to the cost of your airline ticket). $16 for travel within the Netherlands Antilles.

DRIVING: Traffic travels on the right side of the road, as in the US, Canada, and most of Europe. Valid foreign and international driver's licenses are accepted. International road signs are used. Right turns on red lights are not allowed.

ELECTRICITY: The electrical voltage is 110-130 AC (50 cycles). Most outlets accept the same plugs used in North America. Electrical items from North America will function on this voltage, but not perfectly. Timing devices will not be accurate and heating appliances, such as hairdryers, may overheat. Use a surge protector for computers, and charge underwater strobes and videos at dive or photo shops with regulated systems. Most plugs are the same as those in North America, though older hotels may have European plugs. Adapter plugs are available on the island.

EMERGENCY: Police and fire department (☎ 911), ambulance (☎ 912), hospital (☎ 910), and Coast Guard (☎ 913).

GAS STATIONS: Gas stations are conveniently located on the ring road around Willemstad and along the main roads throughout the island. Pay before you fill up. Most stations accept credit cards and will convert prices to US dollars and accept dollars as payment. Only a few stations stay open late in the evening or on Sundays, so fill up Monday-Saturday between 7 am and 9 pm.

GOVERNMENT: Curaçao is the capital of the Netherlands Antilles, which includes Bonaire, Sint Maarten, Saba, and Sint Eustatius. Willemstad is the capital of Curaçao. The Netherlands Antilles is an autonomous part of the Kingdom of the Netherlands, which includes Holland and Aruba. Citizens of Curaçao and the other islands in the Kingdom are Dutch nationals and carry European Union passports. The governor of the NA and the lieutenant governor of each island is appointed by the ruling monarch of the Kingdom. Each island's parliament is elected by popular vote, and citizens may vote at the age of 21.

HOSPITAL: St. Elisabeth Hospital, at Breedestraat 193 in Willemstad, is well equipped and uses up-to-date treatments. The modern facilities include beds for 550 patients and a recompression chamber. ☎ 462-4900. In an emergency, dial 910 (hospital) or 912 for an ambulance.

LANGUAGE: The official language is Dutch, but locals speak Papiamento (spelled Papiamentu on Bonaire). Many are multilingual and also speak Spanish, English, and German.

LEGAL AGE: 18 for drinking and gambling.

MONEY: The Netherlands Antillean florin (NAfl) is the official currency, and US $1 = NAfl 1.78 or NAfl 1 = 56¢. The dollar is widely accepted. Exchange only a small amount of money to pay for taxi fares, tips, and small purchases. Stores will convert prices for you at a good rate, about NAfl 1.75 = $1, although change is given in local currency. Major credit cards are accepted at large resorts and restaurants, and many stores, but smaller establishments may require cash. The florin is also called a guilder. The old square nickel and newer square 50¢ piece are popular souvenirs.

PHARMACY: Pharmacies are called boticas. Most are open Monday-Saturday, 8 am-7 pm, and on-duty pharmacists rotate 24-hours-a-day throughout the week. Check with your hotel for the botica nearest you. Most common prescription and over-the-counter medications are available on the island.

POPULATION: 170,000, with more than 40 nationalities represented.

PUBLICATIONS: These magazines are available free in hotel lobbies and at many restaurants and tourist attractions: Curaçao Holiday, Curaçao Nights, Curaçao Visitors Guide, K-Pasa and Curaçao Explorer.

SAFETY: Curaçao is generally safe. However, downtown Willemstad, especially the narrow back roads of Otrobanda, is known to have drug problems. Be cautious walking off the beaten path in the city, even during the day. The waterfront and most tourist areas are safe, but take common-sense precautions to avoid theft, especially from cars parked at beaches. Many car rental agencies issue anti-theft gadgets for cars that do not have alarm systems. Use them.

SHOPPING HOURS: Some stores open on Sunday when a cruise ship is in port. Otherwise, hours are Monday-Saturday, 8:30 am-12:30 pm, and 2-6 pm. A few shops may stay open during the lunch hours, especially when cruise-ship passengers are in town. Supermarkets usually are open Monday-Saturday, 8 am-8 pm, and Sunday, 8 am-noon.

TAXES & TIPS: A 5% sales tax is added to most purchases. In addition, hotels charge a government tax of 12%. A 12% service charge may be added to hotel and restaurant bills, but the money may not go to your maid or server. Leave a bit extra for good service. In addition, a $3 per-day, per-room energy charge is added to hotel rates. Ask if taxes and other charges are included in the quoted rate when you book accommodations.

TAXIS: ☎ 869-0747 or 869-0752.

TELEPHONES: The international access code from North America is 011; the country code for the Netherlands Antilles is 599; the island code for Curaçao is 9. To call Curaçao from North America, dial 011-599-9, plus the seven-digit local number. If you are calling Curaçao from Europe or most of the rest of the world, dial 00 + 599 + 9, then the seven-digit local number. On Curaçao, dial only the seven-digit local number.

Buy a phone card at hotel shops to make long distance and local calls on public phones. To call internationally from Curaçao, dial 00 plus the country code. (The country code for the US and Canada is 1.)

International cell phones may be rented at many hotel reception desks. Your cell phone from home will not work on the island.

TIME: Curaçao is on Atlantic Standard Time (AST) year-round, which is one hour later than Eastern Standard Time and four hours earlier than Greenwich Mean Time. The island does not observe Daylight Savings Time, so Curaçao's time is the same as Eastern Daylight Savings Time.

TOURIST INFORMATION: ☎ 800-328-7222 (in North America); www.curacao-tourism.com. Curaçao Tourism & Development Bureau, 19 Pietermaai, PO Box 3266, Willemstad, Curaçao, Netherlands Antilles, ☎ 434-8200.

WEBSITES: Dozens of sites offer information about activities, accommodations, and travel. The best general information sites are: www.curacao-tourism.com; www.dutch-caribbean.net; and www.curacao.com.

Curaçao

Index